The
SALT
ROADS

The
SALT
ROADS

HOW FISH
MADE A CULTURE

JOHN GOODLAD

BIRLINN

First published in 2022 by
Birlinn Ltd
West Newington House
10 Newington Road
Edinburgh
EH9 1QS

www.birlinn.co.uk

ISBN 978 1 78027 791 2

British Library Cataloguing-in-Publication Data
A catalogue record for this book is available on request from the
British Library

Typeset by Initial Typesetting Services, Edinburgh

Printed and bound by Clays Ltd, Elcograf S.p.A.

Contents

Acknowledgements

I am grateful to everyone in Shetland, Faroe, Scotland, England, Iceland, the Basque country and elsewhere in Europe who generously gave me their time and shared their enthusiasm. They have inspired me to write this book. I am indebted to all those who have allowed me to use their photographs and to John Cumming for his masterful sketches. Andrew Simmons and the team at Birlinn could not have been more helpful and supportive. And, to my severest critics and greatest supporters – my wife Wilma, and daughters Hannah Mary and Johanna – you've taught me such a lot.

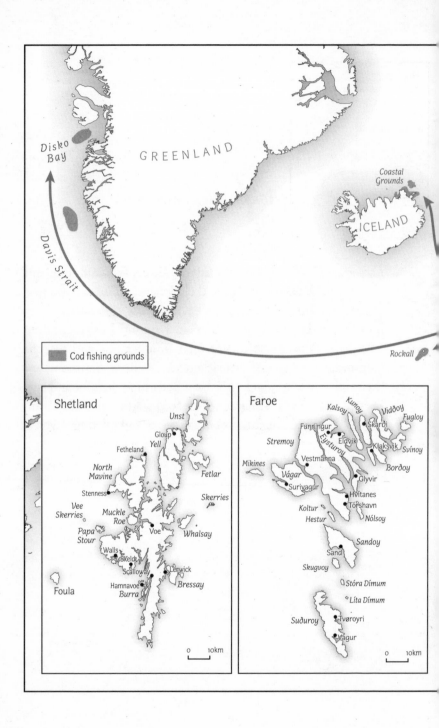

Heglies
Bank

000°

48 miles

36 miles

045°

Raufarhofn   Rifstangi

Axarfjordur   Langanes

ICELAND

0   100 km

Faroe
Coast   Faroe

Faroe
Bank   Shetland

Home Grounds

Wick
Fraserburgh
Peterhead

RUSSIA

St Petersburg

Grimsby
Great
Lowestoft   Yarmouth

Königsberg
Lubeck   Danzig
Hamburg   Stettin

GERMANY

Bilbao

SPAIN

0   1000 km

Prologue – Pitch Dark

It was dark. Not just difficult-to-see-in-the-dark, but impossible-to-see-in-the-dark – the kind of complete blackness that can only be found inside a room with no windows. But this was no darkened room; this was midnight in the middle of the North Atlantic in a hurricane. It was utterly chaotic: everything was moving around, violently and randomly. The old wooden smack, the *Telegraph*, first fell over to one side and then quickly rolled to the other, before plunging headfirst into a black void that seemed capable of swallowing her. The deck was awash with sea-water as one wave after another crashed on board with a weight that made the boat shudder. And, as if there was not enough water on deck, torrential rain was being driven horizontally by the extreme southwesterly wind.

It would have been bad enough, thought James Smith, who was the skipper, if there had even been the slightest visibility. Some idea of where the next towering wave was coming from would have provided a brief warning of sorts. As it was, the *Telegraph* was being bombarded by breaking seas in total dark-ness. She was no longer moving through the sea, her sails having been ripped to shreds by the hurricane five hours ago, just as darkness had come down. At around the same time, what little light that came from the navigation lamps had been extin-guished when they were torn from their mountings by a wall of water sweeping the deck. Total unseeing darkness is unusual at sea; there is usually some moonlight. But tonight, there was no moon, and it occurred to James that it really was as dark as pitch tar. He hated the darkness, and he longed to see a glimpse of moonlight, although he knew that would not happen until the storm passed.

James also knew that darkness was not his problem tonight. His crew were at the mercy of a weather event worse than anything he had ever seen before. The ability of the smack to cope had been seriously compromised when her sails had been torn. If a small area of sail was capturing the wind, the *Telegraph* was able to move ahead and was capable of being steered. The wind in the sail also heeled her over, which provided some stability against the random seas. But with shredded sails, the smack lost her momentum and could no longer be controlled. The two tall masts, now devoid of sail, acted as top-heavy weights, making the boat roll even more erratically. One minute the port rail was several feet under the water, the next the starboard rail was submerged as she wallowed helplessly in the storm.

The crew on deck were exhausted, cold and soaked through with seawater and driving rain. Apart from a few ship's biscuits, no one had eaten anything for more than a day. They all knew how serious things were, although no one wanted to be the first to say so. Even if they had, time had long past when their shouting voices could have been heard above the roar of the wind and the thunder of the waves pounding the deck.

In his time as a fisherman, James had often contrasted being at sea in heavy weather with the gentle greenness of the family croft back home. A greater contrast could not be imagined, but he liked both. When at home he yearned to be back at sea, but tonight, as towering seas rose out of the pitch-black night sky, and as the wind screamed all around, James wished as never before that he was back at Pund, the small croft where he grew up. It is a magical place, nestling right by the shore on the west side of a narrow ridge of land known as Whiteness. All the crofts at Whiteness are on the east side of the ridge except for Pund, which sits by itself facing west. A narrow, almost enclosed finger of sea called Strom Voe runs north from the croft. Unlike most of Shetland's exposed coastline, the sea in this voe never gets rough. This was the secluded, sheltered and idyllic place where the Smith family were raised.

All the Pund children had to do their share of work on the croft, tending to the animals and looking after the limited crops that were grown. But James's real interest was in boats and the sea. Below the croft house is a stone beach, perfect for hauling small boats up and down. Every spare minute that he had was spent with his four brothers in the family boat, in the shelter of Strom Voe, before gradually venturing into more open waters when he was older. As soon as he left school, he became a fisherman, as did his four brothers. Like many men from Whiteness, they found berths on board the growing fleet of cod smacks. His oldest brother, John Smith, became skipper of the *Anaconda* at a young age. As the next oldest, James wanted to emulate his brother's success. He was ambitious. The four brothers, close in age, were regularly competing, but for James there was something more that drove him. Always wanting to be the best, he was strong-willed, sharp-witted and a good seaman. He was confident that he could be as good a smack skipper as his brother – better, in fact.

This ambition and determination, while central to his character, did not always define him. He could be easy-going and he had a sense of humour. Before he spoke, the relaxed twinkle in his light blue eyes would often preface a funny remark – sometimes at his own expense. Whenever he needed to concentrate on a task at hand, however, his demeanour would suddenly change, as his eyes became intensely focused. Always precise in his approach, whether it was catching a sheep on the croft or setting a course on his smack, everyone knew they could rely on him. His blue eyes and high cheek bones were typical of all the Smiths from Pund, as was his dark hair. James had that heady mix of Scandinavian and Scottish genes that characterises so many Shetland families.

After several years sailing as a fisherman on board different smacks, he managed to get a job as mate for a couple of years. In 1877, when he was 27 years old, he got the break he was looking for: one of the islands' most successful cod merchants, Joseph Leask, offered him the job of skippering the *Telegraph*. She was one of the company's largest smacks, carrying a crew of 14. James had been keen to prove himself and he went on to land a bumper catch of cod that year, making her one of the best-fished boats in the fleet. Joseph Leask was happy – his cod smack was making money, confirming that his choice of the young skipper had been a good one.

It was now early September 1878 and James had almost finished his second year in command of the *Telegraph*. They were fishing off northeast Iceland on their last trip of the year. The first two trips had been successful, and he once again had a good catch of cod salted down in the hold. Preparations were being made to set sail for home when word came that another Shetland smack, the *Gondola*, had dragged her anchor and was stranded on a beach. All the crew were safe, but it looked as if the smack would be a total loss. The decision was taken to leave the skipper and two deckhands in Iceland until the owners decided what to do with the wreck, but eight crewmembers asked if they could get back home with the *Telegraph*. James readily agreed. Taking extra food and fresh water on board, they were intending to leave Iceland along with two other smacks owned by Joseph Leask, the *Novice* and the *Destiny*. The smacks owned by the same owner generally fished alongside each other and, if possible, always tried to make the passage home together.

As the crew made ready for their long voyage, the wind had started to pick up and James wondered if the weather was set to deteriorate. There were no weather forecasts, so it was the skipper's observation and experience that determined if a vessel would sail. Black clouds were starting to form in the southwest, a sure sign of worsening weather. But he was torn between this concern and the desire of everyone to leave as soon possible. At the end of a long trip there was always a lot of pressure on a skipper to get home. The crew were tired, and they had all had enough of living and working in a cramped, damp boat for weeks on end. To delay sailing would be unpopular, to say the least, and the skippers of the other two smacks had already told James that they were going to head for home. To stay in Iceland until the weather was more settled, when the other company smacks had left, would be unthinkable. So, he took the only decision that appeared open to him – they would sail for Shetland as well. At least he had plenty of crew, he thought, should he need more men on watch. With the eight from the *Gondola*, there was now a total of 22 men on board.

The crew of the *Telegraph* had worked well together during the season, catching a lot of cod, so everyone was looking forward to a decent pay at the end of this trip. There had, however, been one last-minute change to the crew. Just before leaving home, the second mate had turned ill. One of the skipper's younger brothers, Henry, was taken on as his replacement. He was only 24 years old. The distant-water smacks were generally skippered and crewed by young men, and the *Telegraph* was no exception. Most of the crew were teenagers and only one was married. The Smith brothers, James and Henry, were the oldest on board.

When the three smacks left Iceland on the morning of Saturday 14 September, a strong wind from the southwest was already blowing. As some of his earlier concerns about the weather returned, James reminded himself that they had all sailed through worse, many times before. The sails were fully reefed* and everything on deck was tied down and made secure in preparation for a rough passage. As night came down, the

---

* A method of reducing the sail area, essential in strong winds.

Telegraph plunged through an increasingly angry sea. When daylight broke the next morning, it was clear that conditions had deteriorated. The wind had increased during the night and had now reached storm force with the seas becoming ever more threatening. Visibility was so poor that the *Destiny* and *Novice* could no longer be seen. Heavy rain and endless spray meant that the men on deck were constantly soaked through. As one watch replaced another, the cramped conditions below deck soon became a chaotic scene of discarded wet clothing as the worn-out crew tried to get some rest in the damp berths. Rest might have been possible, but sleep was out of the question. As the salt water slowly dried on their faces, turning them white, the teenage crew looked like terrified old men.

There was no abatement as the day wore on. The smack dived violently into the depths of the troughs between the waves before slowly managing to lift her bow up on the next wave. She was sitting so heavy in the water with her large cargo of salt cod that it sometimes felt as if she did not have enough buoyancy to defy the gravitational pull of the ocean. The *Robert Kirkwood*, one of the smacks belonging to another fishing company, was sighted in the distance. While it may have been of some comfort to both crews to know that another smack was at hand, this comfort was illusory as there was nothing any one vessel could do to help another in such terrible conditions. With darkness falling on the second night, it was plain that both smacks were now at the mercy of a hurricane, the like of which neither skipper had seen before. By this time, they were well south of Iceland and, with no shelter near at hand, they had no alternative but to keep going until the weather improved.

The storm was at its fiercest around midnight. Although a gale was still blowing when dawn came, the worst had passed. The skipper of the *Robert Kirkwood* saw no sign of the *Telegraph* that morning but did not think anything of it. Just as the two smacks had come in sight of each other the day before, so two smacks could easily lose sight of each other during the night. As the weather slowly improved, the crew of the *Robert Kirkwood* were able to raise more sail and begin to make better speed on their way back to Shetland. When they arrived in Scalloway, they were surprised that there was no sign of the *Telegraph*. The other two smacks belonging to Joseph Leask, which had left Iceland at the same time, had made it back safely, although both had suffered damage to their bulwarks and rigging.

As the crews of the smacks went about their work that day, they found themselves regularly looking westward, willing the *Telegraph* to appear among the isles at the entrance to the harbour. Despite the ferocity of the storm, they reassured themselves that James Smith was an able skipper, with a good crew and a large smack. But she never came that day, nor the day after. As time went on, worry was replaced by concern, before anxiety finally took over. It was an agonising time for everyone but none more so than for the families of the crew. Hope is difficult to extinguish; sometimes it is all that people have left. But, as each day passed, the reality of the situation eventually stole what little hope remained. The families faced the appalling realisation that none of their men were ever going to come home.

It was a double tragedy; the crews of two smacks had been lost. There was much speculation as to what might have happened. Other smaller smacks had survived the severe storm, so something serious must have overcome the *Telegraph* during that second night at sea. With her torn sails, she was at the mercy of whatever the North Atlantic could throw at her. It is likely that an exceptionally powerful wave tore off the hatches to the fish hold or accommodation, with the next breaking wave flooding the vessel. She would have immediately developed a list with a catastrophic loss of stability. Until this time, the crew would have hoped that, once the hurricane had passed, they would make safe passage home. When she started to flood, this hope would have been replaced in the blink of an eye with the horrific fact that they were sinking. For these few last confused minutes before she went down, every crewmember would have had his private terror. A dread of drowning, perhaps, maybe a longing for the family he would never see again, or even wishing that this nightmare would all end quickly. Some might have prayed; others may have cried. It would have been a desperate scene. The Smith brothers were on deck together as she started to flood. Looking at James, Henry recalled how, as a child, he had always looked to his older brother to sort out problems and find solutions. For James, the aching realisation that he would never see Pund again was punctuated, not for the first time, with bitter regret at his decision to leave Iceland when he had harboured his private doubts about the weather.

The loss of the *Telegraph* was not an exception. Many smacks were lost at sea as they sailed around the North Atlantic in search of cod. It was a time of one tragedy after another for many fishermen and their families. Despite these losses, the drive to catch cod never lessened. There was money to be made, and it was all the result of an insatiable demand for salt cod in Spain. Why had salt fish become so important?

I

The Dutch and the Basques

Sitting at the desk in my office, I am holding a fillet of dried salt cod. It feels strange, as if I am handling a delicate historical artefact. There is a strong smell of slightly rotten fish, but it isn't decayed in any way – it just has that very strong pungent smell that all cured protein does. This is a smell that we no longer recognise, thanks to the odourless, plastic-covered food we pluck from supermarket shelves. The fillet is stiff but not heavy since most of the moisture has been removed during the drying process. It reminds me of a piece of balsa wood; making the same kind of wooden noise when I gently knock it on my desk. A dusting of salt crystals falls and sparkles white, like winter morning frost in the light that is streaming through the window. This is only a small proportion of the salt, most of it remaining attached to both sides of the fish, forming a crust that has the texture of sandpaper. At last, I decide to find out what it tastes like, tearing a bit away with my teeth. Not surprisingly, the sensation is mostly of salt and only slightly of fish, a flavour that does not change during the long chewing process. This is no subtle eating experience; it is the taste of well-preserved protein.

Amid all the electronic equipment spread around the desk, my fillet of salt cod seems strange and not of our world anymore. It only has historical relevance in the same way as an Iron Age nail might have. And yet, confined to home because of the pandemic, it occurs to me that I cannot eat any of my electronics. In contrast, a piece of salt fish is a meal and, if I had enough stored away, it could keep my family alive for a long time. Most people today have never eaten salt fish; its hard texture, rotten smell and salty taste does not appeal to our modern palate. So used have we become to pasta, blueberries and avocado that it is hard to believe that salt fish was once an essential part of the weekly diet for most people.

Before food could be preserved by freezing, fresh protein could only be eaten for a short time after an animal was killed. Unless the meat and fish could be cured in some way, it would be lost as decay rendered it inedible and eventually dangerous to eat. In medieval societies where hunger was common, and famine not unknown, the rotting of scarce food was a disaster that had to be avoided at all costs. For most people, life was precarious and survival during the winter months depended on how much food it had been possible to preserve. All surplus protein had to be cured. There were two main methods: drying or salting, or some combination of both. Salt fish therefore became an important part of the medieval insurance policy against hunger. Amongst the many kinds of salt fish, two species came to dominate the diet of Europeans before the age of freezing. In northern Europe herring was king, while cod became the queen of the Mediterranean. To successfully cure fish is not easy and the techniques were first discovered by two of Europe's great seafaring nations, the Dutch with herring and the Basques with cod. They both used their newly acquired expertise to build up huge fishing and trading enterprises that fed much of Europe.

***

Herring are a shoaling species that often swim very close to shore, which means that very large quantities can be caught even when using the most primitive of nets. It is also an exceptionally oily fish that deteriorates very quickly. This combination of large catches and rapid spoilage meant that an effective preservation technique was vital in order to make best use of the fish – in far too many cases, the largest proportion of a bumper catch would have to be used for fertiliser once everyone in the locality had eaten all the fresh herring that they could. Many people had tried salting herring, but it was a Dutchman, Willem Beukels, who is credited with perfecting the technique in the late 15th century. Previous attempts to preserve herring had involved taking out all the fish intestines before adding salt. This seemed the obvious thing to do as fish start spoiling in the gut before spreading to the flesh. It was therefore somewhat counter-intuitive that Beukels only took out some of the internal organs, leaving the liver and pancreas in the gut cavity. By doing so, he discovered that the salted herring tasted much better and, crucially, could be kept for up to a year. It is now known that the liver and pancreas release important enzymes that are essential to the curing process.

Having discovered the secret of preserving herring, the Dutch saw a business opportunity and wondered how they could best realise the potential of catching and salting herring. The answer was the herring buss, a two-masted, decked boat that was able to venture far out into the North Sea, where it was possible to catch larger quantities of herring in drift nets that were set each night. It was a very wide vessel with plenty of space below decks for gutting and salting the herring. A buss would remain at sea, catching and processing, until its hold was full of barrels of salt herring. This could often take months. By the early 16th century, a fleet of more than a thousand busses fished throughout the North Sea, with the fishing grounds east of Shetland being particularly important during July and August. Once they had fully supplied their domestic market, the Dutch looked eastwards, towards Germany, Poland and Russia, where there was a huge demand for cured fish. Before long, a barrel of salt herring became an essential source of protein for most households in eastern Europe during the long cold winters that swept in from Siberia.

The Dutch had a monopoly of the salt herring trade for a long time. Huge profits were made, and this partly accounted for the period of prosperity associated with the Dutch Golden Age. Shetlanders used to say that the building of Amsterdam was financed by the catching of herring 20 miles east of Lerwick. Undoubtedly an exaggeration, but, like all hyperbole, there may have been a kernel of truth buried somewhere. By the early 19th century, the Dutch monopoly was being challenged by Scotland and Norway. These two newcomers copied the Dutch model, apart from one very important difference: instead of curing the herring on board, the Scottish and Norwegian fleets landed their catch to curing yards, where thousands of women gutted and packed the herring into barrels. This made sense as they were fishing their own herring stocks near the coast. For the Dutch, who sent their busses to the other end of the North Sea, onshore curing was never a possibility.

Most of the salt herring from Scotland and Norway was also exported to eastern Europe. In the period before the outbreak of the First World War it is estimated that upwards of two million barrels were shipped every year from Scotland to Baltic ports. An extensive transport network was developed from these ports to thousands of small villages and towns throughout Germany, Poland and Russia. The distances involved were vast, particularly in the Russian steppe. Before the age of railroads, salt herring could only be transported if there was snow, the barrels being carried on horse-drawn sleighs. In those years when the snows came late, this distribution network collapsed. For as long as these so-called 'green winters' lasted, barrels of salt herring were stuck in the Baltic ports, while the rural population, many miles from the sea, went hungry.

Herring was not only eaten in eastern Europe; it was also a popular food throughout the north of Europe. Eaten several times a week, it became an integral part of the culture and diet of many countries. In Scandinavia, salt herring is used to make *sursild*, a type of pickled herring that is eaten raw. It is still popular, with the *sursild* option remaining part of the breakfast buffet in most Scandinavian hotels. In the Netherlands, while many types of preserved herring are eaten, the favourite is *maatjes*. This is a herring that is very fat and has only been cured in salt for a few days. The word *maatje* comes from the Dutch word for 'virgin' (*maagd*), presumably named since these are the young herring caught at the beginning of the summer. Like *sursild*, *maatjes* are eaten raw. Preparation is very simple: the head, guts and spine are removed, leaving two herring fillets still joined by the tail. If you are Dutch, there is only one way to eat this: you hold the fish firmly by the tail, tilt your head back and slowly lower the raw fillets into your mouth. Two important things to remember: don't eat the tail and finish with a long cool beer. This very Dutch custom can still be seen at the many *maatje* festivals throughout the Netherlands every June.

In Scotland, the culinary tradition was much more basic, with salt herring being boiled (with the water being changed several times to remove most of the salt) and then eaten with potatoes; a staple meal at one time around the Scottish coast. We had salt herring for dinner every Saturday when I was a boy, a custom that was common in the fishing village where I grew up. Salt herring was a cheap source of protein that was eaten extensively throughout Scotland during the 19th century. Aberdeen University students who came from the coastal towns and villages around the Scottish north coast took a barrel of salt herring with them at the start of each term. Since salt herring was inexpensive, buying a barrel made a lot of sense for those families, who were already financially stretched to cover the cost of university fees and lodgings.

Herring is still the most popular fish eaten in eastern Europe. It is now rarely salted, being sold as frozen or canned instead.

The days of a barrel of salt herring in the home of peasants have long gone. But centuries of eating salt herring have left a cultural imprint and it is still eaten in the most unexpected of places, including Israel. Most Jews living in Poland and Russia up until the First World War stayed in the almost exclusive Jewish villages called *shtetls*, which were very traditional communities and highly orthodox when it came to matters of faith. Like most of eastern Europe at the time, salt herring had become an indispensable part of their diet, with a variety of pickled herring dishes being served at the many Jewish festivals. Herring came to feature heavily in the weekly pre-Sabbath dinner every Friday night. The *shtetls* have now disappeared, but the legacy of Jewish pickled herring continues in Israel. Although herring is not a fish that was ever eaten in the Middle East, some Israeli companies now import frozen herring, which they then salt to produce the pickled herring dishes for those recent immigrants from Russia who have taken their salt herring cuisine with them.

***

Turning south, salt cod became the staple of the Mediterranean diet. Cod is a very different fish from herring. It lives longer and grows much larger. It is said that a cod will eat any fish that is smaller than itself, something that can be attested by anyone who has gutted a cod and seen the eclectic range of species in its stomach. This penchant for eating anything is entirely different from herring, which eats nothing but plankton. The flesh of a cod is virtually fat-free. All the fat needed by cod is contained within the liver, unlike herring where the fat runs freely throughout the fish. When eaten fresh, herring is extremely oily, while cod has a much drier taste. This lack of fat in the cod flesh means that, when cured, it can be kept for much longer than salt herring. There are recorded cases of dried salt cod lying forgotten for decades being found again and eaten, apparently tasting as good as the day it was first cured.

The first people to preserve cod were the Vikings. The cold, dry air of a Norwegian winter is ideal for drying cod without salt. Known as *stockfisk*, it allowed the Vikings to eat cod many months after it had been caught, and it was an ideal food to take on a long sea voyage, enabling them to range across the North Atlantic in their longships. While it can keep for many months, *stockfisk* does not cure as well as cod that has been salted before it is dried. The Vikings simply did not have enough salt to develop the dried salt cod cure. Another seafaring people, the Basques, living at the opposite end of Europe, did however have access to plentiful supplies of good quality salt. This, together with their early discovery of the Grand Banks fishing grounds near Newfoundland, led to salt cod being produced in the Basque region before anywhere else in Europe.

The Basque fishermen first caught cod off Newfoundland during the 16th century. Some argue that they were even fishing there before Columbus discovered America. Such was the unbelievable productivity of the Grand Banks that they kept its location secret. You did not want other fishermen sharing your good fortune, and for a long time no one knew where the Basques caught their cod. They also perfected the technique of splitting and salting cod on board their ships. On returning to the Basque country, these salt cod were unloaded and laid out in the sun to dry, and thus the dried salt cod product was invented. Once salted and properly dried, it is almost entirely protein. Simple to store, easy to transport and cheap to buy, it became an essential guarantee against hunger in the same way as salt herring had done in northern Europe.

The Basques, with their secret fishing grounds and their effective way of curing cod, had a head start over the rest of Europe. Producing more than they needed themselves, they began to export salt cod to the rest of Spain as well as to Portugal and Italy. This market then got an unexpected boost from an unusual source, when the Roman Catholic Church redefined fasting days as days when you should not eat meat, as opposed to not eating at all. The readily available alternative to meat was salt cod. For obvious reasons, there was a much greater observance of this meat-free exhortation than there ever had been for complete fasting. Encouraged, the Church began to increase the number of meat-free days and, before long, every Friday, the 40 days of Lent, the four weeks of Advent and many other religious holidays were all included. This amounted to almost half the year, ensuring that salt cod became firmly embedded in Mediterranean cuisine.

According to Mark Kurlansky, who has written extensively about the Basques and their obsession with salt cod, this unique community has the most highly developed salt cod cuisine in the world. For many people, the Basques are those Spaniards who live in a coastal province of northern Spain. But the Basques would be profoundly offended by such a notion since they do not regard themselves as Spanish at all. Their language, Euskera, sounds strange to our ears and looks very different, with what appears to be an excessive use of 'k's and 'x's. It is unrelated to any other European language, and linguists believe it to be a very ancient tongue, prompting speculation that the Basques have been in Europe longer than any other people. They have a fiercely independent and vibrant culture that is, to a large extent, defined by their fishing and maritime tradition. The Basques are said to be as much at home on the sea as they are on the land, and their seafaring skills have always been in demand by the Spanish Crown. So much so, that a large proportion of the crews on board the Spanish Armada were from the Basque country.

As would be expected from a people with such a maritime tradition, the preparation, cooking and eating of salt cod is central to their identity. At one time, salt cod was a basic food but, by the 19th century, it was being used to create elegant dishes served in the finest of restaurants. For these recipes, only the best part of the dried salt cod is used: the *lomo*, which is the succulent centre cut taken from the head rather than the tail of the cod fillet. 'Bacalao a la Vizcaína' is the most famous of all these dishes. The starting point is to soak the salt cod, to remove all the salt. This takes anything from 36 to 44 hours, with the water being changed every eight hours, although the top chefs still argue over what soaking time is best. Vizcaína sauce – a complex mix of onions, choricero green peppers, ham, butter, olive oil and garlic – is then prepared. After poaching pieces of desalinated cod (skin side up) for about five minutes, the Vizcaína sauce is poured on top. The result is a dish that still defines what it means to be Basque.

Demand for salt cod kept growing. The Basques could no longer supply this market by themselves, and it was not long before merchants in Iceland, Norway and Shetland saw the economic opportunity. Based on catching cod in the North Atlantic, a new export trade in salt cod was established. Reaching its peak in the late 19th century, it was based on copying what the Basques had perfected. Every crewman on a cod smack fished with a hand line that had two baited hooks – a simple catching method that was first used on the Grand Banks. The cod were headed, gutted, washed and split on deck before being salted in the hold, again as first done by the Basques. After fishing trips lasting several months, the salt cod was then laid out to dry on stone beaches. The drying process in northern Europe probably owed more to the wind than the sun and took longer than it did in the Basque country, but eventually an acceptable product was produced.

***

As we have become accustomed to our modern world of supermarket shopping, with its 'just in time' supply lines, it is difficult to appreciate just how important salt fish once was in shaping the economies, societies and cultures of much of Europe. Salt herring and salt cod was regularly eaten by millions of people and huge industries were based on catching, curing and selling it. The enormous demand for salt fish brought employment and prosperity to hundreds of small fishing communities dotted around the North Atlantic. In some cases, these settlements would not have existed at all had it not been for the salt fish trade. Almost everyone worked in the salt fish business, and it dominated every aspect of life.

The Icelandic Nobel Prize-winning author, Halldór Laxness, often tackled important philosophical questions in the most ordinary and mundane of settings. His novel *Salka Valka* is a story about a precocious young woman called Salvör Valgerður from the fictional fishing village of Oseyri. Published in 1932, it deals with the very contemporary issues of gender and feminism, subjects that were rarely addressed then. It is also about salt fish. The salt fish trade is the reason why Oseyri exists in the first place, and it is how everyone makes a living. Laxness was not being in the least ironic when he wrote that 'when all is said and done, life is first and foremost about salt fish'. He was simply, in his direct manner, explaining how it is, or at least how it was, for a long time in many Icelandic villages.

The tradition of eating salt fish has now almost disappeared. Even in places like Iceland, Norway and Shetland, younger people rarely eat it. I was part of that last generation of Shetlanders who grew up eating salt fish several times a week. People often ask me if I liked it. It is probably the wrong question. It was dinner and there was no alternative. Salt fish remains hard and salty, no matter how long it is boiled. But with potatoes and melted butter it is good, and I still eat it from time to time. The salt fish fare of my Shetland childhood, however, was nothing like the elaborate and complex salt cod dishes still eaten by the Spanish and Portuguese. Known as *bacalao* in Spain and *bacalhau* in Portugal, this is a cuisine which has spawned hundreds of recipes.

Salt herring and salt cod are very different eating experiences, and I sometimes wonder if the dishes have taken on the different characteristics of the Dutch and the Basques. Herring is a matter-of-fact fish, usually eaten as a snack or as a starter; it never features as a main course. Its predictable taste and texture appeal to the Germanic and Slavic peoples. Perhaps salt herring is a bit like the Dutch themselves – dependable, predictable, getting on with life without making a fuss but always making money. In dramatic contrast, *bacalao*, which is served as an elaborate and extrovert main course, is distinctively Basque. The many and varied *bacalao* dishes are so much more than food; they are a metaphor for the Basque culture in their uniqueness and individuality. A dinner of *bacalao* is usually eaten by extended family groups late into the evening, along with bottles of full-bodied merlot wine. It is a noisy and sociable affair quite unlike the eating of herring, which is often a solitary experience, undertaken seriously and quietly with a glass of cold beer.

Diana Feliciano is a postgraduate student from Portugal. As she explains in her faultless English how she has come to study at Aberdeen, I guess that she misses the Mediterranean sun, particularly during the cold, dark Scottish winters. When I told her that I was visiting the university to undertake some research on the salt cod trade, I was surprised by Diana's reaction – salt cod is, after all, not to everyone's taste, either as a foodstuff or as a topic of conversation. However, her brown eyes lit up as she told me that she always brought salt cod with her to Aberdeen so she could make *bacalhau*. It was impossible for her not to eat *bacalhau* every few weeks, she explained – it was the Portuguese national dish and central to her culture. Most of all, it reminded her of many happy family celebrations back home. Some of her university friends had initially regarded her liking for salt cod as rather exotic, while others thought it downright strange. But that all changed after she treated them to Portuguese *bacalhau* cooking. As far as she knew, she was the only student who had ever come to study at Aberdeen University with her personal supply of salt fish. The link between Aberdeen University and salt fish goes back a long way, I explained, telling her about the Scottish students who used to arrive with their barrels of salt herring.

The salt fish saga involved many communities, and their stories are often similar. This book is primarily about Shetland and how salt fish came to dominate life in, and shape the culture of, the islands for hundreds of years. During this time Shetlanders would have regarded Halldór Laxness's observation that 'life is first and foremost about salt fish' as simply stating the obvious. Shetland has had an enduring relationship with both salt cod and salt herring. This is the story of how and why Shetlanders first embraced queen cod then abandoned her in favour of king herring. Shetland's adventure with cod began in 1818 with a dramatic chase to the cod fishing grounds and a failed attempt to keep the location secret.

2

The Great Cod Race

In January 1818, William Thomson was approached by a merchant who had an idea for a new fishing business. His plan was to convert his cargo vessel, the *Don Cossack*, into a fishing boat to catch cod. To begin with, Thomson was sceptical, thinking that this was a half-baked idea, apparently based on a chance catch of cod in the previous year. He was, by nature, a pessimist. He was dour and had a morose sense of humour. Rarely smiling, his gloomy disposition suited his dark features. In Shetland someone with dark hair, brown eyes and a swarthy complexion is often said to be 'dark advised'. Being dark advised does not mean you are also taciturn, but in Thomson's case it did. On the face of it, he did not seem to be the natural partner for a pioneering fishing venture. But the merchant needed an experienced fisherman and skilled seaman, and Thomson was both. Despite his initial scepticism, the offer of an attractive profit share and the position of skipper eventually clinched the deal.

By early April, the *Don Cossack* set off from Weisdale for her first fishing trip. It was a disaster; they only caught four cod despite being at sea for almost a week. The disheartened crew set sail again on 28 April. For the first few days, poor weather prevented fishing. It was a typical Shetland April; not enough wind to abandon the fishing trip and sail home, but far too much for fishing. By the time the wind had eased, a dense fog had descended. The crew was barely able to see the stern from the bow, and the fog also deadened all sound aboard. Their muffled voices contrasted with the shrill screeching of seabirds all around. Hearing, but not seeing the birds, added to the strangeness of the day. It was as if a shroud had enveloped them. There was a sombre mood aboard as the skipper told the crew to bait their hand lines and lower them to the seabed.

Many of Thomson's earlier misgivings returned. Blaming himself for being far too gullible, he was now convinced that he should not have listened to all this nonsense about cod. Who in their right mind could imagine ever catching cod around Shetland? Shetlanders caught mostly ling and tusk with their open boats, and sometimes a few herring. Although he was aware of the stories of the Basques catching cod on the Grand Banks, it was madness, he concluded, to think there could ever be a cod fishery around the islands. He was suddenly shaken out of his pessimism as one crewmember after another shouted that they had fish on their lines. Everyone on board was soon lifting two large struggling cod on board. Looking at each other in astonishment, they quickly rebaited their two hook lines and lowered them back down. The lines did not even get near the seabed this time before the cod struck again and every crewmember was soon hauling another two large cod to the surface. This went on all day and by early evening the crew's initial excitement had turned to exhaustion. They eventually had to stop fishing, not because they were tired, but because they had run out of bait. More than a thousand cod had been caught. In marked contrast, catching 200 ling was regarded as very good for a trip with an open boat. Catching a thousand fish in a day was unheard of.

At some stage, the fog had lifted, although hardly anyone had noticed; there is nothing in the world more focused than a fisher catching fish. As they set sail to return home, spirits were high. Following a dinner of fresh cod, those not on watch could look forward to a few hours' sleep. Thomson was able to confirm that this new fishing ground was around 36 miles southwest from Foula, an area now known as the Papa Bank. As they sailed back, he wondered if it was possible that the cod shoal would still be there when he returned.

Upon arrival at Weisdale Voe, as the crew made ready to drop the anchor, a group of old men and young boys gathered on the stone beach. These were the merchant's employees. Some of them launched a small rowing boat and began to transfer the catch ashore, where the others started splitting and salting the cod. The crew took on board more provisions and water and were ready to sail again within a few hours. Just in case there were still some cod left to be caught, the skipper decided to take more bait than last time. But as this was being loaded on board, he wondered if he was being too presumptuous in assuming the cod would still be there when he returned. Pessimism once more took hold of Thomson, as he began to think that his reward for such over-confidence would be no cod. Expecting the worst, he gave the order to weigh the anchor and set sail.

But the cod were still there when he returned and were as voracious as before. This time, the crew caught over 1,400 cod before running out of bait again. Returning to land his second record-breaking catch, Thomson made a mental note to take on even more bait before he sailed again. He could not believe his good luck. In less than a week he had made two huge landings of cod and was already making plans for a third trip. A moderate southerly wind was allowing good speed to be made and, if it held, it would ensure a quick return to the fishing grounds. It was every skipper's dream, Thomson reflected as he steered ashore; good fishing and fair weather with the prospect of money to be made for both the owner and the crew. He now knew exactly where to catch these cod and he was beginning to regard this fishing bank as his personal property. The quicker he could land this trip and get back to sea, the sooner he would be back

fishing again. As the watches changed, and as the mate relieved
the skipper at the tiller, he thought he detected the faintest of
smiles flit briefly across Thomson's face, but he could not be sure.

However, tales of good fishing are difficult to keep secret in
Shetland. News of the cod bonanza had spread quickly, perhaps unsurprisingly in a community that looked to the sea for
food and opportunity. John Ross, a Weisdale merchant, made
ready two of his vessels and told the skippers to follow the *Don
Cossack* to the fishing grounds. But Thomson had already made
up his mind that he was not going to share his cod shoal with
anyone else if he could help it. Although not realising it, he now
regarded the Papa Bank in the same way as the Basques had
once seen the Grand Banks. He knew the skippers of the other
two boats well, but he was evasive when they asked where he
had been fishing and when he was heading back. Reticent by
nature, he was particularly uncommunicative that day. Hoping
that he could lose his potential competitors during the hours of
darkness, he decided that his best strategy would be to wait until
after sunset before leaving. Although ready to sail by the late
afternoon, the *Don Cossack* remained at anchor. The other two
skippers could not understand why they had not left, but they
had no alternative but to wait as well.

As the sun began to slip into the sea below the western sky,
Thomson suddenly gave orders to haul in the anchor and hoist
the sails. The grinding of the windlass,* as it winched the anchor
chain aboard, and the rustle of the sails unfurling all sounded
much louder than it should have done in the still evening. The
skippers of the other two boats immediately figured out what
was happening and made ready to follow. Before the *Don Cossack*
had reached open water, the night sky had wiped away the last
traces of the fiery sunset. Moonlight shortly afforded some visibility, which allowed Thomson to spend the night scouring the

---

* The nautical term for the winch that is used to haul up an anchor
  chain.

horizon for his potential competitors. Having seen nothing at all, he began to think that his tactic had paid off. But, as the watery light of a new sun rose in the eastern sky around 5 a.m., his heart sank when he saw two sets of sails several miles astern. They were still a long way behind, but he could see them, and that meant that they could see the *Don Cossack*. It was now clear that he was going to have to share his good fortune with others.

The abundance of cod southwest of Foula prompted much interest and there was no shortage of merchants and fishermen keen to take advantage of this new opportunity. Several more vessels joined the *Don Cossack* for the remainder of that year. The following year, 24 cod sloops (as these early decked cod vessels became known) took part in the fishery. These sloops, crewed by eight men, soon established the seasonal pattern that came to characterise this fishery: starting fishing at the end of April, they continued until the end of August, making trips lasting up to a week. Catches were variable but a successful sloop could expect to catch around 1,500 fish most weeks. Although the *Don Cossack* had landed her first catches fresh, it soon became standard practice to gut the fish and remove the heads, before splitting and salting the cod on board, just as the Basques had done. These salt cod were then landed at stone beaches where they were laid out to dry in the wind and sun. As this new fishery developed, these fishing grounds to the southwest of Foula became known as the Home Grounds.

***

This new opportunity provided an alternative to the traditional haaf* fishing, which had been the mainstay of the Shetland economy for more than a hundred years. Small open boats, called sixerns, set long lines on the seabed for ling, tusk and saithe. To the northwest of Shetland they fished at the edge of

---

* An old Norse word meaning 'the open sea'.

the continental shelf, around 30 miles distant. Crewed by six men and a skipper, the sixerns were operated from fishing stations, located where there was an extensive area of stone beach suitable for both drying the salt fish and hauling up and down the boats. Each fishing trip took around 24 hours, after which the catch was cleaned and salted then laid out to dry before being sold to buyers in Great Britain and Ireland. The haaf season was short, lasting from the middle of May to the middle of August. Before May, the weather was never stable or settled enough for the sixerns to fish. After August, there was not enough time to get the salt fish properly dried before the Shetland winter of endless rain and gales set in.

Everything was controlled by the landowners, who were known as lairds. They supervised the fishery, organised the curing of the fish on the beaches and handled all the exports. They also provided credit from their stores so that the fishermen and their families could obtain the essentials of life, paying at the end of the fishing season. Money rarely changed hands in this barter system, known as truck, which was designed to favour the lairds rather than the fishermen. This was the Shetland variant of debt bondage, a pernicious form of exploitation, once found all over the world, that provided an illusion of independence within the reality of perpetual debt.

Central to this system was land tenure. A crofter was only allowed to keep the tenancy for his small croft if he agreed to fish for the laird. The croft rentals themselves were quite low, but the lairds knew they were not going to make money from the land; it was from fish that they would derive their profits. With the crofters forced to fish for them, there was no competition. The lairds set the price for the catch and for everything that was sold in their stores. Cheap fish and dear goods were the consequence of this monopoly. In most years a crofter's earnings from the haaf were used to clear off debts from the previous year. Although this system of credit provided some security for the crofter fishermen from one year to another, it further bound them into an iniquitous system from which there appeared to be no easy escape. Even though the crofters owned their boats and long lines, they were not free agents; selling their catch privately risked their being evicted from the croft. The business model for the lairds, in contrast, was highly successful. The more crofters that could fish for them, the more money they made. Crofts were therefore sub-divided into even smaller parcels of land, so as to increase the numbers of fishermen. This was responsible for Shetland's population increasing by almost half (from 22,000 to 32,000) between 1800 and 1860.

This laird-tenant relationship in Shetland was very different to what was happening in Scotland. In most of the Highlands and Islands, the lairds were finding that they could make more money from sheep ranching than by collecting rents from impoverished crofters. This led to the Highland Clearances, one of the most shameful episodes in Scottish history, where thousands of Highlanders were cleared from their land to make way for sheep. Although this never happened to any great extent in Shetland, the truck system was no less shameful. The Shetland crofters were desperately poor and continually in debt to the lairds. Fishing from open boats was dangerous and many men lost their lives. Even today in Shetland, the words haaf and truck are synonymous with hardship, tragedy and grinding poverty. The life of a Shetland crofter fishermen was little better than that of a serf.

The crofts, with their unbelievably tiny parcels of land, can still be seen in the Shetland landscape. The ruins of a small croft house surrounded by some greener land is a clue to where the staple crops of hay, oats, potatoes and kale were grown. Beyond these little oases of green, is the brown hill land – miles and miles of heather clinging to a thin covering of soil – that was used for grazing sheep. It is not possible to understand this landscape by only looking at the old field patterns. In fact, it is not really an agricultural landscape at all. These tiny crofts, mostly incapable of sustaining a family throughout the year, were the means of maintaining a large rural population, so that there were enough men to crew the sixerns during the summer months. It was a fish economy.

***

The cod fishery seemed to offer something different. With a longer season and with better catches, some fishermen thought it might be possible to make some money and not just clear off debts from the previous year. Early profits encouraged investment in cod sloops. So much so that, by the mid 1820s, more than 40 boats were fishing for cod every year. Most of these sloops were owned by merchants, but several were owned by their skippers. How could it be that some fishermen, who were desperately poor and often in debt, were able to buy their own boats? Some Shetland fishermen, it seems, had been able to accumulate capital from two unusual sources, both involving seafaring many thousands of miles away.

Many Shetlanders regularly found employment on board the whalers from Hull, Dundee and Peterhead that fished around Greenland. These whalers called along Shetland to complement their crews on their way north. It is estimated that between 600 and 1,000 Shetlanders worked on board these Greenland whalers during the early years of the 19th century. The work was undoubtedly hard, the trips long and the pay poor but, after several years working as a whaler, some money could be saved. This was simply not possible when fishing at the haaf.

At the same time, it is estimated that upwards of 3,000 young Shetland seamen had been forced to serve in the Royal Navy during the Napoleonic Wars. Although the naval pay itself was very poor, in those cases where an enemy ship was captured or destroyed, a bounty was paid to the successful crew. In these circumstances, some sailors managed to return home with large sums of money. It was these enterprising ex-whalers and ex-Royal Navy seamen who were able to buy and skipper their own cod sloops. Around a quarter of the cod sloops were owned by fishermen during the 1820s; the first time that they had ever been able to operate independently of a laird. This was even more remarkable given the prevalence of the oppressive truck system at this time. Perhaps doing the bidding of the lairds was no longer the natural order of things?

It is remarkable just how quickly this new fishery developed. The discovery of the Home Grounds, while obviously crucial, does not by itself explain the explosive growth of the cod business. There were two other critical factors. The first was the opportunity that was presented when the Spanish salt fish market was reopened. For more than two decades Europe had been ravaged by the expensive and destructive Napoleonic Wars. Following the Battle of Waterloo in 1815, the much longed-for peace ushered in a period of political and economic stability. Old trading relationships were re-established, and new export opportunities developed. Shetland merchants took advantage of this and began to export salt cod to Spain. The second factor was a very powerful incentive that came from the most unlikely of sources – a government subsidy.

3

Philadelphia

In 1825 the British government paid £8,411 in subsidies to Shetland fishing companies, worth around £9 million in today's money. This is an astonishing fact given that the 19th century was a time of unbridled capitalism and laissez-faire enterprise, with minimal intervention and even less financial support. What on earth prompted such an unusual intervention by the state?

It was all about herring. For several hundred years, the Dutch had been catching herring off the east coast of England and Scotland, particularly around Shetland. In contrast, Scottish fishermen only caught herring with open boats, returning to shore each day with small catches. As far as Shetland was concerned, the fishery for herring was even smaller and was for the most part at a subsistence level. The government wanted British fishermen to adopt the Dutch method of fishing, with its large busses capable of curing herring on board. They saw how this huge fishery, and the resulting export trade, had made Dutch merchants very rich. And the galling thing was that Britain's imperial rival, the Netherlands, had built up this industry by fishing only a few miles off the British coast.

The catching and curing methods were no longer a Dutch trade secret, and the British were as skilled seafarers as the Dutch, so why had Britain not developed its own herring fishery? This question had perplexed the government for years. Britain was leading the world with its industrial revolution and yet, in terms of the fishing industry, it was seriously lagging behind. The government decided to intervene. Despite providing a variety of financial incentives to encourage a domestic herring fishery throughout the 18th century, there had been limited success. Deciding to up their game, they passed an Act of Parliament in 1808 which they believed would finally persuade British fishermen to start fishing for herring with larger decked boats. An unbelievably generous subsidy would be paid to all decked fishing vessels over 20 tons. The subsidy, which became known as the vessel bounty, was initially set at £3 per ton. Astonishingly there was no stipulation that you had to fish for herring; you only had to have a decked fishing boat to qualify. As the Shetland cod fleet consisted of decked sloops, all were eligible for these bounty payments.

So, as the cod fishery began, there was a subsidy for simply owning a decked sloop. It was a fortuitous set of circumstances that enabled this new fishery to become established very quickly. From 1821 to 1828, it is estimated that the vessel bounty accounted for around 40 per cent of the total earnings of the cod fleet. For someone with capital to invest, this was a gold mine waiting to be exploited. Just by buying a decked vessel and rigging her out for catching cod, an owner was guaranteed a government payment, regardless of how much fish was caught – exactly what was needed to encourage investment in this new fishery.

Although the fleet of sloops were all decked and much larger than the sixerns that fished the haaf, they were not large boats by modern standards. Few would have been more than 15 metres in length, barely large enough to accommodate a crew of eight for a week and to hold a cargo of salt cod. Operating mostly from Scalloway, they provided employment for around 300 fishermen each season. The cod catch was, however, very variable for most of this decade, with large fluctuations from year to year. Unlike most other fish species that live on the seabed, cod tend to form dense shoals. Cod is therefore often caught in large quantities or not at all. The *Don Cossack* had proved this to be the case on her first two trips. In some years good profits were made, but in others the cod fishing was a washout. There seemed to be no pattern – sometimes the cod were on the Home Grounds, and other times not. So, the government subsidy compensated for the unpredictable cod catches in poorer years and boosted profits in good years.

With a bounty payment unrelated to catching performance, pursuit of the subsidy often became the purpose of an investment in a decked vessel. This problem was identified by no less a figure than the Enlightenment economist Adam Smith. In his seminal work, *The Wealth of Nations*, he argued that the weakness of the policy of bounties in relation to the herring fishery was that the vessels were fitted out to qualify for the subsidy rather than to catch fish. Adam Smith was correct – the British never did copy the Dutch herring fishery. Possibly because the herring was much closer to home, it was felt there was no need to invest in herring busses that could remain at sea for months. Perhaps it was also difficult to break the Dutch monopoly of the eastern European market for salt herring. In the case of Shetland, it made more sense to take the subsidy and develop a cod fishery instead.

It was the government's eventual realisation that their policy was flawed that resulted in the subsidy being abolished in 1830. They had persisted with this pointless subsidy for 22 years; surely one of the worst of many examples of governments taking the wrong decision and then sticking with it. As far as Shetland was concerned, however, this mistaken policy had inadvertently helped develop a new cod fishery, which in turn laid the foundations for the large distant-water enterprise that would become so important in the latter half of the 19th century.

With the removal of the subsidy, the cod fishery had to survive without any external support. This was a shock, and it had serious consequences for the Shetland economy. In years where the catch was poor, the sloop owners lost money and the earnings of fishermen were meagre. That by itself would have been difficult enough, but there was worse, far worse, to come.

The sixerns, as undecked boats, had not been eligible for the vessel bounty payments. The withdrawal of this subsidy therefore had no impact on the haaf fishing – it looked set to continue as it always had done. Catches of ling and tusk were always more predictable than cod, and the haaf seemed a safer bet than the highs and lows of fishing for cod. It was anything but.

***

As the sun rose on Monday 16 July 1832, there was not a breath of wind. Some crew on schooners anchored in Lerwick harbour remarked that it was so still that their anchor lines were perfectly reflected in the mirror calm sea. This idyllic summer scene was, however, a cruel preface to the rest of the week; a week that would forever be remembered in Shetland for the greatest ever loss of lives at sea. There had been a forewarning of bad weather to come, but not in Lerwick or anywhere else on the east side of Shetland. An unusually heavy swell had been running off the west side – so heavy, in fact, that most of the sixerns from this area had not gone to sea. A heavy Atlantic swell is often an early indication that there is a severe storm raging in the middle of the Atlantic; a harbinger of serious weather to come. On the east side of Shetland, however, fishermen were unaware of this ominous sign. As they gathered at their many fishing stations, they took the decision to go to sea as normal. There was no reason not to; it was a beautiful morning, one of the best in the whole summer. They usually were able to sail to the haaf fishing grounds but, with no wind at all, they faced a gruelling 30-mile row. Normal practice was to set their baited long lines before midnight, haul early the next day and then, depending on how much they had caught, repeat the process, and return home after a full day and night at sea.

Having reached the fishing grounds, some fishermen noticed the sky in the northwest turning very dark but, as it remained calm without the slightest breath of wind, they thought no more of it. By 11 p.m., most sixerns had shot their lines and the crews were hoping to catch a few hours' rest before they started hauling. The storm struck just before midnight. Storms usually build slowly, with the wind gradually increasing over a few hours or even most of a day. But gales from the north and northwest can be very different, with no warning before the wind is unexpectedly raging all around. Within minutes, the late evening calm had been replaced by a screeching wind that was turning the sea into a maelstrom of breaking waves. Writing many years afterwards John Davidson from Unst recalled that 'the wind did not come with a howl but with a scream'. At the same time the air temperature must have dropped by many degrees as a violent hail shower erupted out of nowhere. Fishermen looked at each other in disbelief as the unnaturally large hailstones stung their faces. Breaking seas and hail began to fill the boats.

By now the wind had reached gale force and it was clear that the entire sixern fleet was in peril. In the chaos, a pattern of sorts emerged on board each boat with four men pulling at their oars, desperately keeping the bow pointing into the wind, thereby reducing the risk of a wave breaking aboard and sinking them, while the other two bailed constantly. It was exhausting work, but they kept going in the hope that the wind would eventually ease. This strategy was based on their experience of summer gales that usually lasted no more than a day and sometimes only a few hours. They were not to know that this was no ordinary summer gale. Breaking all the rules, it would rage until Saturday evening. For five long days and nights this fleet of fragile open boats, mostly no more than nine metres in length, were entirely at the mercy of something we would now describe as a hundred-year storm.

The sixern is a classic boat type that is found all around the North Atlantic, from Norway in the east to Iceland in the west. She varies only in detail between each place, and all can trace their origins back to the classic Viking longship. Fast under sail, she can also be rowed very effectively when there is no wind. She is large enough to fish a long way from land but small enough to be hauled on a beach. But, whatever her qualities, an open boat cannot survive a fierce gale for long. Reflecting on the unsuitability of open boats in a storm, the Icelandic author Jón Kalman Stefánsson chillingly describes the Icelandic sixerns as 'open cockleshells the size of a coffin'.

By Tuesday morning the crews were exhausted; they had rowed and bailed all night without rest. Hungry, cold and soaking wet, everyone was worn out. Instead of easing, the wind was getting worse, with even more water breaking on board. Such was the ferocity of the storm that some of the schooners in the shelter of Lerwick harbour had started to drag their anchors. No one held out any hope for the sixern fleet. Over the next few days, boat after boat was sunk. Some were swamped by breaking seas on the first day, others managed to keep their heads to wind for longer. This required a superhuman effort on the oars, but eventually most crews reached the limits of their endurance and these sixerns were also lost. It was ultimately hopeless, and it seemed that the best a sixern crew could do was temporarily postpone drowning in exchange for a few more hours of utter terror. It was a brutal choice.

Some 17 sixerns were sunk with a loss of 105 men. It was astonishing that it was not much more. Against the odds, some crews managed to get their sixerns ashore. By this time these men were so fatigued that they were unable to step out of their boat onto the beach, having to wait until they were lifted out. Several crews were saved by Dutch herring busses that were riding out the storm on their favourite herring grounds east of Shetland. The gale drove many sixerns into the middle of this large herring fleet. Hendrick van Rossen saved George Gilbertson and his crew from Whalsay, while Jacob Don rescued Magnus Leask and his crew from Bressay. In all, 12 crews were plucked from their sinking sixerns by some astonishing seamanship by these and other Dutch skippers. The most spectacular rescue of all was when Jan van Duren managed to save James Robertson of Lerwick, who was clinging to the keel of his capsized sixern, the other crewmembers having perished some hours earlier.

It was only after the end of the storm, as these Dutch busses came into Lerwick with the survivors on board, that the potential death toll started to reduce. The final numbers were catastrophic, but had it not been for the Dutch herring fleet, upwards of 200 men might have been lost. Many families had lost their only breadwinner and some widows and orphans found themselves in a desperate situation. Life, which had been difficult and hard at the best of times, suddenly became impossible for these families. Despite this, some of the lairds insisted that the lost fishing lines, which had been bought on credit, were still charged to the widows' accounts at the stores. The tragedy was widely reported in the British press, and a rich and well-connected Shetlander in London, Arthur Anderson, organised a successful fund-raising campaign, which undoubtedly saved many from destitution. It was a terrible time, and, in an unbelievable example of detached Victorian prose, the appalling situation was summarised by a local minister, the Reverend Watson, when he wrote that 'the grievous catastrophe of 1832 seems greatly to have dampened the spirit of our fishermen'.

One of the sixerns that had been thought lost with all hands was from the island of Whalsay. Today this island is home to one of the most modern fishing fleets in Europe, but in the early 19th century it was just one of many poor Shetland communities trying to eke a living from the sea. Tammy Hughson and his crew – including his two sons, Willie and Lowrie – were tired by the time they had rowed to the fishing grounds and shot their lines. Remarking about the abnormal calm that surrounded them, the skipper was concerned about how warm it was. He felt uneasy; it was never calm and warm like this when you were

30 miles east of Shetland in a boat. With the sudden onset of the storm at midnight, the crew immediately knew what had to be done: four men hauled on oars to keep their head to wind while the other two furiously bailed. It was hard work, with no time to rest or eat. Within minutes every man was soaked through. Hour by hour this continued, as Tuesday morning became Tuesday evening. A combination of sheer terror and a determination to hang onto life fuelled a superhuman effort to keep their boat afloat. But eventually the fuel runs out. By Wednesday morning serious exhaustion had set in and the crew had reached the point of giving up and allowing the sixern to run before the storm, in the certain knowledge that she would broach, fill with water and sink. It was then that they saw a large sailing barque in the distance.

This was the *Edwards*, a Danish ship on her way to America with emigrants on board. Summoning their last reserves of energy, Hughson's crew rowed towards the barque. The captain of the *Edwards* had seen them, and he was able to steer his ship into the wind, allowing the Whalsay boat to come close behind her lee quarter. A rope was made fast to hold her in position while a Jacob's ladder* was thrown over the side. The seas were so mountainous that one minute the sixern was level with the deck of the *Edwards*, and the next it was down at her keel. It was almost impossible to get hold of, let alone climb up, the Jacob's ladder. Ropes were then lowered to haul the crew on board the barque one by one. For some reason one of the crew, Davie Henderson, failed to properly secure the rope to himself. Whether he thought he still had the strength to hold on or, as was more likely, his mind had become addled through exposure and fatigue, he lost his grip and fell to his death into the raging seas.

Once on board, the crew were carried below decks where they were revived with dry clothes, food and brandy. Tammy

---

*   The nautical term for a rope ladder with wooden rungs.

Hughson asked if there was any chance that they could be put ashore in Lerwick. The captain explained that it would take him several days tacking into the storm to reach Lerwick and he was therefore going to maintain his course to pass between Orkney and Shetland on his way to Philadelphia.

By the time they had arrived in America the Shetlanders had fully recovered and were anxious to get back home as soon as they could. But that was not going to be easy; they had no money, and their only possessions were the clothes they were wearing. A Quaker church managed to secure some accommodation and work for them while they waited to see if the British Consul could get them home. Eventually securring a passage on a ship bound for Liverpool, they arrived in late December. After making their way to Leith, they boarded the *George Canning*, which was scheduled to arrive in Lerwick on Christmas morning, which in Shetland fell on Saturday 5 January.[*] Arriving safely in Lerwick harbour that morning, there was incredility that this crew, thought lost in the July gale, had survived. Anxious to return to their families, they tried to arrange a lift with a Lerwick sixern. This was not easy as it was Christmas morning and permission had to be sought from the Church before they could leave.

That same morning on Whalsay, the skipper's old dog, which had pined for her master for the past six months, had become restless and agitated when let out of the barn by the skipper's widow, Charlotte Kay. She had lost her husband and two sons in the gale and was struggling to make a living from their small croft for her seven remaining children. Although there was talk of a relief fund, she had not yet received a penny. The dog set off

[*] At this time, many parts of Scotland still observed the Julian calendar, according to which Christmas Day was on January 5. Recalling the celebration of Christmas on this day remains in the living memory of some old Shetlanders. The islanders of Foula, one of Shetland's more remote communities, continue to celebrate Christmas on 5 January. It is known as Aald Yule.

running to the south, away from the Hughson croft. Charlotte sent two of the younger boys to fetch her back, thinking she had more than enough to cope with on that bleak Christmas morning without an unruly dog. After a long chase over rough ground the two Hughson brothers eventually caught up with the dog. She was running back and forth on a beach, barking at a sixern that was slowly approaching. A small crowd had gathered, having already seen the boat in the distance. No one could think of any good reason why a sixern would have been sailing to Whalsay on Christmas morning.

And then the impossible happened. The entire island had spent six months grieving for the crew and now here they were stepping ashore. Disbelief and shock must have been only two of the emotions experienced by everyone on the beach. These were men who they believed had drowned last July. As word went around the island, and as each man was reunited with his family, there was unbridled joy that was only tempered when Davie Henderson's widow, Merran Shearer, arrived to ask how her husband had met his end.

A few weeks after they had arrived back home, Charlotte received a letter with a Philadelphia postmark. It was from Tammy, explaining they were alive and would try to make their way home as soon as they could.

***

The 1832 gale was an early indication that a fishery depending on open boats in the North Atlantic had severe limitations – but it would take another fishing disaster towards the end of the 19th century before deep-sea fishing from open boats was finally abandoned. The fluctuations in the fortunes of the cod fishery and the 1832 disaster took place against a wider backdrop of profound economic decline that had dire social consequences. In the years after the 1832 disaster there were several harvest failures. The potato crop was ruined by blight for several years in succession while the early onset of winter, with heavy snows, prevented the oat crop being harvested, and many sheep and cattle were frozen to death. Shetlanders, who at the best of times lived in poverty, were on the edge of famine. These poor harvests continued into the 1840s and the accumulated consequences of these years had a lasting impact. For a long time afterwards, this period of great distress was remembered as the Hungry Forties. Such was the level of destitution that the government had to provide food relief. This was not, however, free. In return for a sack of oatmeal, the crofters had to work on a road-building programme that became known as the meal roads.

Somehow, despite all of this, the cod fishery continued. There was even an occasional year when cod were again prolific on the Home Grounds and high landings were recorded. Fishermen are eternal optimists; they must be. There is always the prospect of a better catch next week or next month. But these occasional good years were exceptions in a decade of scarcity. The unsubsidised cod fishery was in the doldrums. One consequence of these turbulent and uncertain times was the disappearance of the skipper-owned sloops. The loss of the subsidy, and the variable catches, had resulted in bankruptcy for many of them. Only the larger merchant companies, with greater resources and diversified interests, were able to survive these loss-making years and remain in business to take advantage of the occasional good years.

All the salt cod was sold to Spain. Unfortunately, it soon became clear that Shetland cod was not fetching anything like the best price. The quality of the fish was poor and not at all comparable to the salt cod from the Basque country. In the days of generous subsidy, this was not so important. But now that government support had been withdrawn, the issue of quality needed to be addressed. Before that could be done, the isles were dealt another heavy blow. In 1842 the Shetland economy would be left reeling from the most spectacular of all bankruptcies.

4

The Hungry Forties

Hay & Ogilvy was the largest merchant company in Shetland during the early 19th century. Owned by brothers-in-law William Hay and Charles Ogilvy, it was one of the first to invest in cod sloops and export salt cod to Spain. William Hay was the driving force of the company – he was always looking for new opportunities to expand and diversify their business, and the company's early success, particularly in the cod fishery, did nothing to temper this ambition. He borrowed heavily to buy land around his country house at Laxfirth, where he aspired to become one of Shetland's main landowners. Some described him as arrogant. Like most merchants, he had been educated privately in Scotland, spoke English and had a privileged lifestyle. Today he would be described as having a sense of entitlement. As the new decade started in 1840, he was on the crest of a wave; unstoppable, it seemed.

By 1842 his world had turned upside down. It was early June and the sailing ship which had taken him back from Edinburgh had just dropped anchor in Lerwick harbour. With the sun shining from an azure sky, it was the kind of summer day that he had always enjoyed. But today his mood was sombre, and he was fighting a losing battle to control his anger. His company had just been declared bankrupt and he was set to lose everything. The future looked bleak for him and his family; the only certainty was that their lavish lifestyle, as one of Shetland's leading families, would soon end. Hay knew that, by the time he arrived back home, all the paperwork would be in place confirming the insolvency. His wife, Margaret Scott, met him outside Hayfield House, their grand Lerwick home. She had known for some time that the company was in trouble but had not realised the full enormity of the calamity about to engulf them. They would lose Hayfield House, he explained, as well as their house and land at Laxfirth. He might have added that they would have very little money left to live on but decided that Margaret had already heard enough bad news for one day.

Incapable of accepting any personal responsibility, Hay blamed his misfortune on his business partner and brother-in-law, Charles Ogilvy, and he immediately set off to confront him. Striding through the hill, almost running, Hay was easily recognised. Always smartly dressed, he had the bearing of a confident and successful merchant. Passing two men working with sheep, he ignored them, as he did with everyone he regarded as his inferior. They kept their heads down, avoiding eye contact, not wanting to get on the wrong side of a merchant who owned and controlled so much of the Shetland economy. By the time Hay reached his destination, his fury had reached new heights.

Ogilvy could see the state that his brother-in-law was in as soon as he opened the door. The relationship between them had always been an easy one, and he was taken aback and confused by Hay's accusations. He leapt to his own defence, saying that they had taken all business decisions together and it was nonsense to argue that the failure of their company was his fault. There was a furious row, which only ended when Ogilvy slammed the door.

As William Hay walked back home, his pace slowed, and his wrath began to subside. Not only had he lost his business and his wealth, but he also realised that he had forever lost the relationship with his friend and brother-in-law. His temper had only made things worse. The sun was still shining as he arrived back at Hayfield House but, as far he was concerned, this was one of the bleakest and darkest days of his life. The two men never spoke again and, very shortly afterwards, Ogilvy and his family emigrated to Australia.

The bankruptcy of Hay & Ogilvy was a direct result of their attempt to establish a commercial herring fishery. This had initially led to a short-lived herring boom during the 1830s but ended in disaster. In Scotland, a herring fishery had developed in the Moray Firth in the early decades of the 19th century. The herring were caught by half deckers, partially decked boats that provided the crew with some shelter and accommodation. Around 12 metres in length, these boats fished during the night, returning in the morning to land their catches to the many curing yards where the herring would be gutted, salted and barrelled. This was totally different to the Dutch fishery, where their much larger busses cured the herring on board. It was rather ironic that this new Scottish herring fishery was not based on the Dutch model, which, of course, had been the entire purpose of the government subsidy earlier in the century. This Scottish fleet did, however, use the same fishing technique – the drift net, which is a curtain of netting with mesh sizes just big enough to trap a fully-grown herring by the gills. It hangs a few metres below the surface and is only effective during the hours of darkness, when the shoals of herring leave the seabed and swim to the surface to feed. These nets, tied together to form an extended line, were made from hemp. Surprisingly expensive, a fleet of hemp nets cost more than a half decker.

In an attempt to emulate the success of this new Scottish fishery, some Shetland merchants bought second-hand boats and nets from Scotland. Hay & Ogilvy was in the vanguard of this new venture. Fishing for herring from May to September, the catch increased year on year, as did the fleet. By 1840 there were around 200 half deckers in Shetland, some 100 of which were owned or managed by Hay & Ogilvy. Not only did this company own much of the fleet, but it was also responsible for curing and exporting most of the catch. The main market for salt herring at this time were the sugar plantations of the West Indies; an indication that the early Scottish herring fishery was as implicated in the business of slavery as were many other parts of the economy.

Hay & Ogilvy also provided much of the credit for the purchase of the boats and their very expensive drift nets through the Shetland Bank, which it owned and managed. The importance of this bank in financing various fishing ventures was such that it became known as the Fishermen's Bank. So, the early herring boom was, to a large extent, the Hay & Ogilvy show. And it could not have happened at a better time, coinciding as it did with the downturn in the cod fishery. It provided a glimpse of optimism, with hopes that this new fishery would continue to expand.

Yet catastrophe lay ahead. When the fleet set sail for the herring grounds off the east of Shetland on Tuesday 9 September 1840, no one could have imagined the catalogue of disasters that would unfold. Although it was windy, and a few skippers decided to remain ashore, most of the fleet went to sea. By the time the boats set their nets for the night, the wind had increased to a full gale from the north-northwest. It was the worst of all possible situations. Had the gale struck before they had shot their nets, the boats could have run for the shore with their nets aboard. As the storm raged, each skipper was faced with an impossible choice: either abandon their expensive nets and try to get back ashore safely or take a risk and try to haul the gear back on board. Most of those who cut their nets away made it safely ashore, but lost all their nets. Those that tried to haul back their nets found that the heavy seas tore everything to shreds. And the half deckers were, of course, only partially decked and not at all suitable for being at sea in such conditions. Five boats sank with the loss of 30 fishermen. Around 30 vessels were driven ashore as the fleet tried to make it back to land. Almost every vessel at sea that night lost its drift nets.

This huge loss of essential and costly equipment in a single night had serious financial consequences for all vessel owners, but particularly for Hay & Ogilvy, which owned upwards of half the fleet and had financed most of the rest. The company suffered serious losses and had to increase its borrowings from the Shetland Bank, making the bank far too dependent on the fortunes of a single company. The Royal Bank of Scotland initially kept the Shetland Bank alive with a loan, but more funds were urgently needed before credit could be advanced to replace the boats and nets that had been lost. Negotiations had dragged on for more than a year before William Hay set off for Edinburgh to try and raise more money. He was confident that his personal intervention would clinch the deal. But the Royal Bank of Scotland had lost confidence in him. Despite all his efforts, both Hay & Ogilvy and the Shetland Bank were declared bankrupt. The Shetland Bank had lost the staggering figure of £60,000, a sum worth more than £57 million today.

This bankruptcy meant there was no longer any source of credit for the replacement of boats and drift nets, while the liquidation of Hay & Ogilvy removed the company that had underpinned and financed this new fishery. The foundations of the herring venture had collapsed. The half deckers stopped fishing and, as they could not be used for either the haaf or the cod fishery, most were hauled onto beaches and abandoned. Shetland would not embrace herring again until the 1880s. But that was a long time into the future and, for the time being, it seemed that there was no alternative to the haaf and the cod fisheries. Indeed, many believed that the catastrophe of 1842 had proved that salt herring would never replace salt ling and salt cod as the staples of the Shetland economy.

The wider consequences of this dual bankruptcy were severe. Hundreds of people were thrown out of work and many small depositors lost their savings. The disappearance of Hay & Ogilvy was particularly serious for the early cod fishery, as the company had been involved at all levels, not only as sloop owners but also as curers and exporters of salt cod. The bankruptcy was something that the cod fishery, which was already struggling to survive through the Hungry Forties, was ill-equipped to bear. The 15-year period from 1830 to 1845 was very hard for Shetland. A sequence of poor harvests, the haaf disaster, the failure of the promising herring fishery and the dual bankruptcy resulted in economic and social hardship for many. On top of all that, the cod fishery had only just managed to survive. An occasional good year kept it alive, but in most years the catches were poor.

∗∗∗

It had been clear for some time that salt cod from Shetland fetched poor prices in Spain, on account of its poor quality. Before better prices could be negotiated, Shetland had to up its game. The man who first realised this, and knew what to do about it, was an enterprising Shetland entrepreneur, Arthur Anderson. Born in Lerwick in 1792, he spent his early teenage years salting and drying fish. At the age of 16 he was, like many young Shetlanders, pressed into service in the Royal Navy. After a decade at sea, he moved to London determined to make his fortune. Specialising in marine insurance and shipping, he demonstrated an early flair for business. Driven by profit, some of his activities verged on the edge of legality. He apparently made a lot of money smuggling guns into the Iberian peninsula during the Carlist Wars. In time he went on to establish the large shipping company P&O Ferries. No doubt his early experiences drying fish on Shetland beaches instilled a strong work ethic which stood him in good stead. He never forgot his roots and, as an older man, he became the MP for Orkney and

Shetland. Funding several good causes in the islands, including the High School in Lerwick, which still bears his name today, he also organised the relief fund in the aftermath of the 1832 disaster.

When gun-running in Spain and Portugal during the 1830s, Anderson saw at first hand the huge potential of the Iberian market for salt cod of the best quality. He was convinced that Shetland merchants could access this market if they produced better quality salt cod. Deciding to lead by example, he established the Shetland Fishery Company and immediately began to make many changes to the curing process.

He saw that it was vital that the cod were properly bled immediately after being caught (achieved through cutting the gills). Failure to do this resulted in blood spots left on the cod flesh, which turned black and unsightly when dried.

The use of better quality salt was important and paying a little more for the best quality was, he believed, an investment well worth making.

Salt cod that still contained moisture would decay, and some cod from Shetland had unfortunately developed a poor reputation in this respect. Recognising this was a major problem, he insisted on a longer drying period.

Having seen an opportunity to get better prices by quality, many entrepreneurs would have guarded these trade secrets, to get an edge on the competition. Anderson did exactly the opposite – he wrote extensively on all these matters in his own monthly newspaper, called the *Fishermen's Magazine*, which was published from 1836 to 1839. This paper was full of suggestions and recommendations for others to take up. He appears to have been genuinely motivated to encourage the Shetland fishing industry to improve and advance.

The changes to the curing process that Arthur Anderson advocated would, in due course, enable the cod fishery to expand and develop. In the fullness of time, salt cod from Shetland would fetch top prices. But even if higher prices could be achieved for better quality, there needed to be greater predictability in catches. What was the point of a bumper cod catch one year if it was followed by a year of scarcity? The limitations of the Home Grounds were clear for all to see. Some far-sighted individuals saw that new fishing grounds needed to be found. These lay a long way from Shetland, but the idea of Shetlanders fishing these distant-water cod banks must have seemed like a pipe dream to many. The realisation of this fanciful hope was, however, much closer than anyone had ever imagined. And the man responsible was the indomitable William Hay.

5

Disko Bay

In the summer of 1862, a large Shetland cod schooner prepared to drop anchor in Disko Bay, near a remote ice-filled Greenland fjord where there was an Inuit settlement. Incredibly blue skies and not a breath of wind provided a spectacular backdrop to this idyllic scene as the Shetlanders wondered why the weather could be so fine when you were this far north. Their quiet pondering about the unpredictability of the Arctic weather was interrupted by the loud splash of the anchor followed by the clattering of the chain rattling over the bow. With the still day, everything seemed much louder than usual.

They should have been fishing but there were no cod to be found, and this prompted the skipper to try and get some local intelligence. Launching a small boat, four crewmembers climbed on board, keen to step ashore after months at sea. Looking as if it was covered in a light sheen of oil, the water was so calm that it seemed wrong to disturb the smooth surface with the oars. Rowing past some small ice floes, glistening brilliant white in the fierce polar sunshine, they were aware of a group of dark-skinned Inuit dressed in white furs gathering on the shore to greet them. There is no record of whether the Inuit could speak English, and it is not known if any useful information was obtained. Probably not, as they eventually returned to Shetland in September with very few cod. This was the last fishing trip that a Shetland vessel ever made to Greenland; the first trips having been made many years before.

How was it that the Shetland cod fishery, which was based on fishing the Home Grounds with small sloops, and which had almost disappeared, become a distant-water operation sending large schooners across the North Atlantic to Greenland? The clue is in the name of the vessel that dropped anchor in Disko Bay, the *Janet Hay*. She was built as a trading vessel in 1840 by Hay & Ogilvy at the company's shipyard at Lerwick. At 30 metres long she was the largest vessel ever to have been built in Shetland. Not only the largest but also the most expensive, at a total cost of £1,400. Being the biggest, and reputedly the fastest, she epitomised William Hay's personal ambition.

When his company folded, the ownership of this new vessel, along with all other assets of the company, were lost. A business that Hay had built up over his lifetime had gone within a matter of a days. The loss of the *Janet Hay* was particularly poignant, as this schooner had been named after one of his daughters, who tragically died of a fever when she was only two years old. Having known personal tragedy and financial catastrophe, many people would have given up. But, despite no longer being a young man, Hay's pride would not allow the humiliation of bankruptcy to be his legacy. Determined to rebuild his business, he set up a new company (called Hay and Company but known simply as Hays) and began the slow process of re-establishing himself as a merchant, sloop owner, fish curer and fish exporter.

His determination became an obsession as he worked 18-hour days to keep costs down; he figured that every hour he worked meant he did not have to pay anyone else to get the job done. Appearing to have lost his earlier impetuous and reckless manner, Hay had become much more prudent in all his business dealings. Perhaps he also became a humbler man, losing some of his former arrogance – it was said that the family never had wine with a meal until his new company started to make money.

Everything is relative, of course. For ordinary Shetlanders at this time, it was all they could do to keep their themselves fed. Most hardly knew what wine was; never having seen a bottle, let alone tasted it. His hard work and business acumen began to pay off as he identified new opportunities. He bought back some of the old company assets and leases, including the two docks in Lerwick harbour and some of the fish drying beaches around Scalloway. One of his smartest moves was to buy the *Janet Hay* for £700 in 1844. With this purchase, he had obtained a vessel that was only four years old for half the price that she had cost to build.

Hay decided to send the *Janet Hay* on a speculative cod trip to the Davis Strait, west of Greenland, even though she had previously been used as a cargo vessel, mostly around Shetland. What prompted this experienced, prudent businessman to take the risk in sending his schooner on a 2,000-mile trip to look for cod? Had his old impetuous nature resurfaced, or did he have good reasons? There is no way of knowing, but the fact that there were hundreds of Shetlanders employed on board whalers at Greenland cannot have been a coincidence. Some of these men were bound to have tried catching cod by hand line and would have seen the potential for a commercial cod fishery there. Returning home, news of these promising fishing opportunities would have been quickly passed on to enterprising merchants such as William Hay. According to Scottish Fishery Board records, the *Janet Hay* first went to Greenland in 1846, returning with over 29,000 cod in September. The crew, many of whom had fished the Home cod grounds, had never seen so many large cod in such quantities. This catch generated considerable local interest, and the Lerwick fishery officer wrote enthusiastically in his annual report:

The master of this vessel informed me that he was 42 days in reaching the fishing grounds having experienced coarse weather and contrary winds, but he was only 23 days on the homeward voyage. The cod fish were in great abundance, on several occasions nearly 2,000 fish were caught by the 20 men on board in the course of 12 hours and the whole quantity was fished in 28 days being an average daily catch of a thousand fish. Some of the fish when taken out of the sea weighed about 80 lbs and the headed and gutted about 60 lbs.

There is, however, some tantalising evidence that the first Greenland trip may have taken place the year before. At this time the Royal Navy was convinced that it was possible to sail from the Atlantic to the Pacific through an ice-free passage around the north coast of Canada, the so-called Northwest Passage. Following many unsuccessful attempts, a well-funded Admiralty expedition, under the command of Captain John Franklin, left London in May 1845 to chart this route, which many believed was just waiting to be discovered. There were two vessels, the *Erebus* and the *Terror*, and by late June they had made it as far as the Davis Strait. In his recent book about this ill-fated venture, Michael Palin describes an encounter with what was described as a Shetland brig. The Shetland skipper explained that 'he was fishing for cod on the banks, a new scheme in these parts'. This was probably the *Janet Hay*. If it was, then her crew of Shetlanders were the last Europeans to see the *Erebus* and the *Terror*. Shortly after this encounter both boats continued their voyage northwards and promptly vanished – it was clear that there was to be no ice-fee passage to the Pacific.

When the *Janet Hay* returned from Greenland with more than 42,000 cod in 1847, William Hay realised that he had struck gold. Having spent a lifetime in the fishing business, he knew it was possible to make a fortune if the right investment was made at the right time. He immediately started looking around for more schooners to buy and he soon had four vessels fishing at Greenland. This was his first big break after the bankruptcy and there is no doubt that this must have restored his confidence.

It is fair to assume that he was drinking wine again. As other merchants began to invest in cod schooners, William Hay was once again seen as the innovator that others wanted to copy. He must have enjoyed that. By 1849 eight Shetland schooners fished in the Davis Strait and around Disko Island. This Greenland fishery had taken the cod industry to new heights, and the merchants had great hopes for the future.

However, after 1850 things began to unravel. The west Greenland cod fishery failed, not recovering again until the early 20th century. The reason for this failure was most probably climate change, which disrupted the currents that transported the cod larvae from Iceland to west Greenland. Catches slumped and by 1852 the Greenland voyages were over; they had only lasted six years. There was, nevertheless, to be one final fling. Perhaps the profits made by the *Janet Hay* persuaded William Hay to have one last try some ten years later, in 1862. Despite the attempt to gather local intelligence from the Inuit, the *Janet Hay* returned from this last voyage with less than 8,000 cod. There were no more voyages to Greenland after this.

***

The Greenland experience encouraged merchants to try other distant-water fishing grounds, particularly around Faroe. By the 1860s, the distant-water fishery at Faroe was developing into a large and profitable enterprise, and it was Faroe, not Greenland, that was to define the halcyon days of the Shetland cod fishery.

The Home fishery continued with around 40 small sloops fishing in most years, but catches remained unpredictable. In contrast, fishing was not only better at Faroe; it was also more predictable. This predictability encouraged investment in the larger vessels needed to fish distant waters. These all had two masts and were called smacks to distinguish them from the single-masted sloops that fished the Home Grounds. By this time the improvements and innovations in the curing process, first advocated by Arthur Anderson in the 1830s, were beginning to pay off. Cod from Shetland was gaining a reputation for consistent good quality. Eventually carving out its own distinctive market niche, the 'Shetland cure' became synonymous with some of the best quality salt cod available, for which Spanish buyers were prepared to pay top prices.

This critical combination of better catches and improved prices boosted profits and the cod fishery expanded year on year. By the mid 1860s fishing at Faroe had become a huge operation with a fleet of more than 60 vessels. Most of these larger smacks were bought second-hand from the south coast of England and were generally between 20 and 30 metres long. This fleet was crewed by upwards of a thousand fishermen and, for a quarter of a century, the Faroe fishing became the islands' largest fishery, with an annual catch of around 10,000 tons. While these larger smacks mostly fished at Faroe, they also started to fish at Rockall and off the northeast coast of Iceland.

The modern fishing industry always makes its greatest profits when good catches are matched by high prices. It is very simple economics, and this was as true in the 19th century as it is now. The cod merchants were lucky to have enjoyed this fortunate combination of both for more than two decades. By this time the Shetland economy was also doing well, in marked contrast to the Hungry Forties, for those who were old enough to remember that desperate and desolate time. While the success of these boom years was underpinned by the good catches at Faroe and the high cod prices in Spain, those involved in the industry became ever more skilled and competent at what they were doing. Skippers and crews became increasingly adept at making passage to and from, and successfully fishing, these distant-water grounds. At the same time, they also became as good as the Basques had ever been at bleeding, splitting and salting the cod on board. And the beach curers honed their skills in producing the high-quality product demanded by the Spanish market. In short, all those involved had become very good at what they did. Shetland became the hub of a large, distant-water cod fishery that was international in its reach, extending from the Arctic waters off northeast Iceland to the warm waters of Spain, where most of the cod was sold.

The distant-water smacks made three trips every year, each lasting several months. Depending on weather conditions, the first smacks would sail for Faroe at the end of March or early in April. The second trip would also be made to Faroe or, from time to time, to Rockall. Many of the smacks would make their last trip of the year to the grounds off northeast Iceland. Returning from this last trip in late September or early October, the smacks were then laid up for the winter. While most fishing trips involved making passage to and from a specific fishing ground, it was not uncommon for smacks to fish more than one area, usually Faroe and Rockall.

There are even some instances of smacks fishing all three distant-water grounds during a single trip. In May 1878 the *James Stevenson* returned to Scalloway with only 3,800 fish. It may have been an unsuccessful trip in terms of the poor catch, but it was one of the most remarkable ever undertaken in terms of the distance travelled. This smack had started its trip at Faroe. Disappointing catches had then prompted the skipper to sail to Rockall but following poor results there they returned to Faroe and then went on to Iceland. Ice cover prevented fishing there, whereupon she once more headed for Faroe before eventually returning home. The *James Stevenson* sailed around 1,700 miles in the search of cod. A non-stop sailing trip like this would exhaust most contemporary sailors on board their comfortable yachts. The smack crews not only made such voyages in uncomfortable and cramped conditions, but they also found time to catch and process cod.

Shetland cod fishermen became renowned for their skills at this time, not only in Faroe and Iceland but also in Scotland.

One of the best Scottish novels ever written is Neil Gunn's masterpiece, *The Silver Darlings*. It is a powerful story of a young boy, Finn, coming of age against the backdrop of the Highland Clearances and the early days of the Scottish herring fishery. About halfway through the book Finn, who is now a skipper, finds himself and his crew lost after an easterly gale. Their small herring boat, the *Seafoam*, had been fishing in the north Minch but was forced off-course by the storm. They fear they might have missed the Butt of Lewis and that they are being driven far out into the Atlantic. As panic begins to set in, a ship appears in the distance. She is making good speed, running westward before the strong easterly wind. Finn realises that this is one of the Shetland cod smacks, famous for making long voyages in bad weather, on its way to Rockall. As this smack draws nearer, the crew of the *Seafoam* begin to wave and shout to attract her attention. Responding to these calls for help, the smack comes alongside the small herring boat. The Shetlanders explain to Finn that they are indeed 40 miles to the west of Lewis, and they must sail back east. As the smack resumes its voyage to Rockall, the crew of the *Seafoam* are full of admiration for the Shetland fishermen who have so willingly come to their aid:

> 'Good for the Shetlanders,' cried Roddie. 'They're brave seamen.'

> 'They have a great trade in dried cod,' said Henry. 'They export it all over the world.'

The navigational and seamanship skills of the cod fishermen were built up over many years, often taught by one generation to another. To learn how to navigate precisely and accurately is the most exact of sciences and can only be mastered with the best of teaching. One of the very best teachers was a polyglot, polymath, poet and Marxist.

6

The Poet

It was late February, and the year was 1871. The nights were still dark and there was no respite from the driving rain and incessant gales. As the wind whistled around the masts of the cod fleet, snugged up in harbour for the winter, the prospect of fine summer days seemed very distant. Despite the weather, however, work had already begun in getting the smacks ready for their first trip of the year. Carpenters, shipwrights and sail makers were rushing around with a great sense of urgency and anticipation. The previous cod season had broken all records with 11,500 tons of cod being cured on the beaches. The thought of another bumper year, with good profits and wages, focused everybody's mind.

There was so much to do. Damaged wood in the hull and deck, frayed rigging and torn sails – all had to be seen to. It was essential that the smacks were shipshape before they embarked on their long voyages. They then had to be provisioned. For the Home sloops, this was relatively straightforward, as these vessels only fished for a week at a time. For the distant-water fleet, however, this involved much more preparation. Upwards of 40 tons of salt for curing the catch, barrels for storing cod livers, bags of shellfish bait, several tons of coal for the onboard stoves, fishing gear, spare sails and cordage, along with food and water for 12 to 15 men for three months was all needed. Vessels preparing for sea also need to be properly trimmed and ballasted. In addition to conventional ballast, supplies of salt at the start of a voyage acted as additional weight and, as this was used up, it was replaced by the weight of fish in the hold.

Making a lengthy passage with a sailing vessel, entirely dependent on the speed and direction of the wind and the prevailing tidal conditions, required navigation and seafaring skills of the highest order. This was particularly so for the smacks operating in the inhospitable waters between northern Scotland and the east of Iceland. With modern satellite navigation systems, it has become easy to navigate; a vessel's exact position at sea can now be found with the flick of a switch. In the 19th century, navigation was about mathematical skill, not electronics. The skipper and mate of a smack needed to be proficient navigators to find the fishing grounds, to fish these for a period of weeks and then make safe passage home.

Navigation is not an art; it is a precise and exact science. And it is not easy. It is all about how you get from where you think you are to where you want to be – when you are out of sight of land and surrounded by the sea. The starting point is to find some way of measuring the distance covered by a ship in a set time. One of the earliest ways this was done was to throw an object over the stern and measure how long it took to run out a length of line. Knots were sometimes tied in the line and the faster a boat was moving the more knots were recorded as the line was paid out. This is how the term knots (which is the measurement of nautical miles per hour) first came to be used.

By the early 19th century, the counting of knots on a line had been replaced by a ship's log. Towed behind a vessel, this was a small brass instrument with blades that made it spin around as the boat moved through the water. This rotary motion was recorded mechanically to provide a read-out of the distance travelled in nautical miles. Deploying this measurement of distance travelled, together with using the ship's compass to steer the boat in a chosen direction, allowed a skipper to plot on a paper chart the measured distance and compass direction steered and so estimate where the vessel was.

That was the relatively easy bit. A navigator then had to adjust the direction steered to compensate for the difference between true north and magnetic north. This is called the variation. It is not fixed, and it varies year by year and by location. Variation is currently only one degree west in the waters around Shetland. In other words, only one degree of difference between true and magnetic north: almost negligible. It was anything but negligible in the mid 19th century when huge variations applied, some 26° west around Shetland and 31° west around Faroe. Off northeast Iceland it was a whopping 38° west. This meant that a smack sailing to Iceland had to be steered 38° east of magnetic north to move in a true northerly direction – it is not unlike trying to steer a supermarket trolley in one direction when the stiff wheels want to take it in another.

A further compass adjustment was then needed to compensate for the distorting effect that any metal on board might have had on the compass reading. This is called the deviation and is a correction that is specific to individual vessels. At the same time as making these adjustments for variation and deviation, a skipper also had to consider the prevailing tidal conditions that can reduce speed (if the tide is flowing against the vessel), increase speed (if the tide is flowing with the vessel) or alter position (if the tide is pushing the vessel to one side or the other). A tidal stream is never constant – its strength varies according to the lunar cycle – and it generally flows in one direction for around six hours and then in the opposite direction for another six. And just as if that was not enough maths, a further adjustment had to be made for the wind in the sails blowing the vessel slightly to the side as well as forward. This is known as leeway.

A skipper and mate would make these complex computations on an hourly basis and plot the resultant positions on their charts. The slightest error or sloppy maths would have been compounded day after day with the inevitable consequence that the smack would not be where you estimated it was. Accuracy was therefore not only desirable; it was essential. To undertake these calculations on board a boat that is pitching and rolling is one thing. To continue with precise mathematics while battling a gale is something else. The only cross-check on the calculation was whenever sunlight allowed a sextant reading to be taken, thereby confirming the exact latitude. As soon as a smack came in sight of land, any positional errors could be corrected by steering on well-known and recognised high landmarks, such as mountains or cliffs.

***

The skippers and mates of the smacks had to be very able navigators. They had all left school when they were only 12 or 13 years old. Despite this most basic of education, they were having to grapple with complicated navigational concepts and challenging maths. Although elementary navigation was taught in some schools, most young fishermen learned the basics of their trade from older fishermen while at sea. There was, however, one exceptional teacher of navigation in Lerwick: James John Haldane Burgess.

He is also one of Shetland's great literary figures, having published many poems and novels, almost all written in Shetlandic. Mark Smith, an authority on Shetland literature, has argued that Haldane Burgess, as he was known, was one of Shetland's most revered people at the time. Few would argue with that. A street in Lerwick was named in his honour and, when he died in 1927, he was given a public funeral. The songs that are sung at Shetland's famous Up Helly Aa fire festival were all written by him. It is less well known that he also taught navigation to fishermen at his home in Queens Lane. Navigation is a very practical and hands-on subject, and the fact that he was blind makes it even more remarkable that Haldane Burgess was able to teach it at all.

He was not born blind. When young, his eyesight was perfectly normal and, from an early age, he was a voracious reader and a brilliant scholar. His intellect was exceptional, and a university education was the obvious option but, like most Shetlanders at this time, his family could not afford this. Encouraged by his teachers to enter a university bursary competition, he came first out of 607 candidates from all over Scotland. Not only that, but he finished some 47 marks ahead of the student who came second. He easily won his place to study at Edinburgh University. When he left Shetland, he had already immersed himself in the politics, philosophy and religion of the day, and it was no surprise that he embraced life at Edinburgh University. Throwing himself into his studies, he found that his MA degree did not tax him as much as he has expected, so he took additional courses and even found time to learn several languages. He was a seriously accomplished linguist by the time he left Edinburgh, fluent in all the Scandinavian tongues as well as having a working knowledge of many other European languages.

His intellectual and academic ascent was, however, cruelly halted when he was struck down by blindness in his last year at university. Despite this, he was able to complete his degree by oral exam at home in Lerwick. Deciding to become a minister, he started a divinity degree, but doctrinal and theological differences with the Church of Scotland led him to abandon this vocation. A radical thinker for his day, he became an early Marxist. Despite his blindness and with the help of his friends, he continued to read and write extensively. Whenever one of his friends asked if he had a certain book in his study, not only could he explain exactly where it could be found but could often quote sections of it from memory.

There were two enduring facets of Haldane Burgess's life: his love of the Shetland language and his socialism. When he was at university, he was told that it was not possible to express profound thoughts or deep feelings in the speech of ordinary people. As a person who was fluent in so many languages, he was well placed to disagree. To his mind, Shetlandic had its own distinctive vocabulary and grammar, a power of description and an edge of humour that English often lacked. He also loved it because it was the language of the crofters and fishermen; the ordinary people that he, as a socialist, identified with.

His house became the gathering place for Shetland radicals. His was not the world of the English-speaking Shetland merchants and lairds. Possibly determined to prove that his university lecturers, who despised local dialects, were wrong he chose to write about the big philosophical issues of life and faith in Shetlandic. This was a radical notion at the time; Shetlandic was regarded as a rough tongue only spoken by the uneducated classes, incapable of being used for intellectual discourse. In one of his best-known poems, 'Scranna', written in Shetlandic, Haldane Burgess takes this condescending attitude apart and turns it inside out.

'Scranna' tells the story of the Devil calling on Rasmie, an old crofter, to try and claim his soul. This powerful work describes Satan as a well-dressed, articulate and educated man who speaks perfect English. The suggestion that English was the language of the Devil must have been challenging at the time. Rasmie, in contrast, is poor and speaks only Shetlandic, but he is the intellectual match for his unexpected visitor. The poem takes an unexpected turn when Satan explains that he is a church minister: 'Look at me, I've been years in the kirk . . . I dispense the Communion, I preach, I baptise / You can manage it all with a few handy lies.' Exposing the ultimate hypocrisy, this imagery is still arresting and must have outraged many. Shetland was, like most of Britain at the time, a very religious and deferential society. Some argue that the point of all art, however, is to challenge prevailing orthodoxies and to make people think in new ways. Even to shock. Haldane Burgess certainly achieved that and, according to Mark Smith, this seminal work extended the intellectual reach of Shetlandic and laid the foundations for future generations of Shetland writers.

Looking at old black-and-white photographs of Haldane Burgess, this slim and handsome young man must have been conscious of the prevailing fashion, given how he is dressed. He also sports a bushy handlebar moustache that was very popular at the time. Somewhat unexpectedly his eyes appear to be full of life and enthusiasm, almost denying his blindness. Another Shetland poet, Jack Peterson, famously described Haldane Burgess as 'the blind man who saw in the dark; who could not see across the road but saw across the centuries'.

Writing poems in Shetlandic and discussing socialism could not, however, pay the bills. Having rejected a possible career in the ministry, he needed to find another way of supporting himself. His home in Queens Lane is a short distance from Lerwick's waterfront and Haldane Burgess had grown up very much aware of the extent to which seafaring and fishing were the lifeblood of Lerwick and Shetland. As a young man he had spent many hours speaking to fishermen from all over Europe, in their own languages, when their boats were packed into Lerwick harbour during bad weather. On these stormy days the small port of Lerwick was transformed into a cosmopolitan maritime community where Norwegian and Dutch were spoken more than English. He saw an early gap in the market, as it were, and decided to teach himself navigation so that he, in turn, could teach fishermen and seafarers. For anyone who has studied even the basics of navigation, the challenge of self-teaching this subject as a blind person, let alone then teaching students, almost defies belief. And yet, by all accounts, he was an excellent teacher and many young Shetlanders who sailed the grey and unforgiving waters of the North Atlantic learned their trade from this blind poet.

Navigation was essential to make safe passage to and from the fishing grounds. But that by itself did not make a successful cod fisherman. You had to be able to catch fish. And that was not as easy or straightforward as you might think.

7

Brains in Their Fingers

Having successfully navigated the smack to the fishing grounds, it was the responsibility of the skipper to find enough cod to fill the hold. A skipper had to be a good fisherman as well as a competent navigator – very different skills. The method of catching cod, a simple and inexpensive hand line, had not changed since the Basques had first pioneered its use on the Grand Banks. At the end of every line was a lead weight which was pierced by an iron rod. Two separate, lighter lines, each with a hook, were then attached to each end of this rod. All fisherman fished with their own hand line, and a smack had as many hand lines deployed over the side as there were crew on board.

The hand line is one of two methods of fishing with hooks; the other is called the long line. It is so called because it has many hundreds (sometimes thousands) of baited hooks along its length. It lies anchored on the seabed for several hours before it is hauled back. The sixerns at the haaf fished with long lines, which were ideal for catching bottom-feeding fish such as ling and tusk. In contrast, a hand line only has two baited hooks and must be hauled back to the surface whenever a fish is caught. On the face of it, the long line is the more efficient technique; fishing with a hand line requiring a disproportionate amount of effort to catch only one or, at best, two fish. It is, however, an ideal method for catching a shoaling species such as cod.

Different from its bottom-dwelling cousins, cod can form into shoals above the seabed, sometimes well up through the water column. While the long line can only catch fish that are on the ocean floor, the hand line can be fished at any depth, depending on where the cod are swimming. Sometimes the line needs to be on the bottom, at other times it can be used many metres above the seabed. It was this flexibility of the hand line that allowed a cod shoal to be fished so efficiently by the cod smacks. With good fishing, the expectation was that there would be a cod on each of the two hooks before the line was hauled back to the surface. When every crewmember was catching two cod at the same time, all the time, the hand line was very efficient.

Line fishing declined rapidly during the early 20th century, being replaced by the much more efficient method of trawling. For a long time, fishing was all about catching as much as possible, as quickly as possible. This changed when it became clear that unregulated fishing can overfish stocks. It is now all about catching fish in the most sustainable manner; something that civic society demands and is often described as the social licence to fish. This fundamental shift in attitudes has resulted in a revival in line fishing. Many argue that fishing with hooks is more sustainable than trawling as only larger fish are caught, there is no by-catch (which usually needs to be dumped) and no adverse impact on the seabed. Some fish in supermarket shelves and in restaurants are now labelled as line-caught; this term becoming synonymous with sustainable seafood.

This recent revival in line fishing bears little resemblance to the long lines and hand lines used in the 19th century. Both have been mechanised and computerised. Norway has a fleet of autoliners operating from west-coast fishing ports such as Måløy and Ålesund. These large steel vessels set miles of long lines on the seabed to catch ling and tusk. The hooks are baited automatically (hence the name autoliner), and the lines are hauled back by a specialist hydraulic hauler. The hand line has also had a revival with small boats from Iceland, Norway, Faroe and Shetland fishing with up to six hand lines (or jiggers) per vessel. Each jigger is operated by a computer that instructs a hauler to haul the line to the surface when it detects that a fish has been hooked. Unlike their ancestors on board a cod smack, contemporary hand line fishers from Shetland can enjoy a coffee while the computers and hydraulics do all the work.

This would all have been regarded as fanciful nonsense back in the days of the smacks. A crucial choice to be made when fishing with hooks is what bait to use. While fish will generally eat anything if they are hungry enough, there is no doubt that fish, like us, have their preferences. The cod fishermen mostly used shellfish, either horse mussels or white whelks. Sometimes enough were salted down to last a full trip. However, fresh bait was always preferred as it was believed to fish better. To have a plentiful supply of live bait, perforated wooden boxes filled with shellfish were towed behind some smacks as they left Shetland. Sometimes a cod shoal can be so dense that a feeding frenzy occurs and the kind of bait used becomes irrelevant or even even unnecessary – so voracious are the cod that they can be caught on a bare shiny hook. When the *Janet Hay* made her first trip to the Davis Strait, the fishing was so intense that most of the cod were caught on bare hooks.

Feeding frenzy or not, the catching of a cod is not that exciting, at least when compared to catching some other kinds of fish. A mackerel, for example, will continuously tug on the line desperately trying to escape, right until it is hauled on board. Cod are different. The first sign for a smack fisherman was a series of small tugs on the line, an indication that a cod was nibbling at the bait. A good fisherman would immediately react to this by yanking the hand line, which was looped round his hand, thereby embedding the hook in the cod's mouth. That was the excitement over; the cod does not fight to escape. All that remained was the very heavy work of hauling one (or two) large cod to the surface. Catching the first few might have been exhilarating, but this excitement was eventually replaced by the routine of endlessly hauling heavy fish up from the sea floor. Monotony then developed into tiredness. Add in the relentless wind, the driving rain, the bitter cold and a moving deck, and you start to imagine the life of a cod fisherman.

Most smacks operated a three-watch system of eight hours on deck and four hours below. For a smack with a crew of 12, that meant that there were eight on deck fishing, with four resting below at any one time. This system would be maintained under normal fishing conditions for as long as possible, as it ensured that the crew got eight hours of rest (in the form of two breaks of four hours) every day. But whenever a smack encountered a large cod shoal and there was intensive fishing, the watch system was abandoned, and the entire crew came on deck to fish. It was essential that every hand line was used so that the largest possible catch could be taken. Fishing has always been opportunistic and, if you do not take full advantage of an opportunity, it may be a long time before another one presents itself.

Sunday was the only guaranteed rest time; unlike today, religious observance was not an option, it was compulsory. But there were few crewmembers who objected to a day of enforced rest, whatever their private religious views. The only other possible rest time was if extremely bad weather forced the skipper to anchor in a sheltered Faroese or Icelandic fjord. At the end of every distant-water trip, each fisherman would go home for a few days or, at most, a week. It was over far too quickly. In no time at all they had to be back to take on board provisions before setting sail on the next trip.

Amongst the few written accounts of what life was like on board a cod smack, the most authentic is that written by Captain Halcrow in *The Sail Fishermen of Shetland*. His narrative is authoritative and reliable for the simple reason that he worked on board cod smacks as a young man. Although written more than 70 years ago in a style that is clunky and old-fashioned, his description of the catching and handling of a large cod catch cannot be matched: 'After two thousand cod had been hauled, split, cleaned and salted down . . . it was a crowd of blood-splashed, half-frozen automatons with gashed and salt scarred hands, who stumbled rather than walked below to fall asleep at the foot of the ladder, on their chests, anywhere, before removing their oilskins.'

Towards the end of the 19th century, the Faroese developed their own cod fishery using, until the 1950s, the same two-hook hand line that the Shetlanders had used. I spoke to a retired Faroese fisherman about his experience of fishing for cod one incredibly misty day in the village of Tvøroyri. Dense fog is common in Faroe, and it was so thick that morning that we could only see each other and nothing else, not even the shop that we were standing outside. We were both dressed for the Faroese mist, which can be as wet as a heavy rain shower, so neither of us were in a hurry to go inside. We were also enjoying our discussion.

I explained that there was a marked variation in catches of Shetland smacks. Some could return from Faroe with more than 25,000 fish while others caught only a few thousand. The distribution of the cod on the fishing grounds, poor weather and the ability of a skipper to find the cod, all determined this fluctuation in catches. He told me that it was the same for the Faroese cod fleet, and then he said that there was also the huge difference between what each fisherman caught. Recognising that I had not fully grasped what he meant, he said that in his home village 'you always knew which fishermen would catch most cod, even before the boat had left the pier'. Assuming he had expressed himself clumsily in his broken English, I asked if he meant that it was not possible to know how much cod anyone had caught until the boat returned. He looked at me as if I was stupid and slowly repeated what he had originally said. There was clearly nothing wrong with his command of English, but I remained sceptical, wondering aloud how some fishermen could always catch more than others when they were all fishing with the same hand line. With typical Faroese confidence he shrugged his shoulders and smiled. 'Well, that was how it was with the Faroese fishermen – some were much better at catching cod than others.' As if to emphasise the point, he then told me that some fisherman regularly caught twice what others did, trip after trip. I thought this was absurd but said nothing – which was wise as I was subsequently proved wrong.

When I started to investigate further, it was clear that some fishermen regularly and consistently caught more than others. Since Faroese fishermen were paid according to how many cod they caught, a record of individual catches was kept. This was done by cutting off the barbel underneath the mouth of every cod. These were counted and recorded each day by the mate. These daily tallies confirmed what I had been told. As soon as I accepted this surprising fact – which was not easy to explain – I began to wonder if it had been the same on board the Shetland smacks.

A proportion of the fisherman's wage on board the Shetland smacks was related to individual catches as well, and the method of recording this was also the collection of cod barbels. In all the archives I looked at there were no records of these daily counts. But that was to change when I travelled to the island of Unst to examine the records of A. Sandison & Sons, a large haaf fishing company that operated two distant-water smacks, the *Silver Lining* and the *Thomas Henry*. For two centuries this family company dominated the economy of Unst, controlling the large haaf fishery, owning land and operating several merchant stores. They are still an active company, amongst other things running a factory in Lerwick that makes boxes for the fish-farming industry.

After a long drive and two ferry trips, I arrived at the main shop in the village of Baltasound, still run by the Sandison family. Over a welcome cup of tea with Duncan Sandison and his wife, Jan Fraser, I was told that she had looked out all their cod fishing records for me to examine. Someone had already explained that Jan was a trained librarian who, in her retirement, had organised the family archive with great precision. Her expertise was immediately apparent when I went upstairs where the archives were stored. Laid out on a large table was the most perfectly complete record of all the activities of their two cod smacks. There were crew lists, every kind of detail about the two vessels, the numbers of cod landed at the end of every trip, information on where the exports of dried salt cod were sent, how much money each shipment made and the settling sheets which showed the earnings of every fisherman for each season. At the far end of the table were several well-worn small ledgers, each with the intriguing name 'Nippling Book' written on the outside cover. Never having come across this term before, I was not sure what I might find as I started to flick through the first one. It was what I thought I would never find, a record of the individual catches for each Unst fisherman, recorded and signed by the mate. These books confirmed that some fishermen on board the *Silver Lining* and *Thomas Henry*, like their Faroese counterparts, consistently caught double the tally of other crewmembers.

I was curious to find out more. A similar variation in catches was also known to exist amongst the Basque, Spanish and Portuguese fishermen when fishing on the Grand Banks. They referred disparagingly to those fishermen who caught less as the 'bait wasters'. The best fishermen were, in contrast, held in the highest esteem on board their cod schooners.

How could it be that one fisherman was better than another when using the same hand line? Could it have been an uncanny ability to feel a cod nibbling at the bait? Or was it that these successful fishermen concentrated solely on fishing and did not daydream? In Iceland it is said that the best hand line fishers think like a cod, such is their skill and determination to catch them. This struck a chord with me as I have heard it said in Shetland that you get some people who are fishers and then you get others who go to the fishing. There are many reasons why people go fishing. Maybe it is because the money is good or because it is what the family have always done and that is what is expected of the next generation. But, for others, fishing is an obsession. They eat, sleep and breathe fishing. For them there is no alternative career that they would consider. I am pretty sure that it was these guys that always caught most cod on their hand lines. The famous seafaring author Alan Villiers once went on a six-month trip to the Grand Banks with the *Argus*, one of the last Portuguese schooners fishing for cod with hand lines. During this time, he came to know and admire these banksmen from Portugal. It became apparent to Villiers that some of the crew always caught more than others and when he asked the skipper why this might be the case, he was told that 'the best cod fishermen had brains in their fingers'.

Cod are generally caught on relatively shallow fishing banks. Those that were fished by the smack fleet in the 19th century are still fished today, mainly by trawlers. All are clearly marked on fishing charts and easily located – all apart from one fishing bank with the strange-sounding name of Heglies Bank. It seemed to have disappeared and no one knew where it was.

8

Heglies Bank

The Vikings spoke about the sea road when they described an ocean voyage. The sea was how the Vikings got around, using well-known sailing routes to connect their northern archipelago. The cod fishermen also had their sea roads to their favourite fishing grounds which they used year after year.

It is difficult for us to get into this way of thinking, dependent as we are on road, rail and air transport. Places that we now regard as remote were often very accessible in the past by sea. For a Shetlander today, travelling to Faroe or Iceland is complex, expensive and time-consuming. On a recent occasion, when travelling from Shetland to Faroe, the only available route took me first to Aberdeen, then London, on to Copenhagen and then finally to Faroe, flying above Shetland on this last leg. During the 19th century it was quite different. Upwards of a thousand Shetlanders sailed to Faroe and Iceland on board cod smacks several times a year. Most of these men would never have been to Aberdeen, let alone London. With a good sailing wind, it took little more than a day to make the passage to Faroe. The record time for a trip was 17 hours, recorded by a cod smack returning from Faroe to Shetland in near perfect sailing conditions.

Perception of distance is as important as actual distance, sometimes even more so. Shetland has a modern transport network, connecting us to Scotland and the rest of the UK. But all roads

(or, at least, ferries and flights) lead south. Our connections with
the north have been lost. Most Shetlanders, who think nothing
of flying to Scotland for the weekend, see Faroe as a faraway
place, even though it is closer than Edinburgh. Likewise, few
realise that the east coast of Iceland is nearer to Shetland than
London is.

Back in the 19th century, Shetland was a fishing hub with
spokes pointing both north and south. This created a confidence
within the islands that Shetland, if not at the centre of the world,
was at least central to much that was happening in the North
Atlantic. It is very different today. At best, Shetland hangs onto
the northern edge of maps of Britain. At worst, the isles are
simply omitted. This is standard practice on most TV channels
and newspapers. Even the National Trust for Scotland, which was
established to cherish and preserve Scotland's landscapes, continues to produce the most ridiculous maps with Shetland placed
in little boxes, sometimes in the Moray Firth and sometimes east
of Orkney. They claim that their maps are representative rather
than absolutely accurate. I wonder how long that lame excuse
would last if Edinburgh was shown where Glasgow is.

Although I had a lot of fun debating this with the National
Trust, there is a serious point to this geographical obsession
of mine. Generation after generation of Shetlanders have seen
their home islands clinging on to the edge of a map of the UK
or discarded into a box in the wrong place. It is a cruel mani-
festation of a narrative which says that the islands are remote
and inconvenient, being located where they are. So much so
that it is acceptable and permissible to change their location.
This does nothing to foster a confident community, comfortable with its pivotal position in the North Atlantic. Instead, it
accentuates a sense of dependence on the UK and a belief that
we can only look south for opportunity and support. Despite all
the privations of the time, this was not something that afflicted
Shetlanders during the 19th century.

The Scottish government, to its credit, recently made a commitment to show Shetland in its correct geographical location in all its publications and communications. No one even expects the UK government to understand how important all of this is, let alone follow suit. Waiting for others to correct their errors is not good enough, and Shetlanders should be much more vocal in explaining where the islands really are.

A few years ago, a local radio station, exasperated by the Shetland-in-a-box syndrome, produced a T-shirt that had a map of Shetland with the UK in a box (in the wrong place and scale, of course). A similar perspective is shown by the folk of Tory Island, which lies off the west coast of Donegal. With their quirky humour, they describe Ireland as a large island that lies to the east of Tory.

***

The cod fishermen not only had an excellent knowledge of geography, but they also had to know the seabed, which can have a topography as varied and dramatic as any mountainous terrain, in order to know where to fish. Cod prefer to live and feed on shallower areas of the seabed, from 50 to 100 metres deep, and these extensive areas are known as fishing banks. It was the shoaling of cod on the Papa Bank that kick-started the cod fishery. Expanding into more distant waters, similar cod banks were fished around Greenland, Faroe and Rockall. When fishing off Iceland, the cod smacks fished off the northeast coast, close to the point of Langanes. When I was growing up, I often heard the story about how a Shetland cod skipper, called Aald Heglie, had discovered a new cod bank at Iceland, much further offshore, and how this became known as Heglies Bank.

Aald Heglie was christened John Johnson, but nobody knew him by that name. At this time there was a limited range of surnames, many of which were patronymic (ending in 'son'), as is the case throughout Scandinavia. The range of first names used was even smaller. Most men were called Andrew, William (or Willie), John (or Joanie), Robert (or Robbie), Magnus (or Magnie), Thomas (or Tammy), Laurence (or Lowrie) and James (or Jeemie). There were no Kyles, Kevins or Kelvins in 19th-century Shetland. One consequence of this limited nomenclature was that many people had the same name. There were probably hundreds of Joanie Johnsons. Another more defining characteristic was therefore essential to better identify individuals. Some were called after the boat they sailed on; others were named after the croft they came from. So, Joanie Johnson, who lived on a croft called Heglibister, was always known as Joanie a' Heglibister; the croft name replacing his surname.

This practice continues today in some parts of Shetland. In the island of Whalsay I have a good friend called John Anderson. If you were to ask where John Anderson stays, you would be met with a look of incomprehension. If there is a little more explanation and some context provided, the mystery will be solved and you will be told: 'Ah, you mean Joanie a' Hamister.'

By the time Joanie a' Heglibister was skipper of the *Clipper*, he was in his fifties and had become known as Aald Heglie – it was unusual for a man of this age to still be fishing. It was said that he had such a liking for the cod fishing that he was reluctant to give up. Despite having sailed on smacks most of his working life, he never lost his boyish enthusiasm for striking a cod shoal. Sometimes when he was off watch, sleeping below, younger crewmembers would repeatedly strike the deck just above his bunk with their hands. This made the same noise as several large cod hitting the deck. It did not matter how many times this trick was played, he always rushed on deck convinced that this was the start of a good fishing.

I remember being enthralled by the story of Heglies Bank. Whenever I asked where it was, no one seemed to know, other than it was somewhere off Iceland. There is certainly no fishing ground by that name to be found on historical or contemporary fishing charts. Perhaps this was a story that became exaggerated over the years; possibly there was no such bank; or maybe the knowledge of where it was had been lost. I was pretty sure that this was just a fanciful story until I read *The Sail Fishermen of Shetland*, by Captain Halcrow, who devotes several pages to Aald Heglie.

According to Halcrow, in the autumn of 1889, a severe south-westerly gale forced the Shetland cod fleet that had been fishing off Iceland to take shelter in a bay to the north of Langanes. Concerned that this bay was becoming dangerously congested with too many smacks swinging at anchor, Aald Heglie decided to allow his smack to drift slowly before the wind by lying hove-to. This was a technique commonly used by sailing vessels to ride out a storm, involving a particular set of the sails and the rudder. It took several days for the gale to abate, and, by this time, the *Clipper* was out of the sight of land. Lying becalmed, somewhere northeast of Iceland, there was little to do until the wind picked up and they could sail back to re-join the rest of the fleet. Possibly out of boredom rather than anything else, one of the crew threw a baited fishing line over the side. Surprise at finding the water was shallow quickly turned to astonishment when two large cod were caught. The rest of the crew started to fish and there was soon a cod on every hook. It was a bonanza. Halcrow does not say how many days the crew kept fishing but, in the event, they had to stop after they had caught more than 20,000 cod, having used all the salt they had on board. Aald Heglie generously passed on the details of where to find this new fishing bank to the other Shetland smacks when he sailed past them on his way back to Shetland. As fishing was poor off Langanes that day, most of them sailed north to try out this new bank. None were disappointed and they all returned home with full holds. From then onwards this new fishing ground was called Heglies Bank.

So far, so good; Halcrow's written account tied in with the story I had been told. But where exactly is Heglies Bank?

The starting point is the bay north of Langanes where the *Clipper* was hove-to and began to drift slowly before the south-westerly gale. According to Halcrow, the *Clipper* drifted for 'several days'. Taking several days to mean three or four days, and assuming that she would have drifted at around one knot (one nautical mile per hour), the smack would have ended up between 72 to 96 miles northeast of Langanes. Laying these distances on a chart, she would have been into deep water, nowhere near any fishing bank. The only part of the seabed shallow enough to be a fishing bank, according to a modern Icelandic fishing chart, is an area called Þistilfjörður Grunn. But this is only 30 to 50 miles from Langanes and, if the *Clipper* had drifted for several days, it would have long passed over this bank.

I realised that this was beginning to resemble a detective story, and I wondered what the next confusing clue might be. One afternoon, I found myself sitting in the home of retired skipper Davie Smith, from Scalloway. Having been a fisherman most of his life, he had been part owner and skipper of the *Evening Star*. Most fishermen have a passing interest in fishing history, and some are very knowledgeable, but Davie is different. He is an expert. A fellow skipper once told me that what Davie does not know about Shetland fishing history is not worth knowing. I would not disagree. He is one of these men who, had he not been a fisherman, could easily have been a history professor. With a knowledge of fishing and maritime history that is encyclopaedic, I reckon he must have a photographic memory. Davie looks at history through the eyes of a fisherman.

As we sat chatting, I looked out of his living room window. The strong wind that had blown all day was now a full gale, tearing the white tops off the waves and effortlessly throwing them into the air. It's the kind of day where you are better to be ashore, Davie joked. I explained my problem in trying to work out if Heglies Bank was in fact Þistilfjörður Grunn. He was as perplexed as I was, thinking that the account by Captain

Halcrow must be wrong. But hold on, Davie suddenly inter-jected, what if Aald Heglie had used a sea anchor[*] that night. If you were really wanting to slow the drift of a vessel before the wind, you would use a combination of hove-to and a sea anchor, he suggested. We discussed this idea for some time, and eventually concluded that, if both had been used, then the drift would have been reduced to around 0.5 knots. I quickly redid the maths. With the *Clipper* drifting at this reduced speed, the minimum distance travelled over three days would have been 36 miles, with a maximum of 48 miles over four days. Laying these distances on a chart, the *Clipper* would have ended up right on top of Þistilfjörður Grunn. So, perhaps it could be Heglies Bank, after all? Davie and I were pretty sure that we had solved the mystery, but we both agreed that some external validation was needed to confirm our theory.

I had always been told that Faroese fishermen, some of whom were employed as crew on board the Shetland smacks, had con-tinued to use an adapted version of the Shetland name for this fishing ground when they started fishing there with their own vessels. I had no idea if this was true or not until I came across a log entry from the Faroese cod smack *Westward Ho*, which referred to fishing the Hegglebanken off northeast Iceland in 1913. The log entry read: *Fiskede på Hegglebanken, vi drev frem og tilbage hele dagen.* ('Were fishing on the Hegglebanken, we drifted back and forth the whole day.') This confirmed that the Faroese were still using the name Hegglebanken at this time, but was this the same fishing bank that the Icelanders call Þistilfjörður Grunn?

The Faroese had continued to fish around Iceland right up to the 1970s, by which time trawling had long replaced hand lining for cod. I needed to find one of the last Faroese fishermen who had fished around Iceland, and several people suggested

---

[*] A sea anchor is a contraption (often made of wood and canvas) that is deployed to slow a vessel's drift.

that I should speak to Mortan Johannessen when I was next in Faroe. He had started fishing after leaving school and soon became a skipper. Although now over 80, and long since retired, he was not easy to get hold of. Every time I phoned, I was told he was not at home. It transpired that retirement for Mortan meant he was fishing for cod with automatic jigging machines on board his small boat when the weather allowed, and then processing his catch at home when he was not able to get to sea. His wife said I might get hold of him at one of the small piers in Tórshavn, where he had a stall selling his catch.

It was a cold and windy March morning as I made my way down to the harbour to see if I could find him. It was one of those days where everyone was in a hurry; doing what they had to do quickly so they could get back to their warm homes. Standing next to brightly painted hardware stores and sheds, I scanned the many piers that form the town centre of Tórshavn, but there was no one to be seen. Making my way across to a group of fishermen sheltering next to the offices of the Faroese Fishermen's Union, I asked them if they knew Mortan Johannessen. 'Sure,' said one. 'He is the guy over there who looks like Santa Claus.'

And there he was at the end of the pier, a large, jovial-looking man with red cheeks and a white beard, dressed in an orange survival suit selling his catch and speaking on his mobile phone. As he sold cod roe, fresh cod fillets and salt cod to discerning customers, and as he spoke to other fishermen on his mobile phone finding out who was catching most cod and where, I could not believe this was a man in his eighties. He had the energy and enthusiasm of a 20-year-old entrepreneur. Engaging with his customers, persuading some to buy more, giving others a discount, I could see Mortan was a born trader. It took some time before I was eventually able to introduce myself and explained that I wanted to know the exact location of Heglies Bank.

When I took out my fishing chart and pointed to where I believed the bank was located, he immediately confirmed that

I was correct. I could see that he was wondering why a Shetlander was interested in a fishing ground he had last fished in 1975. He explained that the name Hegglebanken had never appeared on a fishing chart but had been handed down by one generation of Faroese fishermen to the next. While we were having this discussion, cod continued to be sold, money handed over and change given out. The Faroese skippers wrote this name in pencil on their charts, he explained, never using the Icelandic name of Þistilfjörður Grunn. Hegglebanken was probably an old Faroese name, he suggested. It was only when I explained who Aald Heglie was, and how this bank had been discovered, that he began to give me his full attention. Despite the cold and wind, we spent the next hour talking about the salt cod days in Iceland, Faroe and Shetland. As Halldór Laxnes said, when all is said and done, life is about salt fish.

9

Beach Boys

Today, fish processing is all done indoors, in specialist factories. From the outside, they look like large warehouses and, unless you go inside, you would not know that these buildings had anything to do with fish. It was very different in the 19th century. Instead of fish processing factories, salt fish was laid out to dry on the stone beaches of Shetland. Nowadays, these beaches look as if they have never had any economic value. Many are remote and are, for the most part, deserted. In the 19th century they were the economic heartland of the islands.

The challenge of drying salt fish on a beach during a rainy Shetland summer was the job of the beach boys; teenagers, mostly aged from 11 to 14. Not yet old enough to be fishermen, they were old enough to cure fish. The culture of these beach boys was as different from the sun-kissed Californian Beach Boys culture of the 1960s as can be imagined. Instead of sun, surf and cars, the Shetland beach boys had to cope with rain, wind and mind-numbing drudgery.

Going for a walk around Shetland's stone beaches, their aesthetic value is immediately apparent. They are rarely straight, often forming beautiful arcs which inspire great photography. Never flat, they all slope into the sea at different angles, shaped and moulded by the sea that they play host to. Even on a calm day there is the energising noise of breaking waves, followed by the distinctive rumble of the sea as it runs up and down the sea-worn smooth stones.

In recent years these beaches have become adorned by hundreds of miniature stone towers, one stone delicately placed on top of another, patiently constructed during the summer months. Few survive the winter gales, but that is not the point. As much pleasure is derived by building them again the next year. Some stone beaches have recently become a popular location for agate hunters. The fluorescent and translucent colours of these tiny silica-rich stones attract passionate geologists and jewellery designers in equal numbers. The beaches are also wonderful places to walk, sit and listen. On a busy day there might be some other people, but most times, it is a solitary experience. Surrounded by the noise of birds and the sea, they are peaceful without being quiet. It is difficult to believe that this was where thousands of tons of salt fish were dried every summer.

Another huge difference between then and now is plastic. Walking along one of my favourite Shetland beaches, I reflect that there has always been rubbish washed up. Dead and decomposing seaweed is not new; it is as old as the beaches themselves. What is new is the tideline of plastic that has become so depressingly commonplace in the past half century. The waves cannot distinguish between seaweed and plastic, and they are thrown together in the confused mess I see lying just above the high-water mark. The seaweed strings range in colour from brown to black and are dull; organic-looking, in fact. In alarming contrast, most of the plastic is over-bright and garish. Hundreds of pieces of synthetic twine, a few inches long and frayed at both ends, use their bright green, red and yellow colours to scream for attention.

The fragments of broken plastic boxes and bottles are less lurid but no less harsh, as they all seem to have sharp and serrated edges where they have been broken by the power of the sea. Wondering where the other parts of the plastic boxes might be,

I remind myself that this process of disintegration does not get rid of plastic; it actually makes the problem worse. The pieces of plastic get smaller and smaller until they can hardly be seen. Even when the plastic is reduced to microscopic fragments, it remains indestructible. That is when it does its greatest damage as it is eaten by fish and enters our food chain. In contrast, seaweed has been part of the marine ecosystem for millions of years. It has always had a purpose; as food, as a habitat for marine life, as well as being the marine equivalent of the rainforest in capturing carbon dioxide. When seaweed dies, it is torn from the seabed by waves and washed up on beaches, making an excellent natural fertiliser. Plastic is the opposite. In return for a temporary utility, we are left with something that cannot be destroyed and will never disappear.

The intertwined and jumbled mess of seaweed and plastic could be a metaphor for much of our contradictory world; the ancient and the modern, the biodegradable and the indestructible, the benign and the malignant – all mixed together. The scale of the problem is simply staggering, with an estimated eight million tons of plastic dumped into the ocean every year. According to a report produced by the Dame Ellen McArthur Foundation, by 2050 there will be as much plastic in the sea, by weight, as there is fish. That is less than 30 years away. What a toxic legacy is being left to the next generation, the most pernicious evidence of our own greed and foolishness.

***

Back in the 19th century there was no plastic, only seaweed. This had to be removed every day to keep the beaches as clean as possible during the drying season, starting in April and ending in October. An older man, experienced in the science of drying fish, was in charge but it was the teenagers who did the work. Their first job, every morning, was to lay out every salted fish, skin side down, on top of the stones. Anyone who has enjoyed a

Shetland summer will appreciate that the process of drying fish would have been an endless battle against the prevailing weather conditions. At the first sign of rain, the fish had to be collected and built into cube-like towers, called steeples, and then covered up with a tarpaulin to keep everything dry. After the rain had passed the cod were laid out again, one by one. On a rainy day the gathering into steeples and then laying out again might have happened four or five times. Before dusk all the fish were gathered into steeples for the last time and covered to protect them from dew during the night. It was all back-breaking work. Most of the day was spent bending over, one eye on the beach, the other looking to the sky for signs of rain. Never has a generation of teenagers been so expert at forecasting rain.

Insofar as the exacting Spanish market for salt cod was concerned, around six weeks drying time was required. Once judged to be fully dried, the cod were carefully placed, one on top of another, in large jute bags, which was how the product was shipped to Spain. Smacks were always arriving to land their catch, and the aim was to get as many six-week cycles as possible fitted into the drying season.

While beach drying of fish took place all over Shetland, the drying of salt cod was concentrated in the area between Scalloway and Skeld. Some beaches were large, others were small. Some were easy to get to, others more difficult, involving a long trek through the hills. The largest and most accessible were used all the time, while those less suitable were selected only when there were heavy landings. Most beaches had buildings, where the dried cod was stored prior to export, but only a few had piers. The smacks generally anchored offshore and discharged their catches into small rowing boats. In a similar way, the finished product was rowed out by small boats to the anchored cargo vessels.

One of the largest cod-drying beaches was at Hirpa. Located at the southern tip of the Whiteness peninsula, this was an important place. There is an extensive area of stone beaches, the walls of several large (now roofless) buildings and the ruins of a substantial pier.

To get to Hirpa, you drive to the end of the road then take a short hike through the hill. It was a warm day the last time I walked there, the dry weather ensuring that the ground was firm underfoot. The first lambs had arrived; the newest ones sticking with their mothers while the older ones were becoming more adventurous and independent. The sky was full of the cries of Arctic terns – or tirricks, as they are called in Shetland. Migratory birds, they only come to Shetland to nest and rear their young. Their arrival in the first week of May marks the beginning of the summer for islanders. People talk of seeing their first tirrick as a harbinger of the long summer days to come; a signal that the dark winter is over. Once the summer is past, they leave Shetland to undertake one of the longest annual migrations on Earth. Travelling an incredible 60,000 miles every year, these tiny birds fly to the Antarctic where they spend a few months before coming back to Shetland in early May the following year.

With their long-pointed tails and their red beaks that are as sharp as a spear, they dart around the sky, bursting with boundless energy. Making a shrill noise as they fly high above, you hear them before you see them. Each tirrick releases a series of high-pitched, rapid-fire clicks followed by a screech. If you say tirrick very quickly four or five times in succession, you get an idea of what their call is like. More than a hundred birds doing this together created a cacophony that was the backdrop to my walk down the hill. I knew enough about tirricks not to go anywhere near their nests. Anyone doing so is subjected to a fierce aerial attack. The speed of their almost vertical descent, together with their manic screeching, reminds me of the footage of Stuka dive bombers from Second World War newsreels. Just when it seems they will use that sharp red beak to inflict serious damage, they veer away. Occasionally their wingtip will clip your head, but most often all you feel is a draft of wind as they pass inches away. It is nevertheless a scary experience that is made worse for those who have watched *The Birds*, the famous horror movie directed by Alfred Hitchcock. The only way to feel safe is to hold a stick above your head.

As I neared the beach, I was aware of an unevenness under my feet. Looking down I saw that I was standing on beach stones, partly hidden by grass – a remnant of the beach boys' activities. Such was the need for drying space that beaches were extended by moving stones into new areas. Despite the recolonisation by grass, the extended beach area was clear to see. It probably doubled the natural beach drying area.

As I was thinking about the physical effort needed to move a beach, I began to imagine what I might have seen had I been standing on this spot in the middle of the 19th century. A smack was lying at the pier with its crew busy landing their catch while the beach boys were laying cod out to dry, keeping a weather eye, as always, in case of rain. The entire beach area, natural and extended, was already glistening white with salt cod from earlier landings. All around there was the noise of people in a hurry, the crew of the smack rushing to finish landing their catch so they could get home for a few days before their next trip to Faroe. Joking with each other, the beach boys were laying out fish as fast as they could, enduring the shouts of the supervisor, who was running around checking that everything was being done properly.

I also imagined a large Spanish schooner anchored in Whiteness Voe waiting to load its cargo of finished product, which was lying in jute bags in the wood-lined store, having been made ready a few weeks earlier. Most of the Spanish crew were Basque, and they were observing the Shetland operation with a critical eye; they were, after all, the experts. The Shetland fishermen and beach boys were working in their shirts, it was so warm. The Basques, in contrast, were wearing their woollen jackets; this fine Shetland summer day was not their idea of warm.

The cry of the tirricks suddenly brought me back to the Hirpa of today; a remote and deserted beach covered in plastic rubbish. As I walked back up the hill, it struck me that the scene I had imagined had an entirely male cast. The crew of the smack and the Spanish schooner, as well as all those working on the beach, were men and boys. It would not be until the end of the century that women would come to play a direct role in the fishing industry, when they gutted and packed the herring.

But their place in the cod fishery, although not one of direct employment, was no less critical. While their husbands and older sons were fishing for cod, and their younger sons were working as beach boys, the women had to run the family croft. Looking after a cow and lambing sheep, tending the crops, fetching home peats, as well as looking after young children, was hard. Although being a cod fisherman allowed the family to earn some money, most of their food still came from the croft. The long summer days were filled with unending toil and responsibility for these women. Apart from a few days between long trips, the men were not home until it was almost winter, by which time most of the hard work on the croft had been done.

The hill seemed steeper as I walked back. Pausing to rest, I looked back down at Hirpa. While this was one of the largest beach drying areas, there are hundreds of similar beaches around the isles. The laying out of each fish side by side, but not on top of each other, needed a lot of beach space. Many visitors to Shetland at this time wrote that every beach on the islands was sparkling and glistening white like snow, with acres of salt fish spread as far as the eye could see.

***

The beach boys not only dried cod: they were also responsible for the salting and drying of the catch from the haaf fishery. The haaf operation was mostly based at fishing stations located at the extremities of Shetland, the nearest points of land to the sixern fishing grounds. These stations consisted of stone beaches, large enough for drying the fish as well as for hauling up the sixerns. Unlike the cod fishery, all the fish were split and salted ashore before being laid out to dry. The fishing stations in the far north of Shetland were a long way from the crofting townships. Here, the sixern crews and beach workers stayed in temporary seasonal lodges for the duration of the haaf season, the fishermen sometimes walking home at weekends.

Two of the best preserved and largest of these fishing stations are at Fethaland and Stenness, both located at the northern extremity of the Shetland Mainland. The walk to Fethaland is popular and I try to do it most years. Following a two-hour hike through the bleak hill, this large haaf fishing station eventually comes in sight. Although the roofs from the lodges have long gone, and while some walls have now partially collapsed, it is still possible to see where every building stood. This was once a bustling place with several hundred men and boys living here for the summer. It has two large beaches, one facing west and one facing east. Where the two beaches almost meet each other in the middle are the lodges, home to everyone who worked here, as well as the buildings for storing the dried salt fish. As many as 60 sixerns worked from Fethaland when the haaf was at its peak.

The official historical records invariably focus on the so-called important people. We can read about the lairds and merchants, and there is occasionally a fragment about a fisherman, maybe the skipper of a cod smack or sixern. There is nothing at all about the beach boys. We do not know their names, where they came from or their age. It is as if the thousands of teenagers who worked on the beaches over hundreds of years never existed.

At Fethaland, however, there is a tantalising glimpse into the life of one beach boy. Tucked away and difficult to find, to the north of the west beach, is a large flat rock on which many names and initials are carved. It is a confused jumble of scratches, some very old, some probably quite recent. One of these initials was carved by Gilbert William Guthrie, from the neighbouring island of Yell. He first came to Fethaland as a 12-year-old beach boy in 1867. His life would not have been unusual for the time; a very basic schooling before starting work when he was still a child. From first daylight to dusk the fish had to be tended, but once the fish had been laid out on days where there was no rain, there might have been some time off before gathering the fish back up at the end of the day. It was possibly on a day like that that young Gilbert Guthrie found time to carve his initials and the date – the only official record of his time as a beach boy.

Stenness is the other large haaf station in the north of Shetland. As large as Fethaland, it is, however, much more accessible – only a few minutes' walk from the road. This station has become an important part of Janette Kerr's life. Growing up next to a beach on the south coast of England, she loves the sea. Playing there as a child and going for long walks as a teenager, the power of the sea has been a constant fascination and seascapes have come to define her career as an artist. Acclaimed as a foul-weather artist, she is, according to Brian Fallon of the *Irish Times*, the best painter of the sea in the British Isles. Recalling when she first became aware of Shetland, Janette remembers looking at a map and wondering why this interesting-looking group of islands had been placed in a box. When she found out that Shetland was located much further north than the map-makers had the skill to show, she was determined to visit someday.

The opportunity came when she was awarded an artist-in-residency post in Scalloway. She arrived in February, finding it was not only a long way from home but also dark and windy. She immediately loved it and so began her love affair with the islands, their seas and their history. Shortly after she arrived, she was drawn to Shetland's many stone beaches. Often sitting for hours, she observed and listened to the sea in all its moods. This was eventually the inspiration for a collection of paintings in oil and charcoal of ten beaches that she had come to know particularly well. These are dramatic pieces, her work perfectly reflecting Shetland's extreme weather as she captures the power of the sea framed by dark skies.

After finding out that these deserted and lonely beaches had been the heartland of the 19th-century economy, she began to see these places in a different light and had to find out more. Scouring the archives, speaking to local historians and talking to people who had a family connection with the haaf, Janette started to build up a picture of the fishermen and beach boys who had worked here. Wondering how she could best convey the sights and sounds of a haaf beach in the 19th century, she concluded that she had to find another medium of expression. She teamed up with fellow artist Jo Millett, and they decided to create a sound-and-video installation focused on Stenness.

Entitled 'Confusing Shadow with Substance', this exhibition was premiered in the Shetland Museum. Highly innovative, it features film on three screens and sound from four speakers. The film continually changes from old black-and-white photos of haaf fishermen and beach boys to contemporary footage of boats, the sea and someone gutting and splitting a ling. The effect is one of constant visual change, enhanced by the three screens positioned adjacent to each other. The sound coming from the four speakers is equally eclectic. The noise of the sea in all its moods is interrupted firstly by the rumble of oars moving on the gunwale and then by the sound of oars being pulled through the water. The Shetland voices reading archive texts that appear on the screens are particularly evocative. All these noises and voices are heard from different corners of the gallery, sometimes from one speaker, sometimes from all four. The sights and the sounds are deliberately not always synchronised, further adding to the unique experience. This is an exhibition that grabs your attention, makes you think and leaves you wanting to find out more – art at its best.

Developing this fascination with Stenness, Janette has recently created a sound walk. Another collaboration with Jo Millett, this uses GPS technology, via a smartphone, to take the listener on a guided tour of Stenness beach. This is no stilted tour, instructing the listener where to go and when to listen. The listener is in charge and the narrative of sounds changes in response to which part of the beach the listener chooses to walk to. In a natural evolution from their sound-and-video installation, Janette and Jo have managed to bring Stenness back to life through their imaginative use of the latest technology. In doing so, the haaf fishermen and the beach boys, who had been written out of history, have been given their voice.

10

The Texan Eco Warriors

The global seafood industry is huge. At 180 million tons, fish is the main source of protein for the world's population. Chicken and pork are in equal second place with around 120 million tons each. Beef is a distant third at 70 million tons, while lamb barely registers at 15 million tons. Without fish, the world's population could not be fed; a fact that will become ever more critical as this population continues to increase.

Seafood Expo, one of the main global seafood trade fairs, takes place in April every year. For many years it was held in Brussels and has recently moved to Barcelona. It is vast, with more than 30,000 people attending the four-day event. Whenever I am there, I wonder if it is what a medieval fair might have been like. Thousands of merchants and traders milling around, looking at the goods on offer, searching out deals, comparing prices, haggling and doing business. At the same time, it is anything but medieval. Incredibly modern and technological, many of the stalls have eye-catching backdrops and spectacular video footage of fishing boats working in all kinds of weather. Others show fish farms located in some of the world's most dramatic fjord scenery. Sophisticated chilling cabinets ensure that the fresh fish on display always looks stunning. It is congested with people bumping into one another as they walk around speaking into their mobile phones looking at the fish on offer and not watching where they are going. Energising, inspirational and enjoyable, it is a great place to do business. Every kind of fish and every kind of seafood company is there. A few years ago, I even came across a Norwegian company selling dried salt cod, a reminder that there is still money to be made from selling this enduring seafood product.

Going from stall to stall, I always marvel at the variety and colour of the fresh seafood on offer. Yellowfin tuna from the Pacific, with its unnaturally long and pointed dorsal fin, which often looks more metallic blue than yellow. The stumpy orange roughy from New Zealand, with its permanent bad-tempered expression. Silver, slender and scaly, South African hake always looks very soft. In stark contrast is the firm, fat and round Atlantic mackerel: with its snow-white belly contrasting with its blue and black zebra-striped back, it must be one of the most beautiful fish in the world.

Top-quality seafood is now the default position for all companies. A business selling sub-standard product will not survive long in the highly competitive world of global seafood. It is essential to get fresh fish to the supermarket shelf, fishmonger or restaurant as soon as possible in order to maximise the number of days it can sit on the shelf before its taste and texture begin to be compromised. Not all fish are the same. Oily fish, like herring and mackerel, are only at their best for a couple of days, while most other species remain delicious for a week if kept in a fridge. Flat fish (such as plaice and sole) have an even longer shelf life of up to a fortnight, if properly chilled. For all species the key is to minimise the time between harvesting and processing. Cured, canned or frozen fish can all, of course, be stored for much longer. The quality of these processed products, however, also depends on reducing the time interval between capture and processing.

Many people still assume that fresh fish is always superior to frozen fish. The term 'fresh' implies that the fish has just been caught, whereas the word 'frozen' can suggest a standard that is less than fresh. The reality is sometimes the opposite. Take the humble fish supper, for example. Most of the cod sold to fish and chips shops is frozen at sea, caught by Norwegian, Faroese and Icelandic freezer trawlers fishing the North Atlantic. On board these vessels the catch is gutted, filleted and frozen very efficiently and quickly; the fillets are frozen within 24 hours of being caught. When these cod fillets are fried in batter and served with chips, they are of unsurpassed quality. In contrast, fresh cod served in some of the best seafood restaurants in London will be much older. At best it might be two or three days since this cod was caught, but more likely a week. It's perfectly fine to eat, but not actually so fresh as the frozen cod served in Britain's chippers. It will, however, be much more expensive.

Arthur Anderson was first to recognise that salt cod from Shetland was fetching a poor price in Spain because of its inferior quality. It took many years before his exhortations over quality paid off and Shetland was eventually exporting salt cod that was the equal of any produced elsewhere. Producing good quality dried salt cod was not easy in the 19th century. There was so much that could go wrong: bones in the flesh if the fish had not been properly split; black spots on the flesh if all the blood had not been washed away; taste compromised by too much or too little salt; and the shelf life of *bacalao* being reduced if the fish had not been properly dried.

At every stage of the process there was a set of detailed and exacting quality control checks – even though the term 'quality control' had not yet been invented. The quest for quality began as soon as the fish were caught. The usual pattern, when fishing was good, was for the entire crew to fish and then, when the skipper judged enough had been caught, to start processing. Having made sure that the gills had been cut to facilitate proper bleeding, the next job was to gut the cod and remove the head. The fish then had to be split; a skilled job which was only undertaken by experts, usually the skipper or mate. A split cod is the shape of a heart with the two cod fillets (remaining joined at the belly of the fish) spread out like angel wings and most of the backbone removed. This shape allows the fish to absorb most salt. After splitting, the cod were washed in tubs of salt water, the youngest crewmembers scrubbing away all traces of blood and gut lining. The fish were then carefully passed down into the hold where they would be laid between layers of salt.

Once back in Shetland, the cargo of wet salted cod was discharged and laid out on beaches to dry. The judgement of when the drying process – or pining, as it was called – was complete was of the utmost importance. Dried salt cod was deemed to have been properly cured when the flesh became so white it began to sparkle in the sunshine. This exceptional white colour is caused by the migration of salt to the surface of the cod where it forms a crust. The Spanish buyers expected dried salt cod to be whiter than white. The north of Spain was the destination for salt cod exported from Shetland, with most being sent to the Basque port of Bilbao. The fact that the Shetland cure was recognised as a top-quality *bacalao* product in the Basque country is testimony to how good the Shetlanders must have been at catching and curing cod. It was a bit like sending coals to Newcastle.

***

While ensuring best-quality seafood has been important ever since fish were first caught, a more recent challenge is the question of sustainability. While almost everyone agrees that sustainability is essential, there is a wide range of views as to what this means in practice. A sustainably managed fishery might mean one thing to a fishing company but something quite different to Greenpeace.

Sustainability is all about doing things in a way that is not harmful and, consequently, in a way that can be continued indefinitely. It is not easy. You cannot mine coal or extract oil sustainably – it will eventually run out. You can, however, manage fisheries sustainably. Most agree that this should be measured in respect of the environment, the economy and wider society – the so-called three pillars of sustainability. Some of the more radical NGOs only focus on the environment, neglecting the important economic and social pillars. These are not abstract concepts. Economic and social sustainability is all about keeping fishing communities (many of which are remote and have few alternative employment opportunities) alive. The conservation of fish stocks is obviously essential but if this is only achieved through the decimation of the fishing industry and the death of fishing communities, then the outcome is far from sustainable.

Mike Park's tenacity and frank-speaking is typical of many Scottish skippers. He came ashore some years ago and now works for the Scottish White Fish Producers Association, which represents most of Scotland's trawlers. Like many of his generation he began fishing when there were few restrictions. By the time he sold his boat, fishing had become one of the most regulated industries in Scotland. Fully committed to sustainable fisheries management, he is also conscious of the commercial reality that fishers face every day. To be sustainable in the real world, he argues, environmental needs must be balanced with economic reality. Or, as he puts it: 'It is difficult to be green if you are in the red.'

Increased concern about fish stocks and ocean ecology has spawned a huge number of NGOs, most of which have laudable aims and aspirations. Well-funded, they can employ huge teams of highly qualified researchers, campaigners and lobbyists. Their slick PR campaigns have had a profound impact on public attitudes to seafood and government policy on fisheries issues. Much of this has been necessary and will continue to be essential to create a more sustainable economy in the future. Some, however, engage in a dangerous narrative that *all* fishing and fish farming is bad, and that the ocean needs to be left as a huge marine nature reserve. It always strikes me that these people talk with so much passion about the sea but appear to be utterly oblivious as to how people are going to be fed. Sometimes I wonder if they care.

There are currently 7.8 billion people on our planet. It is estimated that this will increase to more than 11 billion by 2050. Around 700 million people go to bed hungry every night, many of them children. This is almost a tenth of the world's population and it is utterly shameful, particularly for us in the developed world who have so much. Feeding the global population should be the greatest challenge of our age and, if we cannot do this, it will be a catastrophic moral failure for humanity. By 2050 we will need to produce at least 30 per cent more food than we do now. Some argue it will be more than 40 per cent more if we are to eliminate malnutrition around the world as well as feed a much bigger population. Where can all this extra food come from? Cutting down the Amazon rainforest to graze cattle and grow soya, using more fertiliser or accepting genetically modified food are some of the unpalatable alternatives. The sea, as a food production system that covers three-quarters of the globe, is part of the solution, not the problem.

Many of these zealous campaigners see themselves as passionate idealists seeking to save the oceans. For those who see the ocean as a source of protein produced in a sustainable manner, the zealots' reckless actions are at best misguided and at worst hypocritical. And the saddest thing of all is that they are unaware of the contradictions in what they do and say. A few years ago, I attended a meeting in London with a well-known American NGO to discuss the problem of discards. 'Discarding' is the practice where fish are thrown back into the sea because they are too small, there is no market, or they are more than a vessel's quota allocation. Since these discards are all dead, it is an unconscionable practice to which a solution needs to be found. We had a good discussion during which some possible solutions (such as increased mesh sizes on nets to allow small fish to escape) were discussed. I became increasingly annoyed, however, by the hectoring tone of two women who hailed from Texas. Fishers were acting immorally when discarding fish, I was told. Did they not know they were destroying the marine environment? How could they stand by and see all this fish going to waste as it was thrown over the side? It was not an atmosphere that fostered a meeting of minds, but I struggled on, being far too polite.

Anyhow, in the evening we all went out to dinner and I found myself sitting between the two eco warriors from Texas. I tried to keep the conversation relaxed and endeavoured to find some common ground. It was not easy but after a few glasses of wine and some nice fresh fish, a more convivial atmosphere developed. I enjoyed my dinner and, as I had been brought up to do, ate everything on my plate. It was then that I noticed that on either side of me the waiter was taking away fish that had only been picked at. I abhor waste, and it occurred to me that here was fish that had been discarded. Not discarded because of complex quota rules or because of poorly designed trawls, but because it was either not to the taste of the eaters or because they were not hungry. Both are problems associated with privileged people who live in the developed world. Two fish had died to provide them with food, yet the two Texan diners were entirely unaware of their hypocrisy. It annoys me to this day that I did not call them out. Food waste, like obesity, is a problem of the developed world. It is everywhere but is often not visible and is frequently ignored. According to the World Wide Fund for Nature (WWF), over a billion tons of food is wasted every year. That is an astonishing figure that should shame us all. The food wasted by those who have more than they need while hundreds of millions of people do not have enough to eat is a global disgrace that gets little airtime.

Some of the best-funded NGOs are those in North America who oppose fish farming. A frenetic period of effective political lobbying resulted in Canadian prime minister Justin Trudeau pledging to remove all salmon farms from British Columbia. An emotional campaign, devoid of science but expert at social media, demonised fish farming and succeeded in persuading the Canadian government to shut down one of the most sustainable ways of producing protein. It is deeply ironic that most of these salmon farms have been certified as meeting the most stringent environmental standards. That privileged rich people are prepared to curtail one of the most efficient methods of producing food for the sake of an environmental fantasy when hunger still stalks the globe is scandalous. The anti-salmon farming campaign was particularly vicious, with social media targeting fish farmers personally. For some reasons, young women who work for fish farming companies are in the firing line. 'Better for a woman to work in a brothel than on a salmon farm' is only one of many despicable slogans used by these environmental activists.

In this increasingly confused seascape, it is important to refocus on what true sustainability should mean. To my mind the best definition of what sustainability means in a practical sense was first articulated by a Norwegian, from a country which has been, and continues to be, defined by what the sea can provide. According to Gro Harlem Brundtland, sustainability is 'meeting the needs of the present generation without compromising the needs of future generations'. This amazing woman, who was three times prime minister of Norway, went on to become the director general of the World Health Organization (WHO). But it was when she was asked by the UN to chair the World Commission on Environment and Development that she began the discussion about how it is possible to have economic development without environmental degradation. The concept of sustainable development was born and has now become part of our normal discourse.

The Marine Stewardship Council (MSC) was set up in 1997 in response to the debate on how to encourage fisheries to become sustainable. The business model put forward by the MSC is very simple: if the consumer can be persuaded to pay a premium for sustainably sourced seafood, this will create a commercial incentive to manage fisheries better. Underpinning this approach is a comprehensive system whereby the environmental sustainability of fisheries is assessed according to 28 performance indicators covering the health of the fish stock, the fisheries' management methods used and the impact on the wider marine environment. The process is rigorous and scientific. It also has a high bar, with a pass rate of 80 per cent required before a fishery can be certified as sustainable. Once certified, companies can display the little blue MSC logo on their product packaging, thereby informing customers that this fish has been sustainably sourced. This certification process is in effect an environmental audit that defines and measures what constitutes a sustainable fishery. In this way the narrative is defined by science instead of emotion.

Lean, enthusiastic and animated, Rupert Howes is a man with a mission. Since he took over the helm at the MSC, it has grown from a staff of 12 in London to 220 in 20 locations around the world. With 500 fisheries and almost 20 per cent of the global fish catch now certified as sustainable, the MSC has had a huge impact in reducing overfishing. It has shown that there is a much better way – for the fish, for the fishing industry and for the blue planet. Their mission is both moral and ethical, according to Rupert. Sustainably managed fisheries eventually yield a greater catch, and are therefore more profitable, he argues with passion and conviction. There is still much more to do, he acknowledges, with less than one-fifth of global fisheries currently certified. As more people recognise the benefits of managing fisheries sustainably, he is confident that this proportion will continue to grow.

Crucial to this process are the hundreds of Fishery Improvement Programmes now in operation around the world.

These are designed to gradually improve fisheries management practices with the long-term objective of becoming MSC-certified. These programmes, often run by responsible NGOs working alongside the fishing industry, are impressive and are driving real and meaningful change in how the world catches its fish. Rupert Howes is unapologetic when he says that the MSC is both pro-fish and pro the fishing industry. It is possible to be both, he says, explaining that their mission is about food security and livelihoods, as well as environmental responsibility. This pragmatic approach has recently brought the MSC into conflict with some NGOs. It seems that, by making sustainability measurable and scientific, the MSC does not sit well with those who prefer emotional campaigning and leave uneaten food on their plates.

Overfishing was not an issue when fish were caught by hand line. The Shetland cod fishermen were fishing sustainably, even though the word had not yet been invented. Their problem was to catch enough fish so that they could earn a wage. Sometimes catches were very poor, and times were hard. Always enterprising and always resourceful, they were continually looking for new opportunities to earn money. An unforeseen and unusual sideline presented itself in Faroe in the form of brandy. Smuggling brandy from Faroe to Shetland was highly lucrative and many fishermen made a lot of money from this trade. There was one big problem. It was illegal.

II

The Smugglers

Having sailed from Shetland to Faroe in an August gale, I was relieved to stand on the pier in Tórshavn. Twelve of us had chartered the *Swan*, an old wooden sailing boat, for a couple of weeks. As I stretched my legs, I was thankful that I was no longer on a moving deck drenched in spray. Noticing that the wind had gone I looked up and saw that the sun was about to make an appearance. Like Shetland, the weather can change very quickly in Faroe.

Despite having been a regular visitor to Faroe over many years, arriving at the islands still takes my breath away. It is the most stunning of all landscapes. Towering black basalt mountains and cliffs frame the most incredible green grass valleys and coastal strips. The tops of the mountains are often hidden by dense grey fog which clings to these peaks long after the sun breaks through lower down. Brightly painted wooden houses crowd around the many harbours. Every house has its own colour scheme, but most are a combination of white, red, green and black, with some stunning outliers in purple, blue and orange. Faroe has some of the most colourful villages on the planet. Even on a windy and rainy day (and there are many of these), the Faroese landscape is always dramatic and energising.

For some reason I have always felt at home in Faroe. Many other places have struck me as equally beautiful, breath-taking and interesting but only Faroe has always felt strangely familiar. When I am there, I immediately relax and find myself in the same frame of mind as when I am at home. It is as if I have not travelled at all. I have always put this down to the fact that Faroe is very similar to Shetland. Both are small island archipelagos in the North Atlantic struggling with the same inclement weather. Both are also communities that have looked to the sea to provide food and a living. More recently I have wondered if there might be another explanation. Some behavioural scientists argue that such feelings of familiarity can be explained by genetic memory. Apparently, there is now some evidence that a person's attitude and perception can be influenced by events experienced by previous generations which have been passed on through a form of genetic DNA recall. A person can therefore feel a certain way because of the experiences of family members several generations previously. It all seems a bit fanciful, but I find it intriguing, nevertheless.

After a few days sailing around Faroe, we began our journey back to Shetland and decided to spend a day in Suðuroy, the most southerly of the Faroese islands. We tied up in the attractive harbour of Tvøroyri. With a population of around 1,500, it is still a prosperous place, although not as important as it was in the 19th century when it was one of the main fishing ports in Faroe.

Later that day, a few of us went for a stroll through the village. As we walked, we began to talk about the first Shetlanders who came to Faroe to fish. We wondered if some of these cod fishermen, maybe even some of our own ancestors, had walked these same streets more than a hundred years before. Making our way back to the boat, we saw the rest of the crew sitting inside a bar, called Pubbin, in what had once been the Thomsen merchant store, one of the old cod companies in the village. As we joined them, I noticed that our skipper, Magnie Sinclair, was not there. Someone explained that he had stayed on board to hear the latest shipping forecast. Looking around the pub, I could see that there was an eclectic collection of all kinds of things on the shelves and on tables. I realised that all of this – the glass jars, the old tobacco tins, the brandy pigs[*] and the fishing gear – had once been for sale. This is not a pub trying to look old. This is a merchant store that now sells alcohol and food and has not seen any need to clear away the evidence of its previous life.

When we had settled down to enjoy a beer, the lady behind the bar came across to ask if we were from Shetland. Dressed in faded Levi's and a baggy Faroese jumper, she introduced herself with a welcoming smile as Anna Kirstin Thomsen, the owner of Pubbin. Short and slim, with cropped auburn hair, she was both energetic and enthusiastic. She said that she had been brought up with stories of the Shetland fishermen who used to fish around Faroe. Many of them were regular visitors to Tvøroyri and they were well known to her family when they ran their merchant business. She told us there were company records that showed which Shetlanders had come into their shop and what they had bought. 'It was mostly brandy and tobacco,' she added with an impish grin.

I asked if these records were stored in the archives in Tórshavn or Copenhagen. She just laughed and asked me to follow her next door. We went into a room that had once been an office and there, lying on an old table, were company ledgers detailing all the transactions that took place. Although the entries were in Danish it was easy to read which Shetlanders had bought what, when and at what price. Just as I was starting to look through the ledgers, I overheard Magnie shout in the door that he had just heard that a gale was forecast for tomorrow, and we would be best to leave now. So, having just discovered this treasure trove of information about the Shetland cod fishermen, I had to

[*] Brandy pigs are large earthenware containers traditionally used for storing and transporting brandy.

leave them unread. It would be four years before I came back. I barely had time to finish my beer.

In the 19th century, the Danish government did not levy any tax on alcohol and tobacco in Faroe, whereas in Shetland the British excise duty regime was applied in full. Given the proximity between the two island groups, and the development of the distant-water fishery at Faroe, it is not surprising that an illicit trade soon began. With most of the distant-water smacks making several trips to Faroe each year, there were ample opportunities to purchase alcohol and tobacco at duty-free rates and then smuggle this contraband back to Shetland.

Because smuggling was illegal, there is no official information on how widespread this practice was, or how important it became for the local economy. But Shetland folklore is full of tales of smuggling on an extensive scale. I remember as a child sitting in the company of older people, listening with rapt attention to stories of smuggling contraband from Faroe. These events were almost within living memory, about people from my own community and places that I knew well. I recall hearing about Peter Reid, skipper of the *Vixen* from Skeld, who was a notorious smuggler. His crew usually landed their contraband at Culswick, a small inlet near their Skeld base. It was said that an old barn there was often completely full of pigs of brandy.

This practice of discharging brandy before making landfall in Shetland was commonplace. The smacks operating out of Voe, for example, used to arrive on the northwest coast of Shetland as darkness was falling and then launch a small boat to take their contraband ashore to a safe and secluded spot for later collection. A favourite place was the Hams a' Muckle Roe, a remote location that can only be reached by a small boat from the sea or else a long hike of several hours through the hills. Not somewhere that someone from HM Customs and Excise would be likely to drop in. After landing their booty, the smacks sailed into Voe to discharge their catch of salt cod, knowing that the excisemen would find no contraband on board if they decided to search the smacks.

The only evidence which exists about this trade comes from the few incidents where contraband was successfully seized by the authorities. In the official records of the Customs and Excise, it is noted that 81 gallons of brandy was found on board the *Dryad* in 1864 and 48 gallons on board the *Cynthia* in 1866. If these examples are in any way representative of the quantities of illegal goods taken back by smacks every time they returned from Faroe, then this was a large operation.

Once the last distant-water trips had been completed, the fishermen sold their booty. For obvious reasons this trade had to be clandestine. There is one story of a stranger coming to a house on Linga, a small island off Scalloway, and instructing a young boy, who was at home by himself, to tell his father that 'his gear is in the usual place'. Presumably this was the delivery of contraband, in accordance with prior and standard arrangements.

The scarcity of records of fishermen being apprehended conflicts with the many stories and legends of smuggling that survive, even to this day. So, have the stories of smuggling become exaggerated over the years, or was it the case that fishermen were very good at avoiding detection? Suspecting that the Thomsen company ledgers in Tvøroyri might hold the answer, I decided to return to Faroe, this time flying rather than sailing. Anna Kirstin was expecting me and had kindly arranged for several retired fishermen to be there. Most of these men had started their fishing careers catching cod with hand lines, as the Shetland men had done during the previous century. Shaking my hand, one of the oldest men said in halting English, 'Welcome home, Shetlander.'

When I eventually sat down and began to read the ledgers, I was astonished. The scale of the purchases was staggering. Many Shetlanders regularly purchased huge quantities of brandy and tobacco. In 1863 John Williamson of the *Petrel* bought brandy to the value of over £17, while Ross Georgeson of the *Caroline* spent more than £21. At this time, the average annual wage for a cod fisherman was around £18. In other words, some fishermen were spending more on contraband than they earned in a year.

Other purchases were more modest, ranging from £3 to £10 in value, mostly for brandy but also tobacco and occasionally items of clothing. One entry that caught my eye was in April 1864, when William Goodlad bought brandy and three woollen jumpers for the comparatively small sum of £1.65. He was one of my ancestors and was aged 19 at the time. He was drowned eight years later when his smack, the *Turquoise*, was lost on her way back from Faroe.

As I sat at the old desk examining these precious ledgers, I noticed the dust particles in the atmosphere were sparkling in a shaft of bright sunlight that had suddenly found its way through the shuttered window. As this short glimpse of sun disappeared, I became aware of how beautiful the copper-plate ink hand-writing was. No one writes like this anymore; it was entirely legible but much more than utilitarian. The graceful lines and bold capitals spoke of a confident merchant, recording his daily business in a manner that was pleasing to the eye. Looking around at the worn wooden floor and the faded paint on the pine lined walls, it occurred to me that little had changed in this room since Anna Kirstin's ancestors had sold brandy to mine.

Even more surprising than the scale of purchases, was the credit provided. The book-keeping system recorded the date of payment for items, and it was usually a year later. This level of credit reflected the substantial trust placed in the Shetland fish-ermen by the Thomsen family, and a confidence that they would be returning to fish the following year. For the Shetlanders, it was a no-brainer; this arrangement enabled them to sell their contraband at inflated prices back home before even having to pay for it in the first place. It was a unique business opportunity, apart from the small problem of it being illegal.

The scale of the smuggling operation eventually prompted the government to go to extraordinary lengths to try and stop the practice. A new division of the coastguard service was established in February 1879 with the express purpose of ending the trade in contraband. It had plenty of staff and no expense was spared in their war against the smugglers. A few years later, a dedicated cutter was based in Lerwick so that smacks could be stopped on their way back from Faroe.

The penalties for being caught smuggling were severe. The case against the skipper of the *Dryad* eventually resulted in Peter Blance being fined £54, a huge fine that was more than three times his annual earnings. When these excessive fines did not deter the smugglers, incarceration was tried. Four crewmembers of the *Vixen* were each sentenced to six months' hard labour. This was an exceptionally severe sentence, but hard labour in prison might not have been that different to working a cod trip; it might even have been easier. In any case, prison was no more effective a deterrent than the fines had been. As late as 1894, the well-known smack skipper John Inkster, of Burra, was charged with concealing 66 pounds of tobacco in his house. He was found guilty and given the option of paying £50 or serving 30 days in jail. He chose the option of prison.

The failure to deter smuggling suggests that the profits being made were an important additional source of income for the fishermen. It may have been the case that, since only a small number were apprehended, the potential reward of smuggling far outweighed any risk.

Despite the bombast surrounding the arrival of the cutter in Lerwick, she proved to be ineffective at intercepting smacks returning from Faroe. The cod fishermen were as familiar with the geography of the Shetland coastline as they were with the architecture of their boats, thinking nothing of taking a smack into a small inlet in pitch darkness to discharge contraband. The Customs and Excise officers, invariably from Scotland or England, lacked this local knowledge.

Another reason it was not possible to stop smuggling was the fact that the local community provided no intelligence to the customs officers. The man in charge of the Customs and Excise for most of this time was John Gatherer, an appropriate name for someone whose job was to gather excise duty from an unwilling population. His early enthusiasm for the job waned over the years as his lack of success became ever more apparent. He rather wearily concluded that the task of catching smugglers was well-nigh impossible in Shetland because of the general disposition of most islanders to engage in the practice and their almost universal unwillingness to give any information to the authorities. There was no social stigma associated with the smuggling trade, even when large fines or a prison sentence were the consequences.

Despite their failure to stop this lucrative trade, the authorities did have one notable success. One of the fastest and largest smacks in the Shetland fleet was the *Destiny*. One foggy day, when she was returning from Faroe with a large quantity of brandy aboard, she was intercepted by the cutter. Despite being ordered to stop, the skipper of the *Destiny* used her greater speed to leave the cutter behind, which eventually gave up the chase in the poor visibility. This caused an uproar – not only had a Shetland skipper the audacity to ignore an instruction to stop, but he had added insult to injury by sailing his smack faster than one of Her Majesty's ships. The upshot of this was that the Customs and Excise ordered the smack owner, Joseph Leask, to cut 10 feet from the top of the main mast so that the *Destiny* was never again able to out-sail one of their vessels.

There is no doubt that smuggling was taking place on a huge scale under the guise of the cod fishery. This raises the interesting question of what involvement, if any, the smack owners – rather than the crews – had in the contraband trade. On one level, the smack owners had no official connection as not one of them was ever prosecuted. Indeed, a degree of disapproval can be gauged from some of the crew agreements* that specifically prohibited smuggling on pain of forfeiture of annual earnings. Andrew Greirson, the owner of the *Dryad*, was anxious to point out to the authorities that he was not involved in the alleged smuggling of brandy by the skipper, Peter Blance. He pointed out that his crew agreements expressly forbade this practice. But there is no evidence of the smack owners ever taking any action to stop the carrying of contraband, despite these anti-smuggling clauses. It was probably the case that these were only inserted to safeguard the owners from any charges of complicity. This seems to have been the conclusion reached by John Gatherer in his report of 1866 when he wrote that 'with few exceptions I believe the crews of all the vessels engage in it to a greater or lesser extent. The smuggling practices are notorious throughout the islands and are well known to the owners of the vessels who never discharge any of their Masters or men for such offences.'

Smuggling provided an unusual additional source of income for the cod fishermen. But there was also an even more remarkable money-making enterprise that they engaged in. Instead of gutting, splitting and salting the cod, they sometimes kept them alive on board.

---

* These agreements, which were signed by all crewmembers before each trip, set out what was and was not permitted on board and how the proceeds of the catch would be shared after the salt cod had been sold.

12

'A Sight Most Interesting and Curious'

Sitting on board a well boat delivering smolts to our salmon farm a few years ago, I marvelled at modern technology. This boat had loaded these tiny live salmon from a hatchery on the west coast of Scotland two days previously and was now transferring them into salmon pens off Scalloway. Fish are fragile creatures, and it was amazing to see how these salmon smolts thrived in the seawater wells on the boats. I used to think that it is only relatively recently that the seafood industry has become so technologically advanced. But that was before I learned that some of the cod smacks kept part of their catch alive as well.

How could it be possible to keep cod, which had been caught on a hand line, alive in a sailing ship? This seemingly impossible task was undertaken by constructing a seawater well on board. It was built in the middle of the vessel, with the hull forming the sides and two specially constructed bulkheads completing the rectangular well shape. Many holes were then drilled into the hull of the vessel, filling the well with seawater. Effectively creating a storage tank on board, this allowed fish to be kept alive during a fishing trip.

The ceiling of the well was kept as low as possible to maintain vessel stability. It was essential that it was always filled to the top with seawater, thereby preventing any free surface effect. This is the term used to describe the potentially lethal impact on vessel stability of water moving around within the hold, or on the deck, as the boat rolls. This is perhaps best illustrated by the simple example of carrying a half full pan of water from one room to another – the water will surge from side to side. If any water in a well has a free surface, then it will surge to the side at the same time as the vessel rolls. She will then most likely tip over and start to sink. If properly constructed, and filled to the top with water, a vessel with an onboard well is, however, entirely stable.

Seawater wells were first used by fishermen in the Netherlands in the 16th century. This technique was copied by other fishing nations, and, by the 19th century, there were many welled smacks operating from English ports. The first reference to a Shetland welled smack was in 1869. The impetus for constructing wells in boats came from the incredibly high prices that fresh cod fetched at this time. When the only means of preserving fish and meat was by salting, fresh fish was a rare delicacy for which the wealthy were prepared to pay exceptionally high prices. The well-off middle classes in London wanted fresh cod to adorn their dining tables, whatever the cost. It was only possible to properly supply this lucrative market after the rail link between Grimsby and London was completed in 1848. This allowed fresh cod to be sent from Grimsby to London every day. The Humber estuary off Grimsby became the collecting centre for live cod landed from the fleet of welled smacks. Discharged into thousands of large wooden boxes anchored offshore, the live cod were stored until harvested and then sent by rail to London. It was an ingenious way of ensuring that Londoners could buy cod that were only a day old – something that is impossible today.

This intriguing method of storing live cod on an industrial scale fascinated Frank Buckland, a well-known naturalist. Born into a family of academics, he was educated at Winchester public school then Oxford University. Although researching and writing extensively about all aspects of the natural world, it was his lifelong obsession with fish that he is best known for. He authored many academic textbooks which have stood the test of time, including his classic work *The Natural History of British Fishes*, published in 1881. Writing for the popular market and delivering entertaining public lectures, he was well known outside academia, becoming something of a celebrity. In some ways he was the 19th-century equivalent of Sir David Attenborough. He was also incredibly eccentric, even by the exceptional standards of English public-school boys of that time. Short and rotund of stature, his tangled hair and unkempt beard added to his dishevelled appearance. He was also interested in eating exotic meats; his favourites were boiled elephant trunk, roasted porpoise head and stewed mole. Always intrigued by the unusual, and fascinated by all things fishy, he was greatly taken by the cod storage boxes anchored in the Humber. Opening one of these boxes to investigate, he wrote that 'the sight was most interesting and curious; there appeared one solid mass of living cod, all struggling and gaping with immense mouths'.

Although fresh cod could be sold for very high prices, it was not always possible to combine this with the established fishing pattern of the smacks. Making the 1,300-mile round trip from Shetland to the Humber took time and was difficult to fit into the already tight schedule of managing three distant-water trips within the year. As a result, well smacks generally made one trip with live cod each year, after the end of the last voyage of the season, which was usually off northeast Iceland. The live cod were only selected during the last week of fishing. To minimise the time that live cod were kept in the well, the trip to the Humber would sometimes be done first, with the landing of the wet salted cod having to wait until the smack returned home.

The first well smacks to arrive in Shetland were second-hand vessels bought from England. As the commercial benefits of selling live cod became ever clearer, many owners retro-fitted seawater wells into their smacks, and some even built brand-new well smacks. The Shetland Fishing Company invested heavily in this technology when, in 1872, they commissioned the Hall ship-yard in Aberdeen to design and build three large and impressive well smacks, the *Robert Miller*, the *John Walker* and the *Robert Kirkwood*.

Supplying the London market with fresh cod via Grimsby was not, however, without its problems. The challenge was to keep as many fish alive as possible. As a rule, 20 per cent mortality was typical. Although mortalities were higher when the weather was bad, lack of wind could be more serious than a severe gale. If a smack was becalmed in very still waters, the natural circulation of seawater into the well could be reduced and fish would die through lack of oxygen.

If these problems could be avoided, a successful discharge of a cargo of live cod in the Humber hugely boosted earnings. Converting typical prices paid for live cod into today's money suggests that the Grimsby fish merchants were often prepared to pay £9 per kilogram; an astonishing price that is more than double the best price paid for fresh cod in any European fish market today.

For about 20 years the smack owners boosted their profits and fishermen earned good money. But during the 1890s the price paid for live cod collapsed as steam engines replaced sail as the means of propulsion on board trawlers. This transformed their catching efficiency and resulted in huge quantities of fresh cod being landed every day into the trawling ports of Hull, Grimsby and Aberdeen. Fresh cod was losing its niche – it was becoming accessible to the wider population at reasonable prices. Within a few years cod, which had been a luxury food for the rich middle classes, was becoming a staple for the working class in the form of cod and chips. The market for live cod eventually disappeared. The age of steam, which had enabled Shetlanders to take advantage of this niche market, had in turn stolen it away with the development of steam trawling.

The well smacks are a good example of how human ingenuity can respond to a commercial opportunity. They are also a good reminder of why we should not get too carried away with how advanced we think we are compared with our forebears. The cod entrepreneurs of the 19th century were not trapped in an archaic industry. On the contrary, they were innovative, enterprising and always prepared to try something new.

***

The trade in live cod was well documented by the Scottish Fishery Board, which had been recording what was happening in the Shetland fishing industry since opening an office in Lerwick in 1809. Headquartered in Edinburgh, the fishery board posted officers to the many fishing ports and districts around Scotland. These men (and they were all men in the 19th century) recorded the detail of all fish landed, employment at sea and ashore, as well as all kinds of information regarding the export of fish. The board's Shetland archive is a huge statistical treasure trove for the serious researcher but, by its nature, can be rather dry reading.

Their annual reports are sometimes different. Written by the fishery officers, these are a fascinating narrative of the year that has passed. Style and content are variable (some are terse, others verbose) but they all reflect something of the character of each individual author. As government officials, they generally recorded the facts and were not usually prone to proffering their personal opinions and views. One exception was a fishery officer called John Kennedy, who was posted to Lerwick when the cod fishery was booming. He did not like Shetland and was not fond of Shetlanders either. He was also a rather mean man.

He was always complaining. He wrote to the head office in Edinburgh objecting that his lodgings were damp and cold and that his annual allowance to buy coal was insufficient to keep him warm. His remonstrances about the remoteness of Shetland and the poor weather were constant features of his correspondence. Some people are, by natural inclination, optimistic and enthusiastic, while others are pessimistic and negative. John

Kennedy was firmly in the latter camp, but his distaste for all things Shetland eventually created a toxic mix.

Despite all of this, he was an opportunist and he decided to see if he could make some money for himself. In 1860 he invested £50 in the Zetland North Sea Fishing Company. This was a lot of money for a middling civil servant – perhaps it was his life savings? In contrast to all the other cod companies at this time, which were owned by various merchant families, this business was owned by 60 individual shareholders, including John Kennedy. The company did well for many years and the investors received an annual dividend of between 10 and 15 per cent during the 1860s. But disaster struck in October 1872 when the *Turquoise*, a successful well smack that was the company's top earner, was lost with all hands when returning from Faroe in bad weather. This was an appalling tragedy for the widows and orphans left behind. It was also a financial disaster for the business. The directors eventually liquidated the company in 1874.

John Kennedy was furious about the loss of the *Turquoise*, which had been fishing off Iceland before she called along Faroe on the way home to pick up contraband, as was the usual practice. In his annual report to Edinburgh, Kennedy reflected on neither the appalling loss of life nor on the storm that had caused one of Shetland's best smacks to founder. Instead, he believed that the blame lay entirely with the crew who had decided to call along Faroe to buy brandy. His callous assessment of this tragedy, which had shaken the Shetland cod industry to its core, is set out for posterity:

One of the best of the cod smacks belonging to the place was lost in returning from Iceland in the first week of October with her crew of 12 men, it has been ascertained that they called along Faroe on 3 October and that after they left a gale sprang up from the north east ... and the vessel must have foundered ... all conjecture but one thing certain is, had they not called along to Faroe, and come straight home from Iceland, they would have reached home in safety as they would then have been home long before the gale broke out, and there was nothing taking them to Faroe but to serve their own ends.

The decision to wind up the company was the last straw for John Kennedy. The investors only managed to recoup about half of their initial investment, and this loss of money further soured his relationship with Shetlanders. He had been in Shetland far too long and was anxious to return to Scotland. His pleadings with his bosses became ever more desperate. He was hoping that his long years in the north would be recompensed with a senior position in Edinburgh, which would see him through to his retirement. He complained to head office that some younger fishery officers were being promoted ahead of him, something that angered him greatly. At long last, he got a reply confirming that he would shortly be transferred to another post. John Kennedy was elated. But his ticket to escape the islands was not the promotion to Edinburgh that he had hoped for. Instead, it was a posting to the herring port of Helmsdale in the north of Scotland. He was clearly devastated:

> I cannot say that I have much heart for this change . . . it is a cold, out of the way, highland place, which I have never liked, and it comes to be awkward to have to go and furnish a house there now. I have no wish to end my days there. I have no desire however to be troublesome in anyway and if there be not a vacancy nearer my native place for which you think I am suitable; I must try to meet your wishes but I would much rather retire at once.

Whether he took the job in Helmsdale or instead retired, John Kennedy was finally clear of Shetland. It had not been a happy posting for him or for Shetland. They were better off without each other.

13

Vaila Mae

A few years ago, a replica sixern was built by the Shetland Museum. She is called the *Vaila Mae* and is an exact copy of a sixern that was built at the end of the 19th century for use in the haaf fishery. Hauled up on the beach below the museum, it is apparent to even the most casual observer that here is a descendant of the classic Viking longship. Double ended with stem and stern much higher than the middle, she is beautiful. There are few straight lines; almost everything is curved. To build a boat like this you need a good eye, not a ruler. Having been coated with tar, inside and out, as were all the sixerns, it looks as if she was built a long time ago. Her elegant sheer is highlighted by a striking white line painted just below the gunwale. Some 30-foot overall length, the open hull is divided into sections by the five seats where the crew sit. Each section is separated from the others by vertical wooden slats called fiskabrods. In the middle seat is the hole through which the mast can be stepped once she is launched. Named in memory of a 16-year-old girl who tragically died of cancer the year the boat was built; the Shetland community has taken the *Vaila Mae* to its heart.

It was a sunny August day with gusty winds from the north when I first joined the crew for a sail in Lerwick harbour. The core crew – comprising a salmon farmer, a mussel farmer, a doctor and an architect – are enthusiasts, all keen to keep the skills of handling a sixern alive. At the helm was Jim Tait, from Walls, who has been a competitive sailor all his life. Tall and angular, he somehow tucked himself into the kannie, the small steering space at the stern. His eyes never leaving the sail, he told me that the most important job on a sixern was not the skipper but the towsman; the person who controlled the halyard.[*] A skilled towsman, he explained, used the sail to optimise the wind to increase speed, but was always ready to drop the sail in case an unexpected gust heeled the open boat over too far, risking capsize.

Initially surprised at how fast she was and how well she handled, Jim had concluded that, after many hundreds, possibly thousands, of sixerns had been built, the design brief had eventually been perfected. Each skipper and towsman would have suggested certain changes every time a new boat was built, and, through this process, adaptations were made. A minor change in hull shape or sail design could make a real difference in how a vessel performed, in good weather and in bad. From what records are available, it is clear that most sixerns were only used for around ten years before being replaced. This seems a very short working life for a wooden boat, but it certainly afforded several significant changes in design to be undertaken within the working life of a haaf fisherman. The *Vaila Mae* was meticulously built to the lines (or plan) of one of the last sixerns ever built. By this time the design brief could not have been improved; fast under sail, good seakeeping qualities in rough weather but light enough to be hauled up and down a beach by her crew.

There is hardly a part of a sixern that has an English name. The kabe and the humilband, the taft and the tilfer, the rakie and the owsin room, bands and boards, the stammerin, owsekerri and hinniespot are just a few examples. Some people describe these words as poetic, others think they sound downright strange. For many Shetlanders, they remain commonly used and instantly recognisable. Even so, when I speak these words, I feel that I am

---

[*] The rope which raises and lowers the sail.

using an ancient tongue, an almost lost language. These are the old Viking words which are still used for the same boat parts in Norway, Iceland and Faroe. As an embodiment of the Norn language that Shetlanders once spoke, the *Vaila Mae* is much more than just a boat.

Sixerns were originally imported from Norway in kit form then assembled by local boat builders. This export of flat-pack boats was an early Ikea-type venture; the Norwegians getting there before the Swedes did. At the beginning of the 19th century, Shetlanders began to build their own rather than assemble the parts from Norway. It was probably cheaper but, more importantly, the skipper and the builder could discuss possible modifications and changes. And so, the process of evolution began.

Enjoying our sail and watching the crew move the square sail around the mast whenever Jim decided to tack, I was struck by how incredibly small a sixern is. I tried to imagine her making way in poor weather with a crew of six, all their fishing gear and a boat full of fish. There would have been little freeboard* and it is surprising that more boats were not lost at sea. Like Jim, I was also surprised to see how fast we were sailing through Lerwick harbour. Here was a combination of boat shape and sail design that had been crafted together to sail efficiently; essential for a vulnerable open boat to get to and from the fishing grounds as quickly as possible.

***

Shetlanders have always fished. Given the limitations of what can be grown in Shetland's poor climate and meagre soil, fish was a vital part of the diet. The beginnings of commercial fishing date to the early 15th century, back to the days of the Hanseatic League. The Hansa was a confederation of mostly German merchant guilds and trading towns that dominated the

---

* The freeboard of an open boat is the height of the gunwale above the water line.

Baltic economy in the late Middle Ages. Its reach extended as far north as Bergen, which became a large Hansa trading port. It was from there that the German merchants began to do business in Shetland, establishing several trading booths around the islands. Shetlanders sold salt fish and woollen goods and were able to buy lines, hooks, knives, tools, salt, meal, a variety of cloth, as well as brandy and tobacco. Much of this trade was in the form of barter, but what cash did change hands would have been German marks.

As the power of the Hanseatic League declined by the middle of the 18th century, the lairds took over and established their method of monopoly control, based on the haaf fishing and the truck system. The haaf reached its peak in the early 19th century with upwards of 500 sixerns employing around 3,000 fishermen. All working from stone beaches, they tried to make two or three trips every week. Each trip would take around 24 hours, from the time they left the beach till they returned. Baiting their long lines (which had 1,200 hooks) as they set them, the crew would wait a few hours before hauling back and then returning to the fishing station where their catch was cleaned, split and salted before being laid out to dry.

Fish prefer certain areas of the seabed over others. The ability to locate these areas and return there, trip after trip, is what marks out a successful fisher. With modern navigation equipment this is now relatively easy. On board sixerns, there were no electronic aids and the only way to determine location at sea was to use meids. According to Charlie Simpson, author of an authoritative book on this subject, a meid is an observed transect formed by two onshore objects brought into line by the eye of an observer at sea. This ancient positioning technique, based on how the topography of distant land can be lined up, is known to all mariners around the world. In Shetland it had its own special name and was used by haaf fishermen every day. Features that are well defined from a long distance away, such as a sharp hilltop shape or cliff, produce the best results. When two meids are used together the result is surprisingly accurate. Sixern skippers would have used hundreds of meids when fishing the haaf. To master this art, a good skipper needed a detailed knowledge of Shetland's topography, a prodigious memory and keen eyesight. It was not easy and one of the main problems was when the weather conspired to make the layout of the distant land unclear. Under such circumstances, according to retired skipper Davie Smith, it was possible to confuse shadow with substance. Inspired by his poetic turn of phrase, Janette Kerr used this as the name for her sound-and-video installation about the haaf station at Stenness.

Whenever a sixern was out of sight of land, or during times of poor visibility, meids could no longer be used. On such occasions the skipper and crew's detailed and extensive knowledge of the weather and the sea, in all its moods, was essential. One of the navigational aids that the haaf fishermen reputedly used was the Moderdai, or mother wave. This was described as a tidal movement which drives landward regardless of wind direction. It is apparently distinguishable on every ninth wave during a moderate Atlantic swell, and a sixern could make landfall in the densest fog by following this tidal pattern. It was not easy to see, only discernible to the most experienced eye as a slight undulation in the waves.

Despite an unbroken tradition of sailing and rowing open boats since the days of the sixern, the secrets of the Shetland Moderdai have been lost. It is tempting to dismiss this as a foolish notion that emerged during an age of superstition; after all, although the legend has endured, the Moderdai could only have been used (if, indeed, it ever was) before compass navigation became commonplace during the early 19th century – a long time ago. And yet there may have been something, however intangible and difficult for us to understand, that was used to help boats make landfall back then. The sixern crews, venturing into exposed deep water twice a week, must have had a profound

knowledge of the weather and the sea. It is well known that
the ancient Polynesians used wave and swell patterns to help
them navigate the enormity of the Pacific Ocean. I must admit
that I find it rather compelling to believe that Shetlanders may
have had similar nautical skills that we have lost and no longer
understand.

The North Atlantic Fisheries College in Scalloway recently
looked at the Moderdai legend from a contemporary scientific
perspective. Referencing the latest oceanographic research, this
study tentatively concluded that it might have been possible to
identify long swell waves that originate many thousands of miles
from Shetland. According to the author of this study, Dr Ian
Napier, such swell waves can have distinctive characteristics that
distinguish them from locally generated waves. An experienced
and expert eye might have learned to recognise these signs, particularly from a sixern where the crew were never more than a
few feet away from the sea.

Even with fine weather, spending two days at sea in an open
boat was tough; hardly any room to move around (especially
when the boat was filled with fish), no cooking or toilet facilities
and no shelter whatsoever from any rain, wind or spray. I often
wonder how many of us today would have the strength, endurance and skill to sail and row a sixern up to 30 miles from land,
set and haul six miles of line and then return to the same fishing
station, all within a space of a day. And then do the same again
after one night's sleep.

***

Despite the 1832 disaster, within a few years there were as many
sixerns back fishing as there had been before. The lairds had
established a profitable business based on the monopoly they
had created. Any crofter who was not prepared to fish would be
evicted. It seemed that the lairds made all the money and the
haaf fishermen took all the risks.

But the days of the haaf and truck were numbered. The iniquities of the truck system, based on credit and debt, were first highlighted in a government commission report in 1872. Concluding that this system prevented the development of a competitive free market, it was scathing in its criticism of truck. In their evidence to the commission, the lairds defended the status quo. They saw themselves as successful fishing industry entrepreneurs, providing employment for many fishermen. The credit which they made available from year to year was, they argued, an example of their concern 'for the lower orders'. One of the lairds even compared his tenants to 'irresponsible children'. Such attitudes shock us today, but this was a time when landowners regarded themselves as a much better class than the landless poor or impoverished tenants. Their wealth and privilege also conferred political influence, which is doubtless why the government never acted on the 1872 report.

It was probably inevitable that the fleet would again be hit by a severe summer storm as had happened in 1832. It was Wednesday 20 July in 1881 and the fleet of sixerns were at sea as usual. A beautiful morning had developed into a balmy summer's day with nothing to indicate the ferocity of the storm that would strike that evening. With hindsight, some fishermen had remarked that an unusually heavy swell was running, something that was surprising because the weather had been so settled. The storm was unleashed just after nine in the evening. Some vessels had hauled their lines and were on their way ashore, while others had only begun fishing when, all at once and without any warning, a violent storm from the northwest erupted. An eyewitness later described the sudden onset of the wind as being 'like the shot of a pistol'.

Around midnight, the gale was at its height and every sixern in the fleet was struggling to survive as mountainous waves broke alongside, often filling the small open boats with water. The crews were constantly bailing, to try and empty the boats before the next wave broke. With the wind howling around them, it was clear that they would be overwhelmed if more water came aboard. In the 1832 disaster, most crews had tried to keep their sixern's head to wind, to ride out the storm. They had little choice; with a northwest storm and the sixern fleet all fishing to the east of Shetland that day, running before the storm would have taken them further into the North Sea and away from Shetland. In 1881, by contrast, many of the sixerns were actually fishing to the northwest of Shetland, and these skippers therefore had the option of trying to sail ashore before the wind. It was, however, a strategy that ran the risk of the boats broaching and filling with water. Making a long passage running before steep and breaking seas in an open boat requires expert seafaring and sailing skills. One wrong move – keeping her under sail for a few seconds too long, the wrong handling of the helm or not keeping her fully bailed out – could spell disaster: a wall of water would break aboard, sinking the sixern in seconds. In many ways, running before breaking waves must be akin to surfing – riding the wave but avoiding being overpowered by it. A thin strip of sail being hauled up and down with exact precision by the towsman, together with expert steering by the skipper were both essential. To survive, the skipper and towsman's actions had to be properly coordinated every time. One small error and they would be lost.

There are several newspaper accounts of the 1881 disaster. But none of these can match the written account by a crewmember who survived. Born in 1861 at Houlland in North Roe, Charles Johnson was one of a family of twelve. On the night of the storm, he was a 20-year-old crewman on board one of the sixerns. His account, which he wrote many years after the event, contains incredible detail and is written by someone who is clearly very comfortable writing down his feelings and thoughts, such is the power of his narrative. This is remarkable since, like all his contemporaries, he only had the most basic of schooling.

Charles Johnson's story begins with the crew launching their sixern from a stone beach near the island of Uyea in the far north of the Shetland Mainland. Although miles from any road, this area is now one of Shetland's most popular hikes. After several hours walking through the bleak moorland, you arrive at a coastline dotted with small bays, skerries and sandy beaches. The view is dominated by the stunning little island of Uyea, which can only be reached at low tide via a beautiful tombolo. On a sunny day, the white sand and the green-blue shallow waters either side look more Mediterranean than Shetland. No one stays here anymore but during the 19th century there was a sizeable community living here, not because the crofts were productive, but because there was a large haaf fishing station at Roer Mill, about three miles east of Uyea.

Leaving the beach at 5 a.m. on that July morning in 1881, the crew had to row 30 miles to the fishing grounds due to a lack of wind; an exhausting marathon that took nine hours. Using meids to fix their exact position, they baited and set their long lines in the late afternoon. As soon as they started to haul it was clear that it was going to be a good fishing, recalls Charles. With 180 large ling on board by the time the storm struck, the skipper immediately took the decision to cut the long line and to risk sailing before the wind and sea to try to make it back to the land. They were going to surf their way home.

With the skipper on the helm sitting in the kannie, his trusted towsman at the halyard and the rest of the crew bailing water, they were ready to go. A pattern soon emerged with the fully reefed sail hoisted to maintain speed and then lowered to allow a breaking sea to pass beneath the keel and avoid broaching. This was vital said Charles because 'every seaman knows that sails are his life'. The only way they were going to survive this was by the skilled use of sail. He observed how closely the skipper and the towsman worked together, with hardly a word being spoken. On one occasion they miscalculated and the sixern ran too fast

before a wave, with the result that 'the sea rose very high astern
. . . and she took water on both sides'. With the crew furiously
bailing, he describes the white breaking water all around the
sixern 'like a field of snow'.

On another occasion, he stole a glance over the bow as they were
running before a wave. It was, he said, as if the sixern 'was running
over a precipice'. Momentum was everything – if the sixern were
ever to lose speed, she would quickly fill with water and founder.
At one particularly dangerous juncture a large wave broke aboard,
and it was the towsman's ability to get the sail quickly hoisted to
regain her speed through the water that saved them.

For hours they saw no land, but when they did it was obvious
that they were a long way south of Uyea. They finally reached the
shelter of Ronas Voe at 1.30 a.m. on Thursday, some four hours
after they had cut their lines. Covering more than 37 miles in
this time, they had averaged more than nine knots, a speed akin
to the best of modern regatta sailing. Naval architects and keen
sailors have argued for years over the accuracy of this written
account, some refusing to believe that an open boat could
average this speed in such conditions. Others maintain that this
was perfectly possible and point out that, to record this average
speed, the sixern must have been sailing faster than this on some
occasions to compensate for those times when her speed was
less. Such speed could only have been achieved through regular
and repeated high-speed surfing down the backs of large seas.

In my favourite part of his account, Charles reflected calmly
on what must have been the trip from hell: 'I had been brought
up with boating since I was a child, but this was a bit extra.' A
master of traditional Shetland understatement, he never used
more words than were required.

Some visitors to the islands describe Shetlanders as taciturn
and dour. This is to misunderstand a society that is not given
to outward demonstrations of emotion or flowery language.
Charles Johnson's great grandsons are both men of the sea.

Michael Johnson runs his own joinery business but spends all his spare time fishing with his small boat. His cousin, Arthur Johnson, is a full-time fisherman, recently joining the crew of the *Ocean Way*, the latest trawler to be built for Shetland owners. Both, like their great grandfather, know the seas around Shetland and are masters of the Shetland understatement.

Returning to the gale, many more sixerns made land safely than was the case in 1832. Unlike the first disaster, this gale had only lasted one day instead of five. That was vital in reducing the death toll, as was the successful strategy of sailing ashore before the wind. But ten sixerns did not make it and 58 men lost their lives.

Six of these boats, and 36 of those who perished, were from a single fishing station at the north of Yell. Gloup had been one of the largest and most successful haaf stations, partly on account of its proximity to the fishing grounds. Decimated by such a tragic loss of life, this small community never recovered. A tasteful memorial, incorporating a stone statue of a woman looking out to sea, with a child in her arms, now stands hauntingly overlooking the entrance to Gloup Voe.

This second disaster finally shook the long-standing confidence in the sixern and increased the attraction of fishing from a decked boat. Indeed, many saw the 1881 disaster as a clear sign that fishing from open boats should be abandoned. An editorial in *The Shetland Times*, written just after the July disaster, went even further: 'We trust that this disaster will do good in the way of utterly discouraging the deep-sea fishing in sixerns.' But, for as long as a laird was able to evict his tenants, fishing deep waters with open boats was not going to stop, disasters or no disasters. It appeared that nothing would ever change.

But fundamental change often occurs very quickly. As Lenin once said, there are decades when nothing happens, and there are weeks when decades happen. When the Crofters Holding Act of 1886 was passed, the lairds suddenly lost their power. It was an incredibly radical piece of legislation that provided security of tenure to all crofters throughout the Highlands and Islands, including Shetland. No longer could a crofter be evicted by the laird.

The impetus for this far-reaching legislation came from the growing and increasingly vocal opposition to the Highland Clearances, which had forced thousands of crofters to leave their homes to make way for sheep. Press coverage of the worst excesses had resulted in calls for land reform, which eventually prompted the Liberal government to legislate. Even by today's standards, let alone those of the 19th century, this was a truly radical Act of Parliament. Overnight, the previously inviolable rights of private land had been shattered. By legislating to make the tenancy of a croft secure, the state had effectively made evictions illegal. As far as the lairds were concerned, this was an attack on their sacred rights of private property – they could no longer do what they wanted with the land that they owned. But the tenants saw things differently. Security of tenure had fundamentally changed the balance of power between laird and crofter. And even though the iniquities of the haaf and truck played no part in the campaign for land reform, the implications for Shetland were profound. At a stroke, the laird's ability to insist that his tenants fished exclusively for him had been removed. The historian Tom Devine has described the Crofters Act as the Magna Carta for the Highlands. Its impact in Shetland was very different but no less critical as it broke forever the link between the land and sea. Shetland fishermen had also found their Magna Carta.

Fishing remains a dangerous job. In the past it was even more so – especially when attempting to fish many miles offshore with small open boats – and many fishermen lost their lives. The sixern disasters of 1832 and 1881 remain etched in Shetland history and folklore. But while fishing from an open boat was clearly dangerous, there were also no guarantees that fishing from a decked boat was risk free. On the contrary, many of the large cod smacks were also lost.

14

The Old Grey Widow Maker

The Vikings often described the North Atlantic as the old grey widow maker. They spoke of the harsh cold seas devouring young men and making widows ashore. This evocative symbolism was used by Rudyard Kipling in his poem 'Harp Song of the Dane Women': 'What is a woman that you forsake her, / And the hearth-fire and the home-acre, / To go with the old grey widow maker?' The sea can be cruel and those people who make their living from it are aware of the risks they run.

Inevitably, whenever there is any loss of life at sea, the historical record focuses on the tragic event itself. The narrative of those left behind is neglected, almost entirely in the case of the official records of the Scottish Fishery Board. Since all of those lost at sea were fishermen, it is a very male-dominated history. But it was the women and children who had to live with the emotional and economic consequences of a husband, father or son being lost. While time could be a great healer, the crofts still had to be worked and food still had to be put on the table. Not an easy job at the best of times but made much more difficult when the main (and often only) wage-earner was no more. The untold story of those left behind can only be found in Shetland's oral tradition. In Faroe, a community that was scarred in the same way as Shetland by the loss of life at sea, there is a similar rich oral history. Faroe has, however, also recorded for posterity the story of those left behind in a most powerful way through the brush strokes of Sámal Joensen.

Born in 1906, Sámal Joensen was raised on the small island of Mikines, one of the most isolated outposts of habitation in Faroe. He remained very close to his home island, which became a constant source of inspiration for him throughout his working life as an artist. Eventually adopting the name of his island home, he became known as Sámal Joensen-Mikines. He is remembered simply as Mikines, and his art is now as well known around the world as it is in Faroe.

With the dawn of the 20th century, Faroe was establishing its own cod fishery. Hundreds and then thousands of men found employment aboard the growing fleet of sloops.* Living on a small island where almost all the men were fishermen had a profound effect on young Sámal. A promising artist from a young age, he secured a place to study at the Royal Academy in Copenhagen. He was there in 1934 when 43 Faroese fishermen were lost in a violent storm off Iceland. Nine of these men were from the island of Mikines, which had a population of only 150. The young artist would have known all these men; some had been his childhood friends.

Such losses were not uncommon. While 1934 stands out as one of the worst years, Faroese fishermen were lost at sea every year in the same way as the Shetland fishermen had been in the previous century. These were the harsh realities of fishing stormy waters. It seemed that some village or island in Faroe was always mourning the loss of a fisherman, usually a very young man. Tragedy was a regular and recurring feature of every fishing season, and the Faroese were therefore no strangers to grief and death. It was this pain that inspired much of Mikines'

---

* For some reason the Faroese called their large cod vessels sloops, whereas in Shetland they were called smacks. Somewhat confusingly, the smaller Shetland cod boats fishing the Home Grounds on a weekly basis were also called sloops.

art, particularly towards the end of the 1930s. His work from this period has often been described as a door into the dark. And it is dark indeed, with paintings called 'Loss', 'Home from the Funeral' and 'Funeral Procession'. These works are sombre in the extreme, conveying a profound sense of devastation. They also portray what some have called the wordless and soundless grief of the Faroese people. In common with many maritime societies where loss at sea was commonplace, there are no histrionics and there is no melodrama – instead there is a stoic acceptance that this is how things are when you look to the sea for your living.

Although Mikines was an accomplished landscape and portrait painter, he is best known for his work from this dark period. Two of his most famous paintings are based on the theme of waiting women and children. These were painted in 1938 and both are called 'Ships Departing' – an interesting feature of Mikines' work is that there are often two or more very different paintings by the same name. The first of these shows a woman and her two children turning away as three sloops leave Faroe to fish off Iceland. The mother cannot bear to look, fearful perhaps that this will be the last time she will see her husband. The daughter buries her head in her mother's shoulder, wondering if she will ever see her father again. The son, by contrast, steals a look at the sloops sailing out of the fjord. He will soon be old enough to be a fisherman. It is impossible to tell how he feels: is he impatient to get to sea or dreading the day? It is a dark and sad painting, full of foreboding and melancholy.

The second painting is less sombre but equally evocative. A young woman in a blue dress stands at the edge of a cliff watching a solitary sloop in the far distance. We do not know if she is newly married or has a boyfriend on board. We cannot see her face. She is looking directly at the sea, possibly full of hope that all the crew will return safely.

The Faroese are understandably proud of Mikines and his international reputation. Reflecting on his work, the former

Faroese prime minister, Jóannes Eidesgaard, said that 'he paints the women with their children on the desolate shore watching the ships leave for the Icelandic fishing grounds. He paints those who anxiously wait for their loved ones to return, and he describes their dread, despair and sense of loss at the news of a death. He portrays their sorrow but also their hope and faith.'

***

Fishing has always been a dangerous occupation, and loss of life at sea has been, and remains, an enduring feature of the fishing industry. But the loss of life was of a different nature and magnitude in the past. The small open boats fishing the haaf, and the half deckers fishing for herring, were particularly susceptible to bad weather. Even though they were much larger and fully decked, many cod smacks were also lost as they fished some of the world's roughest waters, in the far north. Whenever a cod smack was lost at sea, the entire crew perished, and the wider community keenly felt the impact of the loss.

When the *Turquoise* was lost with her crew of 12 in October 1872, it was believed that she had foundered somewhere between Faroe and Shetland in a northeasterly gale. Some fishermen disagreed. They believed that this gale was nothing that the *Turquoise* had not managed to sail through before. In their view, she had run onto the Vee Skerries as she approached Shetland during the hours of darkness. These are treacherous rocks that lie to the northwest of Papa Stour, right in the path of cod smacks returning from Faroe. The cod skippers always set their course to pass safely to the west of the Vee Skerries, but precise navigation is never easy during a storm. During daylight, the sea breaking over the rocks can be seen from a distance, but at night this danger would not have been seen.

As the *Turquoise* sailed before the northeasterly gale, the crew would not have been aware of anything unusual until the smack shuddered to a halt. They would immediately have known what

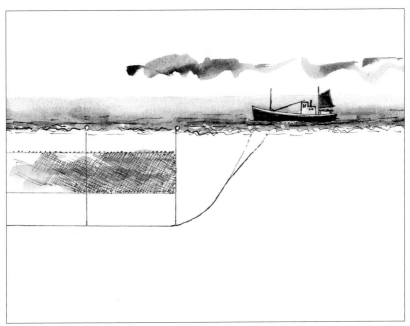

Lying at the drift nets. Sketch by John Cumming

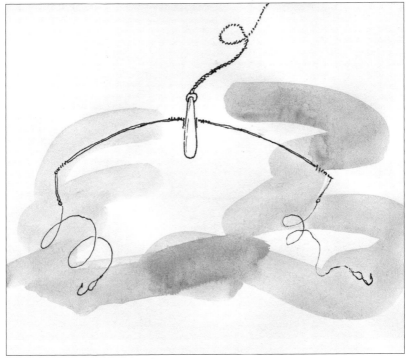

The cod hand line. Sketch by John Cumming

Salt cod laid out to dry on a Shetland beach. Shetland Museum and Archives

The Faroese cod sloop *Johanna* encounters gale force winds. Painting by Hans Skalagard

A half decker hauling back drift nets. Sketch by John Cumming

A sixern setting its long line. Sketch by John Cumming

The crew of a cod smack fishing with hand lines. Sketch by John Cumming

Right. Mortan Johannessen selling fish on the pier in Tórshavn. Photo by John Goodlad

Below. Beach boys laying out salt fish to dry. Shetland Museum and Archives

Dried salt cod for sale at the Seafood Expo. Photo by John Goodlad

Anna Kirstin Thomsen outside Pubbin in Tuøroyri, Suðuroy. Photo by John Goodlad

The crew haul cod on board. Sketch by John Cumming

Heavy weather onboard a Faroese sloop. Faroese National Heritage

The *Vaila Mae*. Photo by Davy Cooper

Ships departing. Painting by Sámal Joensen-Mikines. Reproduced with permission of Kari Mikines

The Swan leaving Lerwick Harbour. Photo by Allister Rendall

Gutters at a herring station in Lerwick. Shetland Museum and Archives

The fleet of herring boats leaving Lerwick harbour. Shetland Museum and Archives

Maggie Adamson, skipper of the *Swan*. The Swan Trust

A night at the drift net with the *Golden Harvest*. Photo by John Henry Goodlad

had happened as the rocks tore through the hull and she began to fill with water. They would also have quickly realised that there was no hope of survival. In the dark of the night, the heavy seas would have begun to tear their boat apart. In desperation, some of the men might have climbed up the rigging. There is no knowing how long it would have taken before she finally broke up: it could have been an hour or two, or it could have taken all night. It would have been the most desperate of all situations, with the crew trying to cling onto life for a little longer in the knowledge that this was ultimately futile. As daylight came up the next morning, the last few surviving men, who had stubbornly clung onto the rigging during the night, would have finally realised how hopeless their plight was. They would have seen that the *Turquoise* was a total wreck lying below. Shortly afterwards, the main mast, which had supported the rigging during the night, would have collapsed into the crashing seas. The only survivors from the *Turquoise* were the live cod which escaped as the boat broke up and the seawater well was breached.

One of the crew was William Goodlad, who had bought brandy in Tvøroyri when he was 18 years old. When the *Turquoise* had set sail in August for her final trip of the year, he was 27 years old, by now one of the oldest on board. His younger brother, Oli Goodlad, was also one of the crew. William had been married to Bella Laurie for five years and they had two sons, aged three and one. She was pregnant with their third child, a daughter, who was born the following year. Left with three young children to look after, Bella faced the bleak and hard future that many Shetland widows endured during the 19th century. She was possibly more fortunate than most, with only three children to look after.

It was only four years later, in March 1876, that the crew of the *John Walker* were getting ready for their first trip of the year. Before leaving, they had to sign the usual agreement with the smack owners. The skipper always signed first; his name was

John Hunter, from Whiteness. Aged 35, he had been promoted to captain one of their finest vessels. Built in Aberdeen only three years earlier, the *John Walker* was a new well smack. Looking forward to his first trip, the skipper reflected that this was a good smack to be in command of. Almost brand-new, with a seawater well, her earning potential was high. He could not wait to get started.

Next to sign the agreement was the mate, Robbie Hunter, the skipper's brother. As he came forward to sign, the pen suddenly slipped from his hand and fell to the floor. If this happened today, no one would think twice about it. The pen would be picked up and the agreement would be signed. But this was a different time. People were superstitious and often ascribed great significance to the most minor of mishaps. Taking this as a bad omen, Robbie refused to sign and go to sea on this trip. This must have created something of an uproar. They had to find a new mate: a process that delayed the start of their trip for a few days. No doubt some of the crew would have chided Robbie for being so superstitious, and the brothers may even have had a row. Within a few days they sailed for Faroe with a new mate. On the face of it, the skipper's brother had acted rashly and foolishly. The *John Walker* was almost new and was one of the largest and most able smacks in the Shetland fleet, the last boat that anyone expected to have a misfortune.

Fishing was poor when they arrived at Faroe. After a couple of weeks, John Hunter was getting impatient. There is nothing worse for a keen fisherman than no fish. The weather was also unsettled, and they often had to lie at anchor sheltering. On one occasion, when they were ashore in Tórshavn, he wrote a letter to his wife, Mary Abernethy, saying that he was thinking of going to Rockall if the Faroe fishing did not improve shortly. This letter was posted on 23 March. When the weather eased, the *John Walker* went back to the Faroe Bank and, after a few days of poor fishing, was one of a group of smacks that once more had to take shelter as another gale passed through. They all rode out the storm that night together. When morning came, the *John Walker* was nowhere to be seen. A combination of mist and rain meant that visibility was poor, so it was thought that she was probably just out of sight. When there was no sign of her over the next few days, it was assumed that John Hunter had finally got fed up and had decided to try his luck at Rockall.

As the smacks began to return home at the end of April there was surprise that the *John Walker* was not already back. As the first days of May turned into weeks, concern began to grow. Despite this, many remained confident that she would soon be coming back from Rockall with a good catch. But these hopes were dashed when the *Sapphire* returned from Rockall at the end of May and her skipper was able to confirm that he had not seen or heard of the *John Walker* among the 17 smacks fishing there. With this news, worry spread throughout the community, and some began to fear the worst.

Mary remained convinced that her husband was still alive, and his smack would soon return home. With each passing day hope faded but, as she kept rereading the letter he had sent from Faroe, she convinced herself that they had gone to Rockall. Although she had three small daughters to look after, she began walking from her croft at Kirkhouse, in Whiteness, to the beach at Hirpa, where she could get an unimpeded view to sea. Knowing that the *John Walker* was most likely to land its catch at Hirpa, she believed that she would see the smack sailing back soon. Her hope probably became an obsession as her anxiety increased. Some days she would walk to Hirpa three times, even though the round trip took more than an hour.

One particularly beautiful Saturday morning, as she set out very early, she saw a smack under full sail in the distance. It was not an unusual sight as smacks were coming and going all the time in the voes north of Scalloway, but she nevertheless quickened her pace. Reaching the crest of the hill above Hirpa, the smack was in clear sight. There was no mistaking her – it was the *John Walker*. With her heart pounding she broke into a run, gathering in her long blue skirt, as she ran down the brae to the beach. By the time she reached the cod stores, the smack was preparing to tie up at the pier. Stopping to catch her breath, her sense of elation began to falter. She read the nameboard on the smack – it was the *Robert Kirkwood*, the sister ship to the *John Walker*. Both built by the same yard in Aberdeen, they were identical. As a result of this cruel case of mistaken identity, Mary Abernethy lost her voice for weeks afterwards.

I first heard this story being told when I was a boy. It was very personal to our family because Mary Abernethy and John Hunter were my grandmother's grandparents. In an age before television and the internet, it was told and retold over the years and, even though this tragedy had taken place more than a hundred years previously, it never felt distant nor without relevance. Whenever I recall that story now, I think of the Mikines painting of the lone woman with the blue dress looking out to sea.

There was no obvious explanation for the disappearance of the *John Walker*. On the night she disappeared, it had been a gale but not a storm – such nights were commonplace at Faroe. Some of the crew on board the other smacks had, however, noticed a large French schooner lying upwind. When daylight came up, she was lying downwind from the smacks. This by itself was unremarkable but apparently a French schooner had called into Lerwick a few days later with a very badly damaged bowsprit. Could it be that the *John Walker* had been run down by this schooner during the night? Perhaps being rammed by a large ship, driven before a gale, might have damaged one of the bulkheads of the seawater well, flooding the smack? It remains an intriguing possibility, but what is certain is that some unusual calamity overcame them during the fateful night they lay sheltering off Faroe.

This tragic loss was made worse by the attitude of the Shetland Fishing Company. A well-funded company, the owners were men of considerable means, and four of the company's six smacks were named after these owners; the *John Walker* being named after the director. By early June, John Walker was still refusing to send a vessel to look for the eponymous smack at Rockall. He said it would be a waste of money, as it was clear the smack was not there and had been lost. This was probably true, but the way the company owners then appeared to wash their hands of the affair led to much anger. A serious difference of opinion within the company became public when one of the managers, Robert Scott, took the unprecedented step of making a statement in the local press:

> The wives, children and relatives of the crew of the *John Walker* were left very destitute, and it was hoped something could be done for them by those interested, but nothing of any consequence has been done for these poor people and they are now appealing to some to help their cause. It being with me that the men were engaged, and most of them all well known to me. Thus, all I can do is to place the facts before the public.

Robert Scott had obviously had enough. He was frustrated at how the company was unwilling to help the families of those who had been lost. Shortly after this, he resigned.

Life was not only lost when a vessel sank. Being washed overboard by breaking seas, or being knocked over the side by booms sweeping across the deck, were not uncommon. In 1876, two skippers were lost in almost identical circumstances when both were flung into the sea as the boom unexpectedly swung from one side of the deck to the other in rough seas.

In 1893, 17-year-old Magnus Laing, of Walls, was lost when a heavy sea swept the decks of the *Hurricane*. Whenever someone was lost overboard in such circumstances, there was nothing that could be done to save them. It would have taken hours for a sailing smack to turn around in heavy weather to look for a crewmember who had been lost over the side. Anyone thrown into the sea in a storm knew that they had no hope of rescue. Young Magnus Laing had possibly been looking forward to going below deck for something to eat or for a rest. He would have heard the crash of a heavy sea as it hit the deck and would then have experienced the sensation of being pulled over the side by the enormous force of the water. His desperate attempts to find something to hold on to failed, and the next he knew was that he was in the icy North Atlantic watching the smack sail away from him, knowing that she would not be able to turn back.

Sometimes lives were even lost in fine weather, as crewmembers undertook the most mundane of tasks. In 1879, the local newspaper reported, in a very matter-of-fact manner, a tragic, but unfortunately commonplace accident, when a young boy was lost at sea: 'The *Foam* arrived in Lerwick from Iceland with 19,000 cod. They had unfortunately lost the cook at Iceland, a young lad from Sound by the name of Smith. He had been drawing water when he was dragged overboard.' Drawing water is the term used to describe the dangerous practice of filling a bucket with seawater. As the bucket is thrown over the side, the attached rope is firmly held by hand. If this is done when a vessel is moving through the water, a great pull is exerted on the rope, more than enough to drag an inexperienced hand over the side.

The similarities and differences between Faroe and Shetland are fascinating. Both communities share so much, especially their relationship to the sea. In both island groups the ocean provided food and money – but at a terrible price, year after year. Each community has described and articulated its complex relationship with the sea in a very different way. Faroe has recorded its cod fishery, and much else, through its art. In every Faroese house, in every public building and even on board its fleet of modern trawlers, there are paintings on the walls. The embracing of art by the wider community has allowed many professional artists in Faroe to make a living from their painting and sculpture. Shetland has gone down a different path: it celebrates its past, present and future through music. A musical style as eclectic as Faroese art, expressed through the most Shetland of all instruments, the fiddle.

15

'Haal in da Drogue'

It was Hogmanay night and we were waiting for the main act to come on in Mareel, Shetland's spectacular arts centre. Having enjoyed all the supporting bands, I was aware of the anticipation in the auditorium before the headline act came on stage. It was several years since Fiddlers' Bid had last played to a home crowd. A Shetland band that has perfected the art of rearranging traditional Shetland fiddle tunes into contemporary settings, Fiddlers' Bid are outstanding. Four stunningly coordinated and talented fiddlers accompanied by guitars and piano on the reels and jigs, they are an explosive force of energy, and they take traditional Shetland music to new places. Watching them play can be exhausting – they leap around the stage, fiddles tucked under chins with their arms bowing back and forth at breakneck speed. Their slow airs and waltzes, in contrast, are haunting, allowing each listener to imagine what the music conveys to them. These sets are perfectly complemented by the sound of the clarsach. Never a traditional Shetland instrument, the plucking of the harp strings nevertheless sounds as if it had been designed to accompany the long, drawn-out bowing of the fiddles. It was a great night.

One of their fiddlers is Maurice Henderson, who is always smiling, his effortless enthusiasm infectious. Growing up in Lerwick, he was a latecomer to music, only starting to play the fiddle when he was 12. Classical music played on the violin is beautiful but can suffer from a reputation of being both exclusive and elitist; it is not the music of ordinary folk. Fiddle music is different – it is folk music. It was not unusual, therefore, for a group of like-minded fiddlers at the Anderson High School in Lerwick to start playing together. That was the genesis of Fiddlers' Bid.

To begin with they were asked to do a few tunes at social events. In Shetland these events often include a traditional music slot followed by tea and home bakes. Maurice recalls that a Cats Protection League coffee morning was one of their first breaks. They played a few gigs without a name and eventually decided that they needed to be called something. A fiddlers' bid is the Shetland expression for a last-minute invitation to musicians, often as an afterthought. As they had been asked to stand in for so many events at the last minute, it seemed very appropriate.

They decided to record their first album by themselves in one of their bedrooms, but the microphones of their home recording equipment kept picking up shortwave radio transmissions from a Russian factory ship that was anchored in Lerwick harbour. One of their first takes was a slow air interrupted by a lengthy soliloquy delivered by a Russian skipper. By the time they released this album they had built up a loyal local fanbase. Regular performances at the Shetland Folk Festival then raised their profile to a wider audience. Their big breakthrough came at the Inter Celtic Festival in Brittany, where they were so popular that they had to play their entire set as an extended encore. On the strength of this international début, they began touring, bringing Shetland fiddle music to Europe, America, Australia and Japan, as well as many UK venues. Going on to produce five more albums, Fiddlers' Bid became ever more accomplished and popular. Highly regarded by fellow musicians, their last album was recorded in Mark Knopfler's private studio in London, and their original, distinctive and contemporary treatment of old

Shetland tunes, fused with their own compositions, has just got better over the years.

Although they still play together from time to time, they no longer tour, and Maurice now works for the Shetland Islands Council. As well as an accomplished fiddler, he is a keen historian and one of the dedicated crew who regularly sail the *Vaila Mae*. Not surprisingly, there are many Shetland fiddle tunes about the sea and fishing, particularly from the sixern era. My favourite is 'Aandowin at da bow', a tune whose rhythm and modality mimics the action of keeping a boat steady at a buoy by careful use of the oars. 'Rowin Foula doon' is probably better known. A poem that has been set to music, it tells the story of a sixern from Papa Stour that was fishing so far offshore that the island of Foula was dipping below the horizon.

Much traditional fiddle music was utilitarian in that it set the pace for Shetland dancing at weddings and other social gatherings. Maurice believes that one of the oldest Shetland dances, the Shetland reel (which is done by three couples), was inspired by the sixern, with different parts of the dance referencing different bits of the boat. One of Shetland's best known and most popular reels is called 'Willafjord', said to have been composed by a Shetlander who went whaling to Greenland. Always wondering if Willafjord was a real or fictional place, Maurice decided to travel to Greenland to find the answer. His quest is retold in his fascinating book, *In Search of Willafjord*. Full of stunning photography, this is the story of a Shetlander and his fiddle, retracing the footsteps of the many Shetland whalers who went to Greenland year after year. He eventually identified the modern settlement of Sisimiut as the most likely suspect for the Willafjord that inspired the Shetland composer.

His determination to discover the origins of this classic fiddle tune impressed me. He was exactly the right guy to help me trace down a fiddle tune from the era of the cod smacks that seemed to have disappeared. It is called 'Haal in da Drogue an Gie da Boys a Buskuit' and is an exhortation in typical Shetlandic idiom to haul in the sea anchor and stop fishing. Maurice had not heard of it but agreed to ask around his extensive musical network to see if anyone knew of it. Finding nothing that resembled this apparently long-lost tune, we were both disappointed. Never one to accept defeat, he suggested that he could always compose a brand-new tune to fit the name. A contemporary take on a 19th-century theme, he said, telling me he could already hear the tune beginning to take shape in his mind.

After a few weeks Maurice was ready to début his new composition. To my ear this new tune perfectly captures the atmosphere on board a cod smack, particularly evocative of the movement of a boat rising and falling on a swell. The first public performance took place at an event in Lerwick and, as word got round that Maurice was going to be playing a new composition about the smacks, I got a call from Robert Anderson, a keen local historian. He asked if he could take his brass fiddle along to the show. Telling me that that this fiddle had been made for a cod fisherman more than 150 years ago, he explained that the instrument was ideal for a long sea voyage, being almost indestructible. Apparently brass fiddles were commonplace on board many smacks, because so many wooden fiddles had been damaged during storms. On the night of the concert, Maurice played a few tunes on it, including 'Haal in da Drogue'. Although lacking the depth of sound produced by a wooden fiddle, it sounded far better than he had expected, and he commented that its slightly metallic sound added a bluesy feel to several of the traditional Shetland tunes. Throughout the evening there was one question that kept coming back into my mind: could it be that someone played the now long-lost tune on this actual brass fiddle? Not impossible, I concluded.

The appeal of the crew to 'haal in da drogue' would probably have been motivated by exhaustion. They might have been fishing for a couple of days without a break and would have been tired, hungry and cold. Whether the skipper actually agreed to haul in the sea anchor and stop fishing is not known, but the experience was sufficient to inspire someone to compose the original tune.

***

Working on board a cod smack is beyond what is imaginable to most people today. Life was tough for most during the 19th century, and few thought it worthwhile to record such hardship. Those few written accounts of life at sea on a smack that exist are, of course, hugely helpful in trying to piece together what life was like at sea. Yet, no matter how good they are, nothing can convey an experience quite like hearing someone recount how it was. For me, this is what makes history come alive. But since the last Shetland cod fishermen died a long time ago, it was clear that I was never going to be able to hear a cod fisherman talk about his experiences at sea – or so I thought.

One day when I was in the Shetland Museum, the assistant archivist, Angus Johnson, came over to tell me that a lady from Kentucky had recently donated something to the archives that might interest me. It was a tape recording that had been made by her grandfather, an elderly Robert Hardie, originally from Lunnasting, on the east Mainland of Shetland. He had emigrated to the United States as a young man. When he retired, he made a recording for his grandchildren about his days growing up in Shetland. Part of the tape was a description of a trip he made with a cod smack in 1900.

I followed Angus into the audio room where he loaded the tape into the old-fashioned tape recorder. A red light came on and the reel began to turn. An elderly man with a heavy American accent began his story. As he described his early days in Shetland, his pronunciation started to change. A few Shetland words and a definite Shetland lilt began to creep into his diction.

It was as if speaking about his young days had taken Robert Hardie back home to Shetland. He began: 'This is December 17, 1955. I am sitting by the window. It is quite cold outside and a lot of snow. I have been on pension from the Central Railroad for five and a half years. Having caught up with the remodelling of our home, I don't have too much to occupy my time. Only make a birdhouse or whatever little chores has to be done around the house or going to the store. So, it gives me time to think of years gone by.'

His early life was hard by our standards but typical for Shetlanders at that time. As one of 13 children living on a small croft, with less than five acres under cultivation, you had to start working at an early age, he explained. By the summer of 1900, Robert Hardie was 14 years old and, like most young men of his age, ready to go to the fishing. He relates that he went to a cod fishing company and got a berth on the *Buttercup*. He then 'went to their store and got fitted out with clothes. We had to have six suits of underwear because we could not wash while we were at sea, high leather boots that came above the knee, and oilskins that we had to wear most of the time. My father and mother helped me to get my things ready. My mother did not want me to go. However, I left home after the middle of March and we spent a couple of weeks in getting the boat ready.'

The smack left Scalloway for Faroe at the end of March. It was not a great start: 'The first night out from Scalloway it started to blow very hard, and I was put on the lookout while the men took off some sails. The waves were coming over us, and I was very seasick and at that time I wished I had paid attention to my mother. Sure was glad when I could go below and get in my bed. Next day the weather was some better and with a fair wind. We made Tórshavn in the Faroes. We all went ashore. Not having a full crew, we hired three men. We left there after a couple of days for the fishing grounds where we fished until near the end of June. Then we left for home.'

After arriving back in Scalloway, the salt fish catch was discharged, and the crew were allowed to go home for a week. Returning with a clean set of clothes, Robert Hardie recounted that, once water and provisions were taken on board, the smack was ready to make its second trip. Having made passage to Faroe, they stayed for a couple of days, before leaving for Iceland where the skipper had decided to fish. This was a trip the young deckhand would remember for the rest of his life: 'We left for Iceland. But before we got there, some of the crew became sick and, before long, more than half the crew was ill. So, the skipper decided to put into some place in Iceland and see the doctor. At that time, I was very sick. The doctor could not speak very good English and did not know what was wrong with us. However, I being the youngest, he did not think I would pull through and the skipper understood the doctor to say the best thing for him to do was to try and get us back home. We started out for home but only got 50 miles in two weeks due to very strong southwesterly winds. During that time the most of us were getting better. So, we went back to the fishing ground and fished until the end of September. Got home around the middle of October. I had my 15th birthday on that trip.'

Living conditions on board the smacks were basic, to say the least. Food was simple and served the sole purpose of maintaining a high calorific intake for working in cold, demanding conditions. Taste and presentation were irrelevant. In common with wider society at this time, most protein was salted. Salt mutton, salt beef and salt pork were standard fare on board. There was always a supply of potatoes and hard biscuits to accompany the salted food. One consequence of such a diet is a constant thirst, and the importance of having plenty of tea, coffee and drinking water is often referred to in the accounts of the provisions taken on board. Fresh cod was always eaten once fishing started, being a welcome change to the endless salt food, and it was of course free. The cook had one of the most important jobs on board when a ravenously hungry crew would come below deck three or four times every day expecting plenty of hot food. It was the cook's job to have this prepared on time, every day.

Conditions were cramped, with the heat from the coal stove and the constant rolling and pitching of the vessel only adding to the difficulty. The layout of each smack was different. Some had a table in the cabin; in other cases, fishermen would have had to eat their meals from plates balanced on their knees. The crew ate with their backs to their sleeping quarters, which consisted of double-tier bunks on both sides of the boat. There was little room and no privacy; yet the crowded and dark cabin must have seemed a haven of rest after long hours fishing on the deck.

Hygiene was basic, with the toilet being over the side and washing undertaken at the end of the trip, as described by Robert Hardie when he was explaining the need for six sets of underwear. Fresh water was a scarce resource that had to be carried on board in barrels and was used only for drinking and cooking. It was far too important to be wasted for washing. For our society where a daily shower is now considered essential, these conditions are difficult to comprehend. No shaving, no washing and only six changes of underwear for a 12- or 14-week trip – the cabin would have been rather smelly, as well as hot and cramped. The opportunity to wash in a cold stream whenever they were ashore in Faroe or Iceland must have been a longed-for treat.

Robert Hardie's memorable two trips on board the *Buttercup* took place in the last years of the cod era. By this time, the haaf fishery was also petering out. There were many reasons for the decline of both fisheries but crucial was the growth of a huge herring fishery that would employ more people, engage more boats and generate more exports than any Shetland fishery has ever done, before or since. It was also very profitable; fishermen were able to earn unheard of wages and soon became boat owners. No one wanted to be a haaf fishermen or go on a distant-water cod trip anymore. Everyone wanted to fish for herring. Well, almost everyone. The last few years of the distant-water cod fishery were marked by one exceptional skipper and a remarkable smack – Josie Peterson and the *William Martin*.

16

'I loved her as much as my own wife'

Once the herring fishery began its meteoric expansion during the early 1880s, fishing for cod started to decline and it became difficult to get crews. Although addressing this problem for a while by employing Faroese fishermen, cod merchants began to wonder if there was any future in the cod business. Many took the view that the cod era was over, deciding to sell their smacks to Faroe, where there were ready buyers. The best cod skippers all left to start fishing for herring. During this period of decline there was, however, one cod skipper who defied the trend. Not only did he not abandon the cod fishery; he kept landing record-breaking catches trip after trip. His name was Josie Peterson, and he was skipper of the *William Martin*.

His grandson, Bobby Peterson, was also a fisherman, only retiring after he turned 70. He first went to sea at the age of 15 and, like so many others, he was seasick and did not like it. He once told me that the first 35 years of being a fisherman are the worst; after that, it is just fine. Bobby never did anything else – he fished all his life. You just got used to the job, he said. Lean and wiry, Bobby always spoke slowly, quietly and deliberately. There was often a trace of a smile on his lips or a cigarette in his mouth, sometimes both. The skipper of the last boat he was on told me that Bobby was exactly the kind of fisherman you wanted to have on board: competent and hard-working, for sure, but also with a good-natured temperament that never varied, regardless of good or bad days, irrespective of the weather. Someone who is reliable and steady is always a valued member of a team, but especially so on a fishing boat, where the last thing you need is unpredictability. A cool head, Bobby never said much, but you could be sure whatever he did say had been well thought-out and was worth listening to. Another master of the Shetland understatement.

For several years he was a crewmember on board the large stern trawler *Sunbeam*, which often fished the Faroe Bank. It was difficult to get Bobby to speak about the bad weather they encountered, or the long hours spent working on deck, when fishing at Faroe. It is simply what a fisherman does, he pointed out, even though such a working environment is far beyond the understanding of most of our desk-bound society. He did, however, allow himself to reflect a little on how his own experiences contrasted with those of his grandfather. He told me that when the *Sunbeam* was trawling at Faroe in the worst of all weathers, he would often remind himself that this was nothing compared to the conditions experienced by Josie Peterson when he had fished there.

He went on to explain that his grandfather might not have become a smack skipper had it not been for a bad storm at Faroe. It was in April 1891, when the crew of the *Violet* were struggling to deal with heavy seas. A boom that had been lashed down had become loose and was being washed about the deck by the seas breaking aboard. As the crew tried to secure this, another mountainous wave crashed on board, throwing the boom against the rail. The skipper, Adam Leask, was in the wrong place at the wrong time; his leg was badly broken. The young mate had to take over and sail the smack back home. His name was Josie Peterson, and he was 29 years old.

The *Violet* was an old smack which needed money spent every year to keep her seaworthy. This latest damage was serious, and the injured skipper was likely to be ashore for a long time. Although the owner, Gideon Nicolson, had the *Violet* repaired and sent back to sea with young Josie promoted to skipper to finish the season, he had already made up his mind to sell her. Every year it was becoming more difficult to get good skippers and crew. There was little point, he had concluded, to keep this old boat. To consider replacing her was out of the question. On Josie's first trip, the young skipper surprised everyone by returning with a full cargo of salt cod. He did the same on his next trip. This persuaded Gideon Nicolson to postpone the sale. With Josie in charge, the *Violet* began to out-fish other smacks. So impressed was the owner at this unerring ability to catch a full load of cod each trip that he eventually decided to replace the *Violet* with a newer boat.

In the spring of 1894, he bought the *William Martin* from Grimsby. She had been built in Rye in Sussex only 11 years previously. At 76 tons, she was one of the larger smacks: stoutly built and in very good condition. The Rye shipyard had a reputation for building strong boats. It was said they had so perfected their technique that all the vessels built in this yard at this time were second to none. Presumably, Gideon Nicolson had been able to buy her at a knockdown price since English trawling companies had started to replace sail with steam. In any case, Josie and his crew now had a large and almost new smack at their disposal.

The *William Martin* was soon fishing well. For several years Josie often completed fishing trips within a month, at a time when some smacks took upwards of twelve weeks. He was in a class of his own. What made a good cod skipper? Knowledge of where and when to fish was obviously essential. A keen crew with brains in their fingers was also crucial. Some have argued that luck played a part. While a lucky cod strike might have been a bonus from time to time, it could never have been good fortune that enabled a skipper like Josie to consistently land more cod than anyone else. Most fishermen take the view that the harder you work, the more luck you have.

His ability to catch cod became even more marked as the industry continued to decline. But the days of cod fishing by hand lines in a sailboat were numbered. It was now almost impossible to get crew, so lucrative had the herring fishing become. It even became hard to get crew for the *William Martin*, the best-earning smack in the fleet. Gideon Nicolson did what every other smack owner did; he employed Faroese fishermen. This began as a trickle, topping up occasional crew shortages, but became a flood as the crewing situation became critical. To begin with, a few Faroese were taken on board the *William Martin*, but as more and more Shetlanders left, the balance shifted, until most of the crew came from Faroe. Eventually, the entire crew was Faroese, apart from Josie. This continued until 1906 when he stepped down as skipper. Perhaps it was the fact that there were no longer any fellow Shetlanders on board, or maybe the lure of much better pay at the herring became too much. It was a decision he regretted. Despite the much better wages and working conditions, Bobby told me that his grandfather never took to the herring, missing fishing for cod at Faroe for as long as he was at sea. After Josie had left, the *William Martin* was sold to Faroe.

***

Many years ago, I was in Faroe taking part in an international fishing conference. Since I was going to be there for almost a week, I tried to get a meeting with the then Faroese prime minister, Pauli Ellefsen. Somewhat to my surprise my request was successful, and, on a brisk windy morning, I made my way to Tinganes, a small rocky peninsula in the heart of Tórshavn, which housed the Faroese parliament in Viking times. Many of the government offices are still there, amongst a medieval jumble of old, red-painted wooden houses with grass-covered roofs.

I was feeling rather pleased with myself – I had secured a meeting with the Faroese prime minister! As he was the most important political figure in this North Atlantic outpost, we would, I was sure, be able to have some very serious and interesting discussions.

'The prime minister is busy right now, but he is expecting you. Come in and have a seat,' an efficient-looking secretary told me with an encouraging smile as she took me through to a large, wood-lined office. As I sat there looking at the many oil paintings hung on the wall, I began to rehearse all the questions I was going to ask the Løgmaður, as the prime minister is called in Faroe. Whenever I have met British government ministers in similar circumstances, they have always entered a room surrounded by many civil servants whose sole purpose seems to be to prevent you asking difficult questions. Not so in Faroe. Pauli Ellefsen suddenly strode into the room unaccompanied and proceeded to introduce himself. He was dressed casually, wearing a brown leather bomber jacket and an open-necked shirt. After a brief welcome and handshake, he proudly told me that it was his grandfather, Daniel Højgaard, who had bought the *William Martin* from Shetland. He was particularly keen to tell me that it was on this boat that he had started his working life as a fisherman. Although he was now prime minister, it was clear that the high-point of his career had been the years when he fished on board the *William Martin*. It was this smack, he explained, along with the many others that had been bought from Shetland, which had established the Faroese fishing industry. We spent the rest of our meeting talking about the Shetland smacks that had fished around Faroe. The Faroese prime minister was as interested in the subject as I was. We never actually got around to speaking about anything else.

On one of my recent trips to Faroe, I stayed at the small family-run Streym Hotel in Tórshavn. After a couple of days, I was finishing my favourite Scandinavian breakfast of cured

herring and rye bread, when the owner of the hotel asked if
he could join me, explaining that he had seen from the hotel
registration that I was a Shetlander. A fit-looking man in his
late 70s, Svend Aage Ellefsen is like many Faroese people who
never seem to think of retiring. He had enjoyed a varied career,
he explained, having been a fisherman, owner of a fishing company, a politician and now a hotel owner.

As the last of the guests finished their breakfasts, and as
the clatter of the dishes being cleared away began to subside,
he ordered some more coffee. After some more small talk, he
tentatively asked if I had ever heard of a Shetland cod smack
called the *William Martin*. I think he had expected a negative
response, so he was delighted to hear that not only did I know
the smack but I was also undertaking some research about the
Shetland cod fishermen who fished around Faroe. In turn, I was
astonished when he told me that it was his grandfather, Daniel
Højgaard, who had bought the *William Martin*. He explained
that his late brother had been the Faroese prime minister – the
same Pauli Ellefsen that I had met many years before. That kind
of serendipity does not happen very often.

As he poured out more coffee, Svend began telling me about
when he first joined the crew of the *William Martin*. As he
recalled these days, he spoke more quietly, almost reverentially.
It was not easy becoming a fisherman when you were still a boy,
he said, recounting that 'after the first few days at sea my wrists
became badly swollen; I was only 14 years old and was completely unprepared for the constant hauling of heavy lines. There
was no respite – fishing never stopped until the deck was full
of cod.' The older crewmembers always impressed on him that
speed was essential when there was a good fishing. Once his line
was hauled to the surface and the cod removed from the hooks,
he was told to quickly rebait and, while the line was plunging
back down to the seabed, to cut the cod gills and then cut off the
barbels to record his catch. By the time the line was at or near

the seabed, two more cod would have been caught and the process of hauling back up began again. And so, it went on, hour after hour, day after day, Svend told me in his characteristically Faroese matter-of-fact style. Breakfast on board the *William Martin* was at 7.30 a.m., followed by dinner at 12.30 p.m. and supper at 6.30 p.m. Breakfast was porridge, and the main meal of dinner alternated daily between fresh cod and dried mutton. There was always plenty of coffee on board, he said, confessing that was where he had picked up his lifelong caffeine habit. Fresh water was at a premium, only used for making coffee and drinking. The crew never washed during a trip and all the cooking was done with salt water.

For more than 50 years, the *William Martin* was an integral part of the extended Højgaard family. Several generations had fished on board, he explained, and, as children, they had all been brought up with stories about her time at sea. During the First World War she was on her way to the Faroe Bank when a warning was received that there was an active German submarine in the area. Daniel Højgaard took the right decision to turn back – five sloops were sunk that day. The crews, who were given time to launch their lifeboats before their sloops were torpedoed, took two days to row back to Faroe.

The *William Martin* was eventually modernised with the installation of an engine and the fitting of a wheelhouse. One New Year's Eve she was lying at anchor when she was struck by another smack. Although she sank and sustained serious damage, she was successfully recovered and repaired and was fishing again within a few months. During the Second World War, like many other Faroese sloops, she began to land her catch in British ports, where high prices were paid by a country desperate for supplies of fresh fish. It was a lucrative but dangerous trade, on account of bad weather during the winter and the constant risk of attack by German U-boats. Many Faroese fishermen lost their lives making this run and it is said the Faroese lost more men, as a proportion of their total population, during this war than did the British. On a trip to Iceland, the *William Martin* miraculously survived a heavy German air-attack which badly injured some of her crew. In typical cod fishing tradition, she went ashore to be repaired and was soon back at sea.

By the 1950s, she was fishing for herring with drift nets during the summer months but still using the old method of hand lines to catch cod for the rest of the year. It is quite remarkable that some of the Faroese fleet in the 1950s was still hand lining for cod, the same fishing method that the Shetlanders had first used in the 1820s. By this time, she was of course hopelessly outdated. This was the era of trawlers – the days of hand lining were over. Her fishing days finally came to an end in 1963.

The relationship between a crew and their fishing boat is personal and profound; a relationship that is difficult for people who are not from fishing communities to understand. Fishing boats are much more than a workplace. They have an identity, character and history all of their own. Different sizes and shapes, boats all have their distinctive hull colour – blue, red, black, green and yellow being some of the favourites. They all have a unique name and registration number, both written in large letters on each side of the bow. Even a casual glance at a harbour packed with fishing boats will show that they are not a generic group; like the crews who sail on them, they are all individuals.

Some argue that boats have their own personalities; some rolling slowly in a swell, others moving around more quickly. Some boats are noted for being dry, deflecting sea spray away from the deck, others are described as watery, seeming to attract seawater aboard. The best accolade a vessel can receive is to be described as a 'good sea boat' – a simple but fundamentally vital characteristic. No one wants to be in the middle of a storm in a bad sea boat.

Fishermen often define their lives by the boats they have sailed on, each providing a backdrop to their experiences. Instead of simply recounting something that they did at a certain stage of their life, they will reference this to the boat they were on at the time. For many, the most memorable parts of their lives are often associated with their boat. A year of exceptionally good fishing and high prices will be remembered as the year that provided enough money for someone to build their house. And, of course, a fisherman will always have a special place in his heart for a boat that has survived a ferocious storm and saved his life. No one gets emotional when describing the years they have spent working in an office block or a factory.

Spending more time on board their sloops than they did at home, the Faroese developed a particularly strong personal attachment to their boats. Svend introduced me to his cousin, another grandson of Daniel Højgaard. Called after his grandfather, this Daniel was too young to have fished on the family boat. He told me that a conversation between his grandfather and the engineer had been recorded on tape, with the two retired shipmates reminiscing about their years on board the *William Martin*. The engineer, Gimmi, said he really loved this boat, she was such a good sloop. Choosing his words carefully, old Daniel Højgaard replied: 'Yes, Gimmi, I can see from your behaviour onboard, that you do that. And to be honest I loved her as much as my own wife, she was such a terrific ship.'

All boats were referred to as females – no ship was ever called 'he' or 'it'. Even if the boat's name was masculine, as was the case with the *William Martin*, the boat itself was always she. Today, many argue that boats and ships should be gender neutral. I can see the force of these arguments and, in the fullness of time, the use of 'she' will no longer be used to describe a vessel. The shipping industry newspaper, *Lloyd's Register of Shipping*, has already made this change. But in the days of the cod smacks and sloops, such a concept would have been met with incredulity and incomprehension. Likewise, 'fisher' is now used as the gender-neutral term for people that go fishing. This makes sense in the modern world, and I now use this term when talking about the modern fishing industry. When looking at history, however, I still use the words that were used then: 'fishermen' and boats described as 'she'.

The *William Martin* was one of 150 sloops in the Faroese fleet. It was this fleet of sloops that lifted Faroe out of poverty. Cod changed everything for Faroe during the early 20th century. It was a society transformed.

17

A Society Transformed

For most of the 19th century, it was no exaggeration to describe
Faroe as a poor peasant society with the most basic of subsistence economies. Cod changed all that. It was the engine that
carried Faroe into the industrial age. The speed and scale of this
transformation is remarkable. There were only 14 cod sloops in
Faroe in 1890 but by 1910 this had increased to 137. The hand
line fishery for cod reached its peak in 1935 when 3,500 fishermen
sailed on board 150 sloops. This investment in the cod fishery,
and the replication of what Shetlanders had done a half century
earlier, laid the foundations for the large and prosperous fishing
industry that underpins their economy today. It also resulted
in a spectacular increase in population. In 1900 there were only
15,000 people. By the Second World War, this had increased to
30,000 – a doubling in only 40 years. Today, the population is
53,000.

Until the middle of the 19th century, the Danish crown
imposed a monopoly on all trading within Faroe. What little
commercial activity existed could only be undertaken through
the Danish crown's merchant stores. Until 1836, there was only
one store, in Tórshavn, for the whole of the islands. This meant
that all goods (such as salt fish, cod liver oil and woollen gar-
ments) had to be transported there to be sold. In a similar way,
it was the only place to buy basic consumer goods and essential

supplies such as tools, rope, hooks and salt. To travel to the Tórshavn store, a sea voyage in an open six-oared boat (comparable to the Shetland sixern) was necessary for most people. It was a lengthy, difficult and often hazardous voyage. In the 1830s, three further stores were opened: one in Tvøroyri on the island of Suðuroy in the south, one in Klaksvík in the northeast and one in Vestmanna in the northwest. While this made it easier and safer to travel to buy and sell goods, the monopoly remained in place, stifling local initiative and enterprise.

While Faroe was struggling under this archaic monopoly, Shetland merchants were investing in the cod fishery. The contrast between the two island neighbours could not have been starker. Someone who quickly became aware of this was an ambitious young man called Christian Pløyen, who had been appointed as the chief administrator of the Faroe Islands by the Danish government. Although he was himself Danish, he was passionate to do everything he could to improve the lot of the Faroese people. Sometimes, when British civil servants sent to administer distant places in the Empire became similarly passionate about local conditions, it was said they had 'gone native'. Perhaps Christian Pløyen had also gone native.

In 1839, together with three Faroese companions, he travelled to Shetland to see what they might learn about cod. In due course, he wrote a book about this trip, which chronicled his frustration at the inability of the Faroese to develop their own fishery. Seeing many smacks landing cod that had been caught around Faroe, he was exasperated, complaining that 'we sit calmly by with our hands in our bosoms vainly complaining that we catch nothing'. Here were the first stirrings of the Faroese determination to establish their own fishery. His visit to Shetland generated much debate back home. Why was it that the Shetlanders had been able to build up a large cod business? Was it the case that the Danish crown's trade monopoly was effectively preventing the Faroese from doing the same? Christian

Pløyen certainly thought so, and he began a campaign to have this monopoly abolished. It took a long time, but his tenacity eventually paid off and the crown's monopoly on trading was finally removed in 1856.

Some shrewd entrepreneurs immediately saw the opportunity to establish independent businesses. In Tvøroyri, for example, an enterprising Dane by the name of Thomas Friedrich Thomsen bought the old Danish crown store in 1856 and set up his own merchants' business. In this way, the Thomsen merchant company, which would in due course sell brandy to Shetland fishermen, was established. Before too long, merchant companies were established in all the Faroese villages. Some of these companies soon saw the potential in setting up cod fishing and exporting businesses. The first decked cod sloop, the *Fox*, was bought from England by Faroese owners in 1872, but it was not until the early 20th century that the cod industry began its meteoric expansion, with many second-hand smacks being bought from Shetland. The development of the cod fishery not only turbo-charged the Faroese economy; it also provided wages for a society where most people had previously lived hand-to-mouth.

Just as the Faroese cod fishery began to grow, many Faroese fishermen found employment on board the Shetland cod smacks. For some this was a culture shock. In 1882, Jóannes Didriksen got a job on board the Shetland smack *Mizpah*. This young man, who had just turned 16, did not actually want to become a full-time fisherman. His aim was to earn enough money from his Shetland cod trips to buy tools to set up a blacksmith business in his home village of Hvítanes. On his first day at sea, he became aware of an unusual smell from the galley. When he went down below, the cook told him he had put on a pot of coffee. Jóannes explained that he had never tasted coffee before, as the cook poured him a cup. Finding the taste to be bitter and strange, he handed the cup back to the surprised cook. By the end of the trip, he was enjoying his coffee along with the rest of the crew.

His introduction to coffee as a teenager was an indication of just how poor some of the Faroese people were at this time. This was to change dramatically. Within a few years coffee had become the staple daily drink on board every Faroese sloop.

Although the cod fishery eventually generated prosperity for the Faroese people, it did not happen overnight. Poverty hung around for a long time. Niels Martin Nielsen was a fisherman from Suðuroy who had a large family to look after. He was the sole breadwinner and took his parental responsibilities very seriously. Standard practice on board Faroese sloops was dried mutton for dinner every second day, and on the other days it was freshly caught cod. Rather than eat his dried mutton dinners, Niels kept his share of meat to take home to his children at the end of the three-month trip. Instead, he boiled several cod heads to eat. For him, it was fish for dinner every day – cod fillets along with the rest of the crew for half the week, and cod heads for himself on the days the crew had their dried mutton. At the end of each trip, he not only went home with his wages but also with three months' supply of dried mutton. This story of the love of a fisherman for his family is also a reflection on how desperately poor some people were in Faroe. This would all change within a generation as the cod fishery continued to expand. Cod provided something that most Faroese people had lacked throughout their history – money. That transformed Faroese society forever.

As their fishery developed, the young fishermen who had sailed on board the Shetland smacks were in great demand as they were the experienced hands who had learned the skills of fishing and processing cod. Many of these newly trained cod fishermen were able to stay on board the smacks they had been working on after they were sold to their new owners in Faroe.

The Faroese fishery eventually became much larger than the Shetland one had ever been. It not only dominated their economy but also profoundly influenced Faroese society and culture in a way that is still apparent today. So many Faroese men had become cod fishermen that this industry came to define what it meant to be Faroese in the early 20th century. They fished the Faroe Bank, but they also developed their own distant-water operation, fishing around Iceland, Rockall and Greenland.

Cod fishing was as dangerous in Faroe as it had been in Shetland, with many men lost at sea. If this had happened, the returning sloop would fly its flag at half-mast. While this was a straightforward method of letting everyone know as soon as possible that someone had been lost, it must also have been an agonising wait for those ashore. Villagers seeing the sloop enter the fjord with its flag at half-mast must have experienced the most profound sense of trepidation, wondering who amongst the crew had been lost. Every mother must have prayed that it was not her son, in the full knowledge that if her prayer were answered, it would be some other poor mother's tragedy. This was the society that was in perpetual mourning, which Mikines so graphically portrayed in his art.

The cod sloops brought both prosperity and heartache. Perhaps that is why there is a unique tradition where a model sloop hangs above the altar in most Faroese churches. A beautiful model of the *William Martin* can be found in the church at Rituvík, the home village of the Højgaard family. Model boats in museums are always viewed from the perspective of a bird, looking down on the deck. It is strange that all these sloops in Faroese churches are suspended from the ceiling, since all that can be seen from the pews is the hull shape below the waterline – the red-painted bottom of the boat. All the interesting detail of the rigging, the masts and the deck layout are hidden. The view from the pews was the same as the cod saw as they were being hauled to the surface.

Brandy became intertwined with the cod fishery in Faroe, as it had in Shetland. Earning money in a way that was unknown in the past, the availability of cheap alcohol soon became a problem. Many Faroese fishermen were drinking most of their earnings at the end of each cod trip. This was alarming large sections of Faroese society and there were calls for the sale of alcohol to be banned. In this religious society, the church was in the vanguard of the campaign, as were some fishermen's wives who had first-hand experience of the hardships that excessive drinking can cause to families. The merchants, who had developed a profitable trade with the Shetlanders and were now selling alcohol to local fishermen, were opposed to the call for prohibition.

The debate between those in favour of a ban and those opposed raged for several years. It was eventually decided that the only way to resolve this issue was to hold a referendum. Held on 6 November 1907, the result was an overwhelming vote in favour of prohibition. From 1 January 1908, all sales of alcohol were banned in the Faroes. It was a ban that would last for most of the 20th century. The days of cheap Faroese brandy were over. Even though women did not get the right to vote in Denmark and Faroe until 1915, all Faroese women had the right to vote in this referendum. And without the women's vote, it is unlikely that there would have been a majority for prohibition. Interestingly, this was the first referendum held anywhere in the world where women had the same suffrage as men.

***

Hand lining for cod continued to be a profitable business until the middle of the 20th century, when trawlers began to replace sloops. In many cases, the companies that had owned cod sloops invested heavily in trawlers. This, in turn, laid the foundations for the modern Faroese fleet, one of the most efficient and advanced in the world. The Faroese success story is not, however, just down to fish. It is also about politics.

Faroe used to be part of Denmark, in the same way that Shetland is part of Scotland. An early home-rule campaign in Faroe had been derided for being unrealistic, and there seemed little prospect that the Faroese would ever obtain more control over their own affairs. But that changed dramatically when Germany occupied Denmark during the Second World War, leaving the Faroese to effectively govern themselves. After the war, things were never going to go back to how they had been, and a new relationship needed to be negotiated between Faroe and Denmark. This was formalised with the passing of the Home Rule Act in 1948, which enabled the Faroese parliament to make decisions on all matters of importance to the islands, including fisheries, while remaining part of Denmark. The Faroese parliament is one of the most devolved legislatures in the world. Retaining all taxes raised in the Faroes from the outset, it has far more powers than the Scottish parliament.

Every time I visit, I can see that this is a very energetic and confident community. Faroe is no remote backwater in the North Atlantic. The bus to Tórshavn from the airport on the island of Vágur is equipped with free Wi-Fi, and the journey to the capital takes only around 40 minutes via an undersea tunnel which replaced the car ferry many years ago. Stunning public art and innovative architecture define Tórshavn, a capital that is clearly proud of its history but also embraces the modern world with enthusiasm and confidence. This is also an affluent society that has one of the best broadband services in the world, full employment, an excellent health service and a first-class public education system. With few resources apart from the sea, how have they managed this? The fact that they have made all their own decisions since 1948 has fostered a belief in themselves and a willingness to make their own mistakes. Political autonomy has worked for Faroe and is now the accepted status quo. Confidence and self-determination are both essential components of the modern Faroe Islands; you cannot have one without the other, and the more you have of one the more you get of the other. No one ever suggests that restoring Danish rule would be a good idea. Such a notion would be regarded as ludicrous.

The political debate within the islands is now about whether Faroe should go further and become an independent nation state. Politics in Faroe is consequently fascinating. The conventional right and left spectrum is divided over the issue of independence. There are two conservative parties, one advocating independence from Denmark, the other wanting to preserve the devolved status quo. On the left there are also two parties, again defined over their differing policies on independence. Coalitions are normal and, as you would expect in a country where fishing is still the largest industry, arguments over fisheries policy are often the defining political questions for this small community. The big issue at the general election of 2019 was a debate on how fish quotas should be allocated. The debate on independence remains unresolved. A seat at the United Nations for a county of 53,000 people! Surely not? And yet this prospect is calmly and rationally discussed by the Faroese people. Whether or not they become fully independent is perhaps less important than the fact that this small, successful and confident island community is even having such a discussion. In Faroe, everything is possible. A well-known politician, Magni Arge, articulates this very well when he says that 'the people of the Faroe Islands have been raised in the belief that we can manage our own destiny'.

Nothing epitomises the self-confidence of the Faroese more than the brand-new arts and performing centre in Tvøroyri. Its origins lie in the salt cod trade. When this industry was at its peak, enormous quantities of salt were needed to supply the fleet of sloops. It was decided to build one huge storage silo to service the entire Faroese fleet and to locate this in Suðuroy, on the outskirts of Tvøroyri. Capable of holding 10,000 tons of salt, this vast concrete and steel structure was completed in 1939. Although it was by far the largest industrial building in the Faroes, its shape was strangely pleasing, resembling an upturned boat. As freezing replaced curing, demand for salt declined and the silo was finally abandoned in the 1980s. When the building began to deteriorate, it was agreed that it should be demolished. The prospect of this iconic part of Faroese history being destroyed appalled Ólavur Rasmussen, who had recently moved from Tórshavn to Suðuroy to take up a position as one of the Lutheran priests in the island. In his view the silo was beautiful, a unique architectural gem in the North Atlantic. But if it was to be saved, what could it possibly be used for? Ólavur suggested that the cavernous silo space would make an ideal concert hall.

There was no shortage of critics who believed the idea was daft. Large performing centres are found in cities, they argued, and the idea that there could be such a venue on a small island of less than 5,000 people was unrealistic. When the cost of converting the silo was estimated to be more than £8 million, the critics were convinced that this mad idea would finally die. But that was to underestimate the vision and determination of this Lutheran priest. He recruited a group of enthusiastic supporters and together they prepared a business plan. Against all the odds, they eventually managed to raise the money. The intervention of Maersk, Denmark's biggest corporation and the largest shipping company in the world, was crucial. The family that owns this company have always supported the arts, and their cultural philanthropy reached new heights in 2005 when they built a brand-new opera house near Copenhagen, presenting it as a gift to the Danish people. Their interest in the Faroese salt silo project, however, was not only motivated by their desire to encourage the arts. It also reflected a debt of gratitude they felt to the hundreds of Faroese sailors who had loyally sailed as captains and officers in the Maersk fleet over many decades. Once Maersk were committed, the Danish and Faroese governments found it difficult not to become co-funders.

The new centre opened in 2017. While most of the original silo has been retained, bold additions of glass within and without provide natural light and optimise the stunning fjord seascape. The interior is mostly given over to a huge auditorium which can seat 400 people. Sophisticated lighting and sound engineering have created an ultra-modern concert hall in the space which once stored thousands of tons of salt. Capable of hosting large international events, art exhibitions and theatre productions, the new venue is best known for its eclectic live music events, including classical concerts, opera, jazz and rock music. Its name, SALT, was carefully chosen. While this is an abbreviation for 'Sounds, Arts, Live, Theatre', it also deliberately evokes the silo's original purpose. What else could it have been called, in a community that cherishes its fishing heritage?

This is an arts centre that any large city would be proud of, and the fact that it has been built on a small island is incredible. There are now few critics, although some complain that people from the rest of Faroe wanting to attend a concert in SALT must make a long two-hour ferry trip from Tórshavn to get to Tvøroyri. That will all change when the Faroese government builds an undersea tunnel to Suðuroy. Scheduled to be completed in 2030, this will be one of the longest tunnels in the world and will complete the long-held national ambition to connect all the main Faroese islands by a subsea road network.

Shetland is Faroe's closest neighbour. The Faroese are acutely aware of this geography, and they acknowledge that it was the Shetlanders who taught them how to fish for cod. They consequently follow politics in Shetland and Scotland very closely. They simply cannot understand why Shetland does not have more political autonomy than it does. Regarding Scotland, they shake their heads in disbelief at those who argue that Scotland is not big enough to be an independent nation state. For the Faroese, who have made a huge success of self-determination, and are now debating the pros and cons of independence, the idea that Scotland is too small or too poor to be independent is beyond preposterous.

Many visitors to Shetland often comment that it is also an energetic and confident community. It undoubtedly is, but not in the same league as Faroe. A couple of years ago I had been telling a friend about Faroe; its history, economy and politics. I worried that I had been over-enthusiastic when he told me that I had persuaded him to visit. When we next met, he had just returned from spending a week there. Always concerned when someone makes their first trip to Faroe that they have endured a week of dense fog and driving rain, I hesitantly asked how he had got on. 'Great place,' he said. 'It's like Shetland on steroids.'

Returning to the 19th century, it was not only smacks and fishing skills that Faroe got from Shetland, and it was not only cod and brandy that Shetland got from Faroe. Both island communities came to realise they shared a linguistic history as the Norn language was lost from Shetland and restored in Faroe.

18

Remnants of Norn

The first time I travelled to Faroe I found the experience strangely disconcerting. It was clear that I was in a foreign country, but in some ways I felt as if I was in Shetland. The high mountains were a contrast to home, but the traditional Faroese boats in the marinas bore a strong resemblance to the Shetland open boats. The constant comings and goings of fishing boats and inter-island ferries were also very familiar.

The language, on first hearing, was strange and foreign. It was clearly Nordic but different to what little Norwegian I knew. And yet, every now and then I suddenly caught a phrase or a word that was Shetlandic. It was clear that we still had many phrases and words in common, something that the Shetland cod fishermen would have been even more aware of all those years ago. For example, the Faroese word for a porpoise is *nýsa*, uncannily like the Shetlandic word 'neesick'. In Shetland, 'tystie' and 'shalder' are the names for a black guillemot and an oyster-catcher. The Faroese names sound almost the same, although spelt slightly differently – *teisti* and *tjaldur*. There are hundreds more examples. The same feeling of familiarity also occurs whenever I look at a map. The place names of Faroe and Shetland are nearly all identical. For example, the Faroese names of Hvítanes, Sand, Fugloy and Vágur are the same as the Shetland names of Whiteness, Sand, Foula and Voe. The name of almost every

Faroese island, village and geographical feature has a Shetland equivalent.

The connections between the two island groups were once very close. In 1405 one of the wealthiest women in Faroe died with no immediate heir to her property. Her name was Guðrun Sjúrðardóttir and she owned land and houses in Shetland and Norway, as well as in Faroe. Her father was from Shetland and was given the nickname Hjaltr, meaning Shetlander, when he moved to Faroe. Six documents, known as the Húsavík Letters, were written regarding her estates and these are a fascinating glimpse into the close ties between Faroe and Shetland at this time. One of these letters was written by Ragnhildr Hávarðsdóttir, from Windhouse in Yell, who wrote to claim part of Guðrun's inheritance for her son, Magnus Erlingsson.

At this time the languages of both archipelagos were one and the same, and this might have continued unchanged had a web . of a complicated marriage plans not conspired to change the geopolitics of Shetland. Having been part of the Viking world for more than 700 years, Shetland was transferred to Scotland in 1469 when a dynastic union took place between the royal families of Denmark and Scotland. At this time, Denmark was a powerful kingdom, ruling over Norway, Iceland and the North Atlantic islands of Faroe, Shetland and Orkney. When Princess Margaret of Denmark was betrothed to marry James III of Scotland, a dowry had to be paid by the bride's family, as was the custom at that time. Presumably following some diplomatic negotiations, King Christian of Denmark agreed to pay 58,000 florins to Scotland. This was a sum that, under normal circumstances, should have been easily afforded by the Danish crown. King Christian did, however, have a reputation for spending more than he could raise in taxes. Any problems he might have had in paying this royal dowry were made worse by the dreadful summer weather of 1468, resulting in a miserable harvest that slashed the crown's income. So much so that King Christian could only afford to pay 8,000 florins against the agreed sum. As an alternative he suggested that Orkney could be given to Scotland instead of the shortfall of 50,000 florins. King James readily agreed. Scotland had been keen for some time to get hold of Orkney with its rich soils and productive farms.

A year later and the Scottish exchequer had still not received the remaining payment of 8,000 florins. When pressed, Denmark offered Shetland instead. This was not met with any enthusiasm as Shetland was, in contrast to Orkney, a rocky outcrop of little value. But there seemed to be no alternative, and, under these ignoble circumstances, Shetland became part of Scotland in 1469. There was no battle, no treaty, no invasion. Shetland's 700-year-old Viking history was ended as part of a grubby deal to settle a bad debt. Had the summer of 1468 been sunnier, the political map of the North Atlantic might have been very different today. History can indeed turn on a sixpence.

For most Shetlanders there was little immediate change. They still spoke Norn, the old Viking tongue, and continued to look to Norway, perhaps not fully realising the significance of what had happened. The first big difference was in 1472 when control of ecclesiastical affairs was transferred from the bishopric of Trondheim in Norway to St Andrews in Scotland. From that date onwards, all the priests and clerics coming to minister to the islanders were Scottish rather than Norwegian. Legal documents then began to be written in the Scots language, instead of Norn, and an increasing number of Scottish landowners, merchants and artisans moved to Shetland, sensing economic opportunity in this new part of Scotland. Slowly but irrevocably, Shetland began to look south to Scotland instead of east to Norway. Despite all of this, many Shetlanders retained their Viking culture and language for a long time. Even to this day, many Shetlanders do not regard themselves as Scottish.

***

Insofar as language is concerned, although Norn was no longer spoken by the early 18th century, the islanders did not speak Scots either. Instead, they spoke Shetlandic (or Shaetlan as many native speakers prefer to describe it) – a distinctive speech that combined both Scots and Norn. This significance of this linguistic change might have gone unnoticed were it not for a remarkable Faroese philologist, Dr Jakob Jakobsen. Born in 1864, he grew up in the heart of Tórshavn. A large red wooden house with a grass roof was the family home, as well as the town's bookshop, which his father owned. Part of this house is now a museum, honouring Jakobsen's work, while the rest of the building is still a bookshop with a recently opened café.

Whenever I am in Tórshavn, I always make time to browse through the well-stocked shelves of this old bookshop. Although I had not intended to buy anything on my last visit, I could not resist a Faroese novel I had been meaning to get for a long time. Outside the rain was torrential and horizontal, flying before a northeasterly gale, so I decided to have a coffee while I waited to see if the weather improved. I watched and listened to the rain ricocheting like bullets off the triple-glazed windows. The noise was deafening, and the windows were trembling. If this was a coffee shop anywhere else, people would be apprehensive and concerned. But this was normal summer weather in Faroe, and no one paid the slightest attention.

Making my coffee last, I tried to imagine young Jakob growing up here. While not in any way ostentatious, their home showed that the Jakobsens had a relatively privileged lifestyle. From an early age, he and his sisters, Ana and Sigrid, were surrounded by books, and it is perhaps not surprising that he read voraciously and developed an early interest in languages. Jakob decided to study linguistics at Copenhagen University, where his roommate was an Icelander who sparked his passion for the old Viking tongue.

Shy and academic, Jakobsen was an unlikely radical. At

university, he joined a small group of Faroese intellectuals who had set themselves the goal of saving the Faroese language. To them it was clear that it was going to disappear under the growing influence of Danish. The language of the church and schools was Danish, which was also used in all legal documents and newspapers. Faroese was the tongue of the poor people, spoken but never written or read. Not everyone in Faroe regarded this as a problem, many seeing Faroese as nothing other than a crude village dialect. To elevate this to the status of a language was pointless. Everyone should speak Danish, they argued, and forget such nonsense. Jakobsen profoundly disagreed. He recognised that Faroese was very close to the original language the Vikings had spoken, as he had discussed many times with his university friend. If the Norse sagas, some of the finest medieval literature in Europe, could be written in the speech of the Vikings, why should Faroese not be the official language of the church, law, culture and literature in his home islands?

He decided to travel to Shetland to study what had happened to Shetland Norn under the pervading influence of Scots and English. Shetland was to be used as a warning signal to the Faroese about what would happen if they allowed their language to die, as the Shetlanders had done with theirs. Travelling throughout Shetland, the place, its people and the remnants of Shetland Norn increasingly fascinated him. Speaking to hundreds of islanders and immersing himself in Shetland culture, he made many long-lasting friendships. One of the closest and most enduring of these was with the blind navigation teacher, Haldane Burgess. These two academics, with their shared love of language and history, had much in common. Jakobsen believed that 'the old Norse language of Shetland is the language of Faroe', and he was saddened to see how diluted it had become.

Like many academics, his subject dominated his life. He possibly became rather obsessed. When asked to give a lecture in Lerwick about Shetland Norn, he reckoned it would take at least six hours to cover everything he wanted to say on the subject. The organisers asked his friend Haldane Burgess to persuade him to make the lecture shorter. It is not known what the result was – two hours, perhaps? These were the days before minimum attention span and the soundbite. He eventually recorded some 10,000 old Norse words, place names and phrases still used by Shetlanders at the end of the 19th century. His work earned him a PhD and was subsequently published as a two-volume dictionary of the Norn language in Shetland. Providing a fascinating glimpse into how Shetlanders used to converse with each other, Jakobsen's work is a rigorous snapshot of a dying language.

While Jakobsen was recording the last traces of Shetland Norn, the Shetland cod fishermen and the Faroese people they met were able to understand each other, at least partially, in a very practical and everyday manner. The Shetlanders had fished around Faroe for half a century – a very long time that spanned several generations. Although Shetlandic was no longer Shetland Norn, the speech of the fishermen was infused with an enormous number of Norn words, phrases and idioms, particularly relating to boats, the weather and the sea. It is therefore not surprising that Shetland fishermen were able to converse, to some extent, with the Faroese. Such linguistic experiments would have been commonplace whenever the Shetlanders were ashore in Faroe, and whenever there was Faroese crew on board the Shetland smacks.

Like Jakobsen, Simun av Skarði was a leading member of the home rule party and an early advocate of the Faroese language, founding the first high school in Faroe where all teaching was done in Faroese rather than Danish. Simun's surname was not actually Skarði, but he was referred to as such following the Faroese tradition of being known by the village you come from – a tradition once very common in Shetland as well. Skarð is a very small village on the island of Kunoy where his father, Johannes Johannesen, was the blacksmith. Fishing vessels often anchored off the village to get equipment repaired. Simun recalled that fishermen from the Shetland smacks visited their house every year. He particularly remembered one Shetlander with a long tawny beard speaking to his grandmother 'in his old Shetland tongue'. They could apparently understand each other and were able to conduct a conversation, of sorts. This Shetlander was James Christie, of Westerwick, near Skeld, who had fished at Faroe for many years.

Returning to Jakobsen, in the introduction to his dictionary, he quotes a verse he recorded which captures the process of linguistic change that he documented so extensively:

Dey vara gud ti	It was a good time
When sona min guid ta Kadanes	When my son went to Caithness
Han kan ca rossa mare	He can call rossa mare
Han kan ca big bere	He can call big barley
Han kan ca eld fire	He can call eld fire
Han kan ca klovandi taings	He can call klovandi taings

This is verse written in Shetland Norn. The father is reflecting on the fact that his son has started using Scots and English words rather than Norn following a visit to Caithness in the north of Scotland. This poem marks the beginning of a process of linguistic change that took several hundred years and continues today. With each generation, Norn words and idioms were replaced by Scots equivalents, and the language that was spoken gradually changed. Within the last generation something new has happened, with both Norn and Scots words being replaced by English. As this continues, the last remnants of Shetland Norn will soon be gone.

Jakobsen used this example of linguistic decline in Shetland as a warning to what would happen to Faroese if nothing was done to save the language. The Shetland experience was recounted repeatedly in Faroe as Jakobsen and his group of radical intellectuals implored the Faroese to always use their native tongue. The campaign was eventually successful, and Faroese was saved from extinction; Jakobsen is still revered in Faroe for his work. It is now the medium of all discourse in the islands. Young people are probably more confident, and certainly prouder, speaking their mother tongue than their great grandparents were. And they are also, like all Europeans, perfectly fluent in English as well.

***

At the other end of the salt cod road, the Basques also managed to save their language. Their ancient tongue, Euskara, was the language of the fishermen who had first fished for cod on the Grand Banks and who had perfected the process of salting and drying cod. A fiercely independent people who love their language, cuisine and culture, they have always stood apart from Spain.

Having fought on the wrong side in the Spanish Civil War, in an attempt to secure an independent Basque homeland, they were to suffer terribly under General Franco. During this long period of dictatorship, political repression took many forms, with all traces of Euskara removed from civil society. It became illegal to publish anything or teach anyone in Basque. For a time, it was even illegal to give babies Basque names. Despite his repressive regime, Franco never succeeded in making everyone speak Spanish, and Euskara continued to be spoken at home and in some workplaces. Usually spoken in hushed tones and only with trusted friends, the very act of conversing in Euskara was nevertheless seen as a way for ordinary people to personally reject the linguistic imperialism of the Spanish state. The Basque fishing fleet was a particular stronghold of Basque speech, since there were no Spanish ears when they were at sea. Nevertheless, suppression of the language over several generations, and a large migration of Spaniards into the region, took its toll on the language. By the time Franco died in 1975 it is estimated that Euskara was only spoken by around a quarter of the population.

This was to change dramatically when the Basque country obtained political autonomy in the post-Franco era. Euskara became an official language and its use in education, the media and public discourse flourished. Some 34 per cent of the population are now fluent Basque speakers. That may sound like a modest increase, but a far more relevant figure is the fact that seven out of ten people under the age of 25 now speak Euskara. As with Faroese, the language of the Basques has been saved and is thriving. It is now cool to speak Faroese and Basque, and it is those who tried to stop these minority languages from being saved whose views are now ridiculed.

Jakobsen could not, of course, save Shetland Norn. It was too far gone. But he did record what remained, and he left Shetlanders a priceless legacy of their linguistic history. But these fascinating linguistic connections between Shetland and Faroe culture during the 19th century have long faded from memory. As Shetlanders started to fish for herring, they forgot about the haaf, cod and Faroe. The inspiration became Scotland, which had built up a huge herring industry that Shetland would soon copy. Within a few years Shetland no longer exported dried salt fish, particularly the salt cod for which it had built up such a good reputation in Spain. Instead, Shetland began to be known for its barrels of salt herring, soon to number in their hundreds of thousands. The queen of the Mediterranean had been abandoned for king herring.

19

The Big Bang

Shetland did not gradually develop its herring fishery. Herring exploded onto the scene. The fisheries equivalent of the big bang, its economic and social consequences were profound. From nothing to a fleet of more than 300 herring boats in less than ten years – it was as if the Californian gold rush had arrived in Shetland. Quickly replacing the haaf and the cod, herring came to dominate the Shetland economy in a way that no other industry had done before or has done since. Exports of salt cod to Spain dwindled, replaced by exports of salt herring to eastern Europe that increased year after year. The origins of this fishery lay well south of Shetland, in the Moray Firth.

The Moray Firth fishery started in the early 19th century when a fleet of half deckers began to fish for herring. Early success saw these boats replaced by larger, fully decked vessels. Mostly around 15 metres in length, they were more seaworthy, could carry more drift nets and were able to hold a larger catch. By the 1870s, this herring fishing was powering an economic boom in the north of Scotland. Boats jostled with each other to get space to land their herring in the many congested ports that were all far too small for the ever-expanding fleet. Wick, Peterhead and Fraserburgh were the main ports, but there were dozens of others, many consisting of little more than a simple pier at the bottom of a cliff. Driving from John o' Groats to Golspie, you are never far from the sea. Someone once suggested that, if I was interested in finding out more about the early Scottish herring industry, I should take every left turn off this road as I drove south. It was good advice, there are more than 20 left turns – all leading to small, well-built harbours that were once full of boats. With magical names such as Latheronwheel, Whaligoe, Papigoe and Keiss, a visit never disappoints.

The ripples of prosperity from the Moray Firth extended as far north as Orkney. For Shetland, however, it was Faroe and Iceland that continued to matter, not Scotland. It is not as if Shetlanders were unaware that herring could be caught around the islands – the hundreds of Dutch busses fishing east of Shetland every summer were a constant reminder. Maybe it was just easier to stick to the familiar haaf and cod. Possibly the scars of the Hay & Ogilvy bankruptcy, and the failure of the herring fishery in the 1840s, were still too raw. It was, therefore, somewhat ironic that it was William Hay's new company that was responsible for re-igniting an interest in herring.

Inspired by the Moray Firth boom, Hay set up a curing business in 1875 and contracted ten Orkney boats to fish for the summer. Unlike the Dutch busses that processed their catch on board, the Orkney boats landed their herring to the Hays curing yard in Lerwick every day. The venture was successful, both for the Orkney fleet and for Hay's first venture into herring curing, and it inevitably led to some Shetlanders asking: if fellow islanders from Orkney could catch and land herring in Shetland every day, why not us?

This question was answered with astonishing speed and extraordinary enthusiasm as this new industry was embraced. In 1876 three second-hand decked herring boats were bought from Scotland. One was bought by a Lerwick baker and merchant, another by a partnership in Cunningsburgh. The third, called the *Lass o' Gowrie*, was bought by fishermen from Burra, in partnership with Hays. Three of these fishermen were brothers:

Tammy, Andrew and Alec Goodlad. What had prompted these three brothers, who had all been cod fishermen, to try something totally new and unproven? It was probably as simple as their wish to emulate the success of the Orkney boats. It might, however, have been partly related to the tragic sinking of the cod smack *Turquoise* only four years previously, when their other two brothers, William and Oli, had been lost.

Unbelievably successful, these three boats not only caught herring most nights, but they all got paid high prices, reflecting the buoyant market for salt herring at the time. The earnings made by these first herring fishermen were unheard of. There is nothing quite like money to drive rapid change, and a headlong rush into herring ensued. By 1883 the herring fleet had soared to 240, and two years later the fleet numbered 319, providing employment for almost 2,000 fishermen. So successful was the industry kickstarted by the *Lass o' Gowrie* that the name Gowrie was used for a long time in Burra and Scalloway as a generic term to describe all sailboats fishing with drift nets. Shetlanders were able to buy second-hand herring boats from the Moray Firth ports very easily as the profits being made there were allowing Scottish fishermen to build new boats. Around the edge of the Moray Firth, dozens of small shipyards were launching decked herring boats as fast as they could build them. Their new owners were able to do this because there seemed to be an insatiable demand from Shetland for their old boats. It was a win-win situation for the Shetlanders and the Scots.

In the same way as the fleet increased, so did the number of curing companies. By 1885 there were 74 curers in Shetland operating 114 curing yards where herring were landed, gutted, salted and packed into barrels on a daily basis. Most of these curers were Scottish companies, already established in the Moray Firth ports, who set up operations in Shetland for the summer herring season. These herring curers had no need of stone beaches and, as the haaf and cod era ended, these beaches began a slow process of returning to nature, no longer being cleared of seaweed and driftwood. Beaches which had been valuable for over 200 years suddenly became worthless.

To cure herring, instead of a beach, a pier next to an area of flat land was required. Very soon, in almost every Shetland voe, small piers were built, like fingers stretching into the sea. The backdrop to these piers was a collection of wooden huts. Some of these huts provided accommodation for the workers, while others were used for storing salt, as essential for curing herring as it had been for curing cod and ling. And everywhere were endless stacks of wooden barrels. This was the new real estate; curers were paying the lairds a handsome rent to secure the land required to build their curing stations.

The language of the fishing industry also changed. No longer was there talk about smacks catching 20,000 cod and the prized Shetland cure then being exported to the *bacalao* markets in Bilbao. Instead, fishermen were now landing crans[*] of herring. After gutting, the herring were graded according to a mystifying set of categories, such as Full, Matfull, Mattie and Spent, before being salted in barrels and then exported to exciting-sounding Baltic ports such as Lübeck, Danzig, Stettin (now called Szczecin), Königsberg (now called Kaliningrad) and St Petersburg.

A daily pattern soon emerged. Boats would sail in the late afternoon, shooting their drift nets as the sun set. The nets were hauled back just after midnight. Depending on how much herring had been caught, this could take most of the short summer night. The crew would haul back the nets over the side of the boat shaking them so that the herring would fall out. Haul and shake – over and over again. Once the line of drift

---

[*] A cran is a measure of volume. Four baskets of herring counted as a cran, with seven crans making a ton. Towards the end of the drift net era, baskets were replaced by small fish boxes, called tins, with six of these counted as a cran.

nets was back on board, it was time to sail ashore. After landing the herring to one of the curing stations, the crew managed to snatch a few hours' sleep as they sailed back to the fishing grounds. The crews all slept and ate in cramped cabins, aft of the fish holds which took up most of the room in these boats.

Most of the early herring boats that came to Shetland were owned by merchants, some of whom had been involved in the haaf and cod fisheries. Scottish curers, establishing themselves in Shetland for the first time, also invested in some of these boats. Ownership of this new fleet was, however, much more fluid than the rigidity of the haaf and the cod. Right from the outset some fishermen became part-owners, as was the case with the *Lass o' Gowrie*. Before too long, fishermen began to see that they could own the boats themselves, no longer needing merchants or curers as part-owners. This was a monumental social change, as profound as it was symbolic for the fishermen who had, for generations, been poorly paid hired hands.

It was not, however, only better pay, and the prospect of becoming shareholders, that persuaded men to leave the haaf and the cod. It was also an easier job. The daily routine of fishing during the night and landing the catch of herring every morning allowed fishermen to be ashore for a few hours every day. This was a world of difference from a long 12-week distant-water trip to Faroe and Iceland, where the only time ashore might have been a quick stop to pick up contraband on the way home.

***

As well as buying herring from the local fleet, the curers also took landings from the large fleet of Scottish herring boats that were now venturing north of the Moray Firth to participate in the Shetland summer bonanza. This combined Shetland and Scottish fleet landed more than 55,000 tons of herring in 1885, a total that accounted for more than a quarter of all landings in Scotland that year.

It was a few weeks after that record-breaking season that the 34-year-old skipper of the *Teaser* told his crew to slip their mooring ropes in Lerwick harbour. Emboldened by their success at the summer fishing, some of the Shetland fleet were preparing to sail to East Anglia. They were looking to extend the herring season by taking part in the English autumn fishery. Lasting from October to Christmas, this was undertaken from the ports of Lowestoft and Yarmouth.

The skipper of the *Teaser* was Robbie Christie, fair-haired and tall with a ruddy complexion. A man of few words, he was quietly spoken and had a reputation for being as steady as a rock. He never rushed to make a quick decision about anything, always taking his time to think things through. The fact that his crew sometimes confused his careful nature with slowness did not bother him in the slightest. Having been a successful cod skipper, he did not need to hurry to make any decision he was not entirely comfortable with.

Robbie grew up in the small crofting township of Symbister, at the south end of the island of East Burra, and his horizons were limited. He had never been anywhere else but his home island when he first went to sea on a cod smack at the age of 14. Since that time, he had spent most of every subsequent year fishing around Faroe and Iceland. When he eventually became a skipper, he already knew the coastline around Faroe and off northeast Iceland like the inside of his pockets. Always calling in past Tvøroyri to pick up brandy on his way home, he was more familiar with this Faroese village than he was with Lerwick. That had all now changed; he had just spent his first summer fishing for herring.

As the wind filled her sails, the *Teaser* began to slowly move through the harbour. Busying themselves around the deck, there was a tangible sense of excitement amongst the crew as they readied everything for their trip south. Robbie, however, felt a little apprehensive. He had only been at the herring for this one summer and he had never fished at East Anglia before. At just over 15 metres long, the *Teaser* was not a big boat. She was much smaller than the cod smacks he was used to, and he still found it difficult to adjust to working with a crew of only six, having been used to crews of 12 and 14 when fishing for cod. Never having been in Scotland before, let alone England, he had no idea what to expect in Yarmouth when he arrived. He had been told that it was a congested harbour at the mouth of a river. Reminding himself that manoeuvring a sailboat was difficult enough in a large harbour like Tvøroyri or Lerwick, he wondered how he would manage to sail the *Teaser* in and out of a river mouth. He had also heard that there were sand banks on the fishing grounds; a real danger to skippers who did not know the area.

In this reflective state of mind, he recalled his early scepticism about herring. When the first herring boats had arrived in Burra only seven years before, he was certain that this new fishing would fail. He remembered his grandfather telling him about the Hungry Forties and how the loss of nets in the September gale of 1840 had resulted in the bankruptcy of both Hay & Ogilvy and the Shetland Bank. His grandfather had been a skipper of one of these early herring boats, one of the half deckers. For a few years he had fished well and invested what little savings he had in some drift nets. Losing their entire fleet of nets on the night of the gale, the crew were unable to buy replacement gear and, within a year, the boat had been hauled on a beach and abandoned; his grandfather had lost both his job and his investment. Lucky to get a berth on a cod smack, he had never forgotten how herring had been his ruin. Robbie had been close to his grandfather, often asking him to recount the events of the 1840 storm, but he now recognised that this bleak family narrative had coloured his early thoughts about herring.

Some of his contemporaries had become herring fishermen right at the outset. At the time he had thought they were being impetuous and rash. He simply could not understand why the Goodlad brothers had bought the *Lass o' Gowrie*. What if the herring fishery collapsed, as it had done in the 1840s? He and his wife, Barbara Ward, could not afford to take such a risk with a young family to look after. His small croft at Symbister was simply not big enough to keep them all fed. He needed to earn as much as he could from fishing. He stayed with the cod, but, as he compared his earnings with the herring crews, it became ever clearer that he had made the wrong decision. The crew pay-out from his last year at the cod was £18 for three long, hard, distant-water trips. Although the bonus for being skipper had taken his total to £27, most of the men who had gone to the herring had taken home between £34 and £40. Against this, he had to weigh the tidy sideline he had always made from selling smuggled brandy. But this was getting more and more risky, and some of those who had been recently caught had been sent to prison. After carefully assessing everything, he decided to try the herring.

His experience at the cod secured him a job skippering the *Teaser*, a second-hand boat recently bought from Scotland by two Lerwick merchants. He was lucky that some of his crew had fished for herring for a few years and, with their help, he soon adjusted to this new way of fishing. It was different to cod in every imaginable way. Short daily trips, no processing on board and the lack of living space on board the *Teaser*, compared with a large smack, were only some of the aspects of Robbie Christie's new life as a herring fisherman.

When at the cod, there was no end to the unremitting toil if there were fish to be caught. Encountering a cod shoal, the crew worked day and night fishing and processing. Rest only came once the cod had disappeared and then the crew settled into a routine of fishing watches. This work routine usually continued until the hold was full of salted cod and the smack began to sail back home. Fishing for herring was different: every night the nets were set and, after they were hauled back, the boats sailed ashore to land their catch. It was predictable. Fishing for cod was like hunting, Robbie thought, whereas fishing for herring was much more passive – a bit like trapping.

Despite these differences, Robbie began to prefer this new daily routine to the long distant-water trips – even though hauling a large shot of herring was back-breaking work, and there were some days where a big catch meant there was not a lot of sleep. Another big difference was the need to lower the main mast every night after the nets had been shot. If this was not done, then the roll of the boat, caused by a top-heavy mast, could badly tear the fragile hemp nets. Lowering the mast was relatively straightforward; it was raising it back up that was difficult. Requiring a complex arrangement of blocks and tackles and a strong crew, it was not easy, especially if it was bad weather and the crew were tired, having hauled a large shot of herring.

For his summer at the herring, he had made almost £40, the most he had ever earned in his life. And now he was going to East Anglia, where he might make the same again. He was already wondering about buying a few nets for next year and, if earnings held up, maybe even seeking to become a part-owner of the *Teaser*. The feasibility of buying his own herring boat, in partnership with other fishermen, had even crossed his mind. The possibilities seemed endless. He shook his head to dismiss these fanciful ideas. It all seemed a bit far-fetched, fishermen owning their own boats. In the world he had grown up in, the merchants and the lairds held all the power. But things were changing fast, and even the cautious Robbie Christie acknowledged that he was living through a time of enormous social change and economic opportunity.

Leaving the shelter of Lerwick harbour, the *Teaser* heeled over as the easterly wind filled her brown sails. Picking up speed, Robbie looked astern to see the impressive wake their greater momentum had created. With the Shetland Mainland on their starboard side, he set his course directly for Yarmouth, having already calculated that the passage should take about four days if the wind held. He would therefore have plenty of time to think everything through.

Something else that was niggling away at the back of his mind was his language. He sometimes found that the Scottish curers struggled to understand Shetlandic, especially when he used a lot of old Shetland words and expressions. The Shetlanders who had gone to East Anglia the year before had told him that the English could not understand anything they said. He was sure that he would work something out, however, and there was always sign language he thought, smiling to himself.

One thing he was looking forward to was the English autumn weather, having been told that it was as good as a Shetland summer, sometimes even better. For a man used to spending every autumn fishing off northeast Iceland, Yarmouth began to look very attractive. There would be few gales and no ice.

Robbie had weighed everything up carefully before he had decided to become a herring fisherman. He was now certain he had made the right decision, and the future looked good. It simply could not get better than this, he thought. But it did.

20

The Herring Capital of Europe

For a few years after the bumper catch of 1885, herring landings declined. But this was only a temporary setback and catches began to increase again. It was almost as if the pace of the expansion during the big bang had been so exhausting that the herring industry needed to draw its breath and rest before its next growth spurt, which was even more spectacular. By 1900 the record catch of 1885 had been exceeded. This continued and in 1905 a total of over 113,000 tons were landed in Shetland, more than double the 1885 figure. Over one million barrels were exported from Shetland that year, a statistic that propelled Shetland into the herring premier league. There were now more than 400 boats, employing over 3,000 fishermen. As the numbers of curing stations increased, it seemed that there was a pier and curing yard in every Shetland voe.

With its large natural harbour, a concentration of curing stations emerged in and around Lerwick, prompting a newspaper columnist, with a tabloid flair for exaggeration, to call it the herring capital of Europe. As one of Europe's largest natural harbours, it was an ideal location for the herring fishery. But even Lerwick was not big enough for the herring boom. At the height of the summer season, it became incredibly congested, and as hundreds of herring boats, sixerns and cargo vessels jostled for limited space, there were many mishaps. According to the local press, 'hardly a day passes without collisions and the carpenters are never without work'.

The nature of the industry also changed. The boats became larger, increasing in length to around 20 metres, able to work even more nets. The line of drift nets was now well over a mile long, nearer two miles for the largest boats with most nets. Bigger crews were needed, some boats having nine or ten men on board. The whole operation became much more efficient when boats began using a buss rope, named after the Dutch herring boats, the busses. For some reason, this name mutated over time into the bush rope. It was a heavy connecting rope that hung from the bottom of the nets, both sinking them to the required depth and making it much easier to haul them back on board. The early masters of the drift net, the Dutch, had first developed this technique.

The first signs of mechanisation appeared when steam powered capstans were installed. These simple winches made the hauling of the bush rope much easier. As it was hauled on board it needed to be coiled into a narrow locker, a space just big enough to hold the rope and the person doing the coiling. This job was given to the youngest crewmember, usually a school leaver, who was also expected to do all the cooking. Cook and coiler became the first job for boys wanting to be fishermen. If no herring were caught, the nets could be hauled back in a few hours. If there was a good catch, it could easily take six to eight hours. Add in bad weather and the hauling time could be more than 12 hours.

Most fishers are seasick when they go to sea at first, but it generally passes after a few weeks. Some young cooks got over this malady quite quickly. For others, it was a horrendous experience. Trapped in the rope locker, hauling and coiling the bush rope all night as the boat lifted and fell on every swell, energy levels became ever more reduced the sicker you were. In order to preserve the integrity of the bush rope it was heavily tarred prior to the beginning of each season. This made coiling a very messy job, with cooks often emerging from the rope locker covered in tar. Older men recalling their season as cook often speak of how isolated they felt, coiling a rope by themselves in this confined space, segregated from the rest of the crew on deck who hauled the nets as a team.

Having survived that ordeal, the cook then had to make breakfast. This was one of the main meals of the day, prepared immediately after the nets had been hauled. Everyone was ravenous. Fried herring was standard, three or more per man, fried to crisp perfection in oatmeal and washed down by gallons of tea. All of this being done in an unnaturally warm galley where the fat in the huge frying pan had to be spitting hot before the herring could be fried properly. Each cook found his own way of wedging himself in a corner to keep his balance with everything moving around, sometimes violently, as the boat rolled its way ashore. If the cook had somehow managed to cope with seasickness while in the rope locker, frying herring usually brought it back.

When the crew had eaten, they managed to snatch a few hours' sleep, but the cook had to wash and tidy up before he got to his bed. It was said that being cook and coiler was a man's job done by a boy. It was not easy for the deckhands, either. Hauling and shaking a fleet of nets full of herring was hard physical work, as was the stepping of the mast before they could sail ashore with their catch. The nets and buoys were hauled into the hold, where the herring were stored in bulk. Before the catch could be landed, the nets had to be hauled on deck to make room to discharge the herring from the hold. Winched out in wicker baskets at the curing stations, the catch was usually gutted within a few hours of being caught.

Two distinctive classes of sailboat dominated the herring fleet at this time – the Fifie and the Zulu. Wonderful and evocative names, they were very different boats. The Fifie, so-called presumably because of some connection with the fishing villages of

Fife, dates from the 1850s. With its vertical stem and stern, this beamy boat became the workhorse of the early herring days. Having two masts rigged with dipping lug sails, they were built to a standard design. The Zulu, on the other hand, was a more stylish and elegant boat. Like the Fifie, she had a vertical stem but had a beautiful raking stern, which created a huge overhang. The result was a vessel that could sail very fast, on account of its reduced keel length. The sail rig was the same as the Fifie: two masts, each carrying a dipping lug sail. The name of this unusual class of boat is both surprising and intriguing. The first Zulu was built in 1879, at a time when Britain was at war with the famous African Zulu warriors. According to the maritime historian Mike Smylie, there was some sympathy in Scotland for these brave Zulus who were taking on the might of British imperialism, and so this topical name was first used for this new boat design. The name stuck and has now become synonymous with this period of Scottish fishing history.

***

By the turn of the century, both the haaf and the cod fishery had dwindled away. Josie Peterson was skippering the *William Martin* on her last trips, having to get his crew from Faroe on account of all the Shetlanders having gone herring crazy. No longer looking north to Faroe and Iceland, Shetland was becoming fully integrated into the huge Scottish herring enterprise. The cod fishery would soon be a memory; nothing tangible would remain. All the smacks sold, no salt cod drying on the beaches, and the Shetland cure, for so long sought after by the Spanish market, no longer available.

One interesting legacy did continue, however. Each boat in the Scottish herring fleet was rigged with two large lug sails, very effective for sailing to and from the fishing grounds but cumbersome to tack, as the sails had to be fully lowered then shifted to the opposite side of the mast before being raised again. The

Shetland cod fleet had all been smack rigged: with a foresail and a main sail attached to a boom, it was much easier to tack as the sails did not need to be lowered and raised. Ideal for sailing in and out of narrow Shetland voes and Faroese fjords, this was the rig that the cod fishermen preferred. So, one of the first things the Shetlanders did when they bought a second-hand herring boat from Scotland was to replace the dipping lug sails with a smack rig.

At the end of the herring season in 1879, another Burra crew keen to invest in the herring boom bought the *Alpha* from Wick. She was rigged with two lug sails, and the new owners wanted to convert her to the smack rig as soon as possible. By early November, the conversion complete, they were ready to leave Lerwick and sail back to Burra. It was a favourable sailing wind, so there was great surprise when she never arrived. After it became clear that she had been lost, some fishermen pointed out that the new sheets and halyards were a tight fit in the wooden blocks. The speculation was that these ropes may have swollen as they got wet with sea spray on the passage. Eventually jamming, it would have been impossible to adjust the sails, possibly leading to her capsize. Six young men were lost, the oldest being the skipper, Robbie Inkster, who was 33.

Although the haaf also went into steep decline once the herring boom began, some sixerns fished for herring at the end of the haaf season. On 22 August 1891, the local press reported that one of these had arrived in Lerwick with a 'sensational shot', caught just outside the harbour. There was astonishment when 38 crans were eventually landed from this tiny open boat. It is difficult to imagine how a sixern, crewed by six men and carrying several herring nets, could carry so much herring: 38 crans being 152 baskets or five-and-a-half tons. There was fortunately no wind that morning as she was slowly rowed into the harbour, the normal understanding of freeboard long gone, with the sea inches from her gunwales. The skipper, Lowrie Isbister, had taken a chance with the fine morning and it had paid off. During these bonanza years, the seas around Shetland appeared to be full of herring. Anything that could float took a few drift nets aboard and went fishing. There are even reports of large shoals coming so close inshore it was possible to scoop herring out of the water with hand nets.

The herring boom allowed Shetland fishermen to earn wages that, a few years previously, would have been regarded as unbelievable. It also provided paid employment for that sector of society that had been entirely excluded from the haaf and cod fisheries – women. Long hours, cut fingers that were unable to heal properly because of constant exposure to salt, as well as pitifully poor wages; women seemed to fit the job specification, according to the thinking of the time. And yet, despite these hardships, working as a gutter provided an opportunity for many young women to escape the drudgery and claustrophobia of the family croft. Leaving home for a few months every year and staying in the gutters' huts offered a taste of independence. There was even the possibility of escaping Shetland altogether by travelling to East Anglia to work in the English autumn fishery. Being away from daily parental supervision and earning your own money was liberation for many. In some ways, it was the university experience of its day for those young women for whom further education was not possible. The opportunities afforded by gutting herring were nothing short of a social revolution in Shetland society.

Organised into crews of three, two women gutted while the third packed the herring into barrels, layer on layer separated by a sprinkle of salt. The gutters stood in front of long wooden troughs called farlins, which were full of herring. With one quick flash of the knife, the guts were removed, and the fish thrown into one of several tubs, depending on its length. This happened in seconds. The packer had to keep pace with the gutters, carefully placing the selected herring into separate barrels. Speed was essential; the arles (contracts) that they had all signed stipulated that no fish could be carried over till the next day – all herring had to be gutted and packed on the day they were landed, regardless of how long it took. Starting at six every morning, sometimes they would not finish until supper time.

The gutters had to find time to cook their own meals in the very basic huts that was their accommodation for the summer. When working at the East Anglian fishery, they stayed in bed and breakfast lodgings where the landlady prepared their dinner in the evening. This was almost always herring. Keen to save money, most took advantage of free herring from the curing yard; one of the few perks of being a gutter. Health professionals now recommend that everyone should eat two portions of oily fish every week to provide the required intake of omega-3 polyunsaturated fatty acids, essential for reducing the risk of heart disease and cancer and so important for mental agility. Having herring for dinner most evenings, these Shetland gutters were ahead of the curve in their healthy eating habits.

The barrels that held the salt herring needed to be well made. Being leak-proof was essential. They also had to be sufficiently robust to deal with the many knocks and bangs that were inevitable when making the long and tortuous journey from a Shetland curing yard to a *shtetl* in Poland. The barrels were made on-site during the winter months by skilled artisans called coopers. They crafted red wood staves, which had been imported from Sweden, into the classic herring barrel – wide in the middle and narrower at the top and the bottom. The wood staves were kept in place by metal hoops of exactly the right circumference. Each cooper could make about six barrels in a day. During the summer, they were kept busy filling the farlins with herring and supervising the gutting and packing operation.

As with salt cod, it was essential to ensure the best quality. Any bruised or damaged fish had to be discarded and exactly the right quantity of salt had to be used. The Scottish Fishery

Board monitored quality by opening and inspecting sample barrels. Provided everything was in order, all the barrels were then marked with the crown brand, assuring the buyers of the quality of the product. This Scottish crown brand became accepted throughout Europe as a trusted guarantee of quality.

***

The history of the Shetland herring fishery was closely bound up with world events. The First World War had a cataclysmic impact. In declaring war on Germany, Britain overnight lost one of its main export markets for salt herring. Unrest in Russia, followed by the revolution, devastated another huge market. There were hopes that the end of the conflict in 1918 might allow the pre-war boom to return. It did not; there was to be no roaring twenties for the herring industry. The German market never recovered, mainly because the Weimar Republic encouraged an expansion of the German fishing fleet to reduce reliance on imported herring. Neither was the Russian market restored; exporting to the Soviet Union was never as straightforward or profitable as the old trade with Tsarist Russia. Most problematic of all was the decline in the mass market for salt herring. As living standards began to edge upwards throughout Europe, salt herring was no longer the only affordable source of protein for most people. Alternatives were available and fewer salt herring were eaten, perhaps once a week instead of every second day.

The Second World War disrupted the herring trade further. One of the best-known Shetland curing companies was J&M Shearer. Established in 1919, it had strong roots in Whalsay, operating a curing station there as well as at Lerwick and other places. Known as Shearers, it mostly supplied the German market during the inter-war period, selling to Jewish trading families in Hamburg and Stettin. The Diamantstein and Finkelstein companies bought thousands of barrels of salt herring from them over two decades. The owners of these companies visited Shetland every summer and became good friends with the Shearer family. But exports to Germany halted following the outbreak of war and all communication with the German importers ceased. As Shearers tried to rebuild its export markets after the war, all attempts to reconnect with the Diamantstein and Finkelstein families failed. Following the Nazi Holocaust, no Jewish trading companies had survived.

The early herring boom had been based on what seemed like an insatiable appetite for salt herring in eastern Europe. By the 1950s, this mass market for salt herring had largely gone. In Shetland during the boom years, every island and every township had its fleet of herring boats and crews of gutters. As the industry began to decline, it was completely abandoned in some areas and began to concentrate in others. Eventually, the two islands of Burra and Whalsay came to dominate what was left of the Shetland drift net fishery.

The herring boom had not only brought prosperity to the islands, but it was also a social and cultural watershed. Enabling fishermen, for the first time, to own their own boats, it also provided the first paid work for women. The historical importance of the drift net era is undeniable, but is this at all relevant to modern Shetlanders? How should a community mark its own history?

21

What Is History?

In May 1900, a brand-new boat was launched from the Hays shipyard in Lerwick. She was called the *Swan* and had been built for two Lerwick fishermen, Thomas Isbister and William Watt. A classic Fifie of some 20 metres long, she was one of the largest boats in the fleet. Fitted with a steam capstan, she was also one of the most modern and efficient. Commenting on her launch, the local newspaper said that the *Swan* was 'acknowledged to be one of the finest boats afloat in the north of Scotland, as regards model, strength and workmanship'.

Hugely successful, the earnings from her first summer herring fishing around Shetland, followed by the autumn fishing off East Anglia, exceeded her build cost of £600. She continued to fish well for many years and, like many boats of her class, made good money. The building of such a boat in Lerwick showed how far the Shetland herring fishery had come. Only 20 years before, Shetlanders were buying second-hand boats from Scotland as they tried to catch up in the herring race. Now Shetlanders were building their own boats which, in the case of the *Swan*, were as fine as any being launched elsewhere. The launch of the *Swan* was symbolic of how Shetlanders had successfully embraced the herring boom and made it their own.

These years have been called Shetland's Golden Age, the history of which is well recorded. The local press is a fascinating resource of weekly articles, outlining how the summer herring season was progressing. Not only fascinating in terms of what was happening locally, but also how world events always seemed to impact the market for herring. Sometimes providing illuminating personal details of individuals, these press reports take the reader back to a very different time. Rather more detached, but equally valuable, is the extensive Scottish Fishery Board archive, which provides statistical detail about the fleet, landings, the curing operation and exports.

By this time photography was commonplace so there are hundreds, if not thousands, of black-and-white photographs of the herring boom, all evoking this era of sail, salt, barrels and herring. The photos of gutters sometimes show the crews at work, heads down, busy and focused. Their hands are usually blurred, the camera shutter speeds of the day unable to capture how quickly the herring were being gutted. Other photos are much more relaxed, with groups of gutters and coopers taking a break, laughing and joking. In the background there are always hundreds of wooden barrels. Empty ones lying on their sides, precariously stacked ten or more high, contrasting with the barrels full of salt herring, ready for export, stacked three high and looking more stable.

Most photos of the herring fleet show the boats lying at piers, the crew working with their nets or landing herring. Less common are those taken at sea, showing the nets being shot or hauled back. One of the most iconic of all these photos captures the fleet leaving Lerwick harbour for the fishing grounds. With hundreds of boats sailing very close to each other, it is impossible to see the horizon. This was a sight that would have been so commonplace every afternoon that most people probably never gave it a second glance. Like so much of history, it only became remarkable after it was no more.

Apart from these images that capture the fishermen and the gutters, the boats and the curing yards, there is now little physical evidence left of this great industry. A skeleton of rusted and bent iron posts, emerging out of the sea, is all that remains of most of the piers where boats landed their herring. The gutters' huts, the salt stores and the farlins have all gone. The once ubiquitous barrels are now rare collectors' items, sold in antique shops. At one time drift nets would have been stored for the winter in the lofts of most houses, having been mended and made ready to be used again the next summer. I recently saw a fragment of a drift net, maybe six corks and a few metres of cotton twine, for sale in a Cornish seaside town. I was shocked when I saw the price tag of £50. My shock turned to incredulity when someone, possibly searching for authenticity, bought it. Was this what history had become reduced to, I wondered, selling overpriced trinkets which neither the seller nor the buyer has the faintest understanding or appreciation of.

Of the fleet of hundreds of sailboats that once employed over 3,000 fishermen, there is nothing left. Occasionally someone might have kept a small reminder of a boat as an afterthought before she was sold or scrapped. Sometimes a nameboard or a steering wheel finds itself displayed in a museum. That this is all that is left of this once great industry always strikes me as profoundly sad. While photographs from this era provide a glimpse into what the herring boom was like, it is only a still image, capturing that millisecond of time. Their value depreciates over time. Sharing an old photo with someone who was there is fascinating. As they identify individuals and boats, tell a funny story and explain what happened later that day, you feel you are part of the photograph. Looking at the same photo without such insider knowledge is a sterile experience in comparison. All the many detailed questions, about who is who and what they are doing, go unanswered. As much as I love looking at old black-and-white photos, it is a bit like reading a menu but never actually eating anything. An interesting, informative but entirely unsatisfactory experience.

If history can only be accessed through dry archives, family stories (that sadly become less interesting to each generation), nostalgic keepsakes and faded photographs, it will eventually become irrelevant. Public understanding and wider community appreciation of local heritage will eventually peter out and disappear. A classic case of managed decline; we forget about something slowly and, within a couple of generations, it is gone. It need not be like this and should not be regarded as an inevitable process about which nothing can be done.

It has been said that the most robust and progressive societies are those that are most conscious of, and fully understand, their past. There is no more vigorous group of islanders than the Faroese and preserving the history of their cod fishing industry became a national priority for them. Public art, models of sloops in churches, an extensive archive and an excellent museum have all played their important part in this endeavour. It is, however, the restoration of two of their old cod sloops, the *Westward Ho* and the *Johanna*, that has done most to make their fishing heritage relevant to young people. These two sloops sail around the North Atlantic every summer, keeping alive the skills of operating large wooden sailing boats and providing a tangible link to their fishing past. Rebuilding and operating old fishing boats is expensive and is a luxury that only affluent modern societies can afford. By the time Shetland was able to consider doing something similar, there were no sailboats left.

That all changed in 1990 when the *Swan* was discovered lying in Hartlepool harbour. She was in poor shape, lying half-submerged and neglected next to the harbour wall. Having been sold from Shetland in 1960 to owners in England who had great restoration plans but no money, she was no longer seaworthy. The vision of capturing Shetland history – in the most real and tangible form possible – prompted a group of enthusiasts to form a trust that took the *Swan* back to Shetland, where she was successfully rebuilt.

Determined that the restored *Swan* would not simply be a floating museum, the trust members resolved to use her to show future generations of Shetlanders how to sail a smack-rigged boat. Painted in her original colours – a dark green hull with a large white cutwater at her bow – she is beautiful. The sight of her underway, the wind filling her brown sails, does more to celebrate Shetland's fishing heritage than anything a museum, archive or old photo can ever do. A volunteer crew have sailed the *Swan* around Shetland, and to many other parts of the North Atlantic, ever since. Watching her under full sail, it is not difficult to imagine what the waters around Shetland might have looked like more than a century ago with hundreds of sailboats coming and going around the isles.

The *Swan* has allowed many people to experience sailing and living on board an old drift net boat. The cramped space, the way she skips along under full sail, how she fares in bad weather, and the dinners cooked in the galley – it all brings history alive for many. Perhaps the greatest contribution that the *Swan* has made to contemporary Shetland culture is the opportunity provided for hundreds of schoolchildren to sail on her. From one-day outings for primary pupils, to lengthy trips across the North Sea for those at secondary school, the skills of sailing a fishing boat have been passed on to the next generation. Other skills are also learned. Many parents have commented that their teenager, who set sail on a *Swan* trip to Norway or Denmark, returned a different person. No longer leaving their room untidy, they seemed to have developed a habit for organisation and an abhorrence of clutter. Some of them had even astonished their parents by offering to help clear up after dinner.

Having enjoyed the *Swan* experience so much, many go on several trips throughout their school years. Others, when they are a bit older, return to become regular crewmembers on board. One of these returners is Maggie Adamson. Not yet thirty and already one of Shetland's finest fiddlers, she is the skipper of the

Swan. The first time we did a trip together, I immediately saw that she was completely at ease on board; it was obvious that she knew everything about the boat – its sails, the rigging and its history. Confident in explaining to the crew what needed to be done, in that engaging and encouraging way that comes naturally to young people, she ensured a textbook departure from the pier. Never stopping looking round, she checked that the sails were properly set as we made passage through a busy Lerwick harbour.

She wanted to start sailing when she was nine, she told me, but had to wait until she reached 11 before she was allowed to sail dinghies in Lerwick harbour. She has never stopped since then, having sailed competitively around Europe for several years. But it is the *Swan* she loves most, and what makes the *Swan* special for her is the no-frills sailing experience; all the crew must work together to handle the sails, keep the boat clean, tidy up the cabin, cook the meals and wash the dishes. There is little personal space, and everyone must compromise. After a few days the crew of individuals (many of whom probably did not know each other in advance) are working together as a team and looking out for each other. Maggie believes that most people become less selfish and more considerate when they are at sea. She reckons this begins to happen when the *Swan* is out of sight of the land and everyone's sleep pattern has been disrupted, as they try to adjust to the watch-keeping system that ignores the daylight-and-darkness routine of life ashore.

The *Swan* was sailing well as we headed north, up the east side of Shetland, bound for Faroe. I went below to make some coffee; in the main cabin some of the experienced crewmembers were getting their gear stowed in their bunks, entirely comfortable with the heel of the boat and her rolling motion. Others, first-timers, were looking a bit disconcerted and nervous, holding onto everything with both hands as they moved around. Reflecting on what Maggie had told me, I could see that, after a couple of days, there would no longer be experienced hands and first-timers. Instead, there would be a single crew sharing the common purpose of sailing the *Swan* to our destination.

Back on deck, as we shared a coffee together, I asked Maggie about her musical career. She first started playing the fiddle and piano when she was eight. Becoming ever more accomplished, she eventually studied both classical violin and traditional fiddle at the prestigious Royal Conservatoire of Scotland, in Glasgow. She is well known throughout the Scottish traditional music scene and has a growing international reputation. For the past nine years the Tbilisi Burns Club, in the Caucasian republic of Georgia, has flown her out to play at their annual Burns supper. The Singapore St Andrew's Society recently booked her to play at their St Andrew's dinner, and this is also likely to become an annual event. Between gigs, she teaches fiddle music but tries to limit this to the winter months so she can have the summer free for sailing.

When you are on a four-hour watch together, everyone takes the wheel for an hour. It was suddenly my turn to steer. As Maggie and I changed places, I asked how she compares sailing and fiddle music, her two great passions. Taking some time before replying, she says that sailing the *Swan* and doing a gig in front of a live audience are challenges that are surprisingly alike: playing a fiddle tune well and enabling a historic boat to sail to the best of her ability are both artistic expressions that can only be achieved through hard work, determination and endless practice. Getting the *Swan*, an old wooden boat of 74 tons, to zip along at nine knots under full sail is as invigorating and energising as playing a Shetland reel. It is also as beautiful. As we heel over further, picking up speed in the freshening wind, I understand exactly what Maggie means.

22

Valkyrie

Catching herring by hanging curtains of net was first done in medieval times by coastal communities in the south North Sea and the Baltic. It was an opportunist fishery; the nets being set whenever herring were seen swimming close inshore. It was not until the 16th century that the Dutch commercialised the operation, creating a huge industry based on selling salt herring. In due course other countries copied the Dutch and by the mid 20th century there was an enormous drift net fishery for herring throughout Europe. From Iceland in the north to the Netherlands in the south, thousands of fishermen went to sea every night setting their fleets of drift nets as the sun set, hoping the herring would rise.

There were some important changes over time. The nets became stronger as hemp was replaced by cotton, which was then replaced by nylon. The other big change was the demise of sail, made obsolete by steam engines and later by motor power. By the early 20th century, it was clear that the first steam drifters had a huge advantage over sail. In light winds, they were always the first to make it back to market, securing the best price. Sailboats, utterly dependent on the wind, were often so late ashore that the curers refused to buy their catch, deeming it too old. On nights with no wind, sailboats were confined to the harbour while steam drifters fished as normal. On the other hand, they were expensive to build and costly to run, consuming large quantities of coal. A cheaper alternative, which Shetlanders favoured, was to instal engines in their sailboats.

Despite these changes, however, the basic drift net method had altered little since the 16th century. Setting drift nets at the same time every night, trusting that herring would swim to the surface and become enmeshed, and then hauling back on board by muscle power now seems archaic and labour-intensive. It was indeed both, and the wonder is that drift netting, which is almost biblical in its origins, lasted for as long as it did.

When changes came, as they did by the middle of the last century, everything happened very quickly. Purse seining was first developed by the Norwegians. As the name implies this net resembles a huge purse, enveloping a herring shoal at depth. Sonar technology, which enabled the accurate location of herring shoals, was invented at around the same time. Mid-water trawling, developed by the Dutch and Germans, also emerged as another alternative to drift netting. The purse seine and mid-water trawl, together with sonar, proved to be a deadly combination. Using sonar to locate the shoal, then targeting it with a purse seine or trawl, meant that herring could, for the first time, be hunted. Drift netting, based on the chance that the herring would rise to the surface, suddenly seemed very inefficient. Within a few years it had become history.

In Shetland, drift netting disappeared as quickly as cod fishing had done, all those years before. Some Shetlanders were eager adopters of the purse seine method, and their early success laid the foundation for today's modern fleet. One of Shetland's first purse seine skippers was Josie Simpson. Together with his crew from Whalsay, he invested heavily in the new technology. It paid off and each of his boats, called *Azalea*, were successful. Although best known as someone who mastered this new technique, and who played a leading role in the Shetland Fishermen's Association over many years, he had also been a drift net fisherman.

Recalling those days, Josie told me that he made an uncertain start. Leaving school at 15, he was, by his own description, exceptionally slender and very young. Taken on as cook and coiler on board the *Ella*, a boat from Burra, he was very seasick. It is one of the worst feelings – beginning as sickness before developing into a debilitating fatigue. Eventually losing interest in all that is happening, all you want to do is lie down. So ill was young Josie that he was unable to haul the bush rope or cook anything when the *Ella* was at sea. Always hoping it would get better, he persevered, but it seemed to get worse. After a few weeks he was forced to give up.

Still determined to be a fisherman, Josie went back to fishing the following year. By this time, he was a year older, a bit stronger and more able. His resolve paid off and, eventually overcoming his seasickness, he began to enjoy the job. In due course, he became a shareholder of a drift netter called the *Fortuna*. Speaking with great fondness about his drift net days, he tells me what he loved most was the teamwork, the hauling and shaking of the nets by a crew working as one: 'When drift nets were hauled properly by a skilled crew it really was something to see.'

Someone else who remarked on the beauty of herring being hauled aboard by drift net was the poet Hugh MacDiarmid. In a poem called 'With The Herring Fishers', he wrote:

'I see herrin" – I hear the glad cry
. . .
O it's ane o' the bonniest sichts in the warld
To watch the herrin' come walking on board
In the wee sma' 'oors o' a simmer's mornin'
As if o' their ain accord.

MacDiarmid is regarded by many as one of Scotland's greatest poets, on a par with Robbie Burns. He was a leading figure in the Scottish literary renaissance during the 1920s. Writing in both Scots and English, his poetry has left a profound legacy on Scottish culture and politics. Although a political radical, he struggled with party politics, being a fierce contrarian all his life. Loving controversy, argument and debate, he was eventually expelled from the Communist Party for being a Scottish nationalist, and from the Scottish National Party for being a communist.

He had a troubled life, particularly when he was a young man. Having moved back to Scotland from London with his second wife, Valda Trevlyn, and their young son Michael, he had no work and was heavily in debt. As he was drinking far too much, some of friends feared for his mental health. Anxious to get him away from the lure of the Edinburgh pubs, they persuaded him to move to Shetland where David Orr, the doctor in Whalsay, had been able to find them a house. He arrived in in 1933 and was soon joined by Valda and Michael. Although the name of Hugh MacDiarmid is now well known both nationally and internationally, it was a pseudonym; a pen name he used for his writing. His real name was Christopher Grieve, and he was always called Chris by his friends and family. In Whalsay, he was known simply as Grieves.

The family was poor when they arrived in Shetland and had no way of making a living. The innate kindness of the Whalsay people made sure that they never went hungry. A constant supply of fish, potatoes, milk, butter and vegetables was provided, with no payment expected. This was not unusual – in fishing and crofting societies, the wider community always looked after those who were less fortunate. Long after they had left Whalsay, Valda still spoke with great affection about the unconditional generosity that they were shown.

Although taking part in all the island's social events, and not in any way reclusive, the family was different. Whalsay folk could not understand how Grieves was able to spend day after day writing poems. That was not work as they understood it.

His intense demeanour, his unruly mop of hair and his owl-like glasses all set him apart as an intellectual. He was not unlike Leon Trotsky in appearance, as well as politics. Their bohemian lifestyle scandalised the islanders. Valda's red painted toenails, their furniture made of driftwood and the garish colours they painted the interior of their small house would not be in the least remarkable today, but they were considered shocking in the 1930s. Fiercely patriotic, Grieves enjoyed wearing his kilt. This only added to his eccentricity in the eyes of the islanders. At this time in Shetland, someone wearing a kilt would have seemed as alien as someone dressed for a fox hunt – both utterly bizarre and having no cultural significance to Shetland.

It is not known what Grieves himself made of Whalsay. Missing the cultural and political milieu of the Edinburgh intelligentsia, he described his time in Shetland as his years of exile. He was probably frustrated that his fellow islanders were more interested in how much herring every boat had caught each night than they were in literature or politics. On the other hand, he and Valda strongly identified with the crofters and fishers of Whalsay; they were poor people who, in his view, had been failed by capitalism.

Living not far from them were Joanie Irvine, his wife Christina Anderson and their seven children. In an echo of the famous smack skipper Aald Heglie, Joanie was known for most of his life as Aald Glibie, on account of having lived for a time at the Glebe. He was a renowned storyteller, having that rare gift of holding an audience spellbound for a long time with an unremarkable storyline that would today be compressed into a 30-second soundbite. Although not a literary man, he was clearly someone who knew the value of words, the importance of a strong narrative and the power of a story well told. It is therefore not surprising to learn that he and Grieves soon struck up a friendship. The Irvine family sometimes looked after young Michael, and their door was always open to the Grieves family.

204 The Salt Roads

Enjoying Grieves' company, Aald Glibie took him around Whalsay in his small boat, pointing out places of interest, telling stories and recounting folklore. They spent some time together on Linga, a small uninhabited island to the west of Whalsay. It is said to be the inspiration for one of MacDiarmid's most famous poems, 'On a Raised Beach'.

Aald Glibie was a fisherman all his life and was skipper of the *Valkyrie*, one of the last sailboats still fishing from Whalsay. Immersed as Grieves was in Scottish history and culture, he would have known how important the herring industry was for much of Scotland. It may have been this awareness, or perhaps some curiosity as to what most of his fellow islanders did for a living every night, that prompted him to spend a night at sea with Aald Glibie and his crew. He would also have been looking for inspiration, as he always was, for his writing. There is no question that he would have known that the *Valkyrie* was one of only a few sailboats still left in a Scottish fleet that had once numbered upwards of 10,000. The poignancy of this would not have been lost on Grieves, and he would have known that his trip to sea with Aald Glibie was an opportunity to experience the last years of the sail era.

Spending a night at sea with a crew speaking to each other in Shetlandic, with its rich vocabulary of the sea, must also have been a wonderful literary experience for this poet. He was passionate about the Scots language and must have enjoyed listening to the rhythm and cadence of Shetlandic being spoken as they sailed to the fishing grounds that evening. He would have recognised many old Scots words, maybe some that had fallen from use in Scotland, but he would also have been aware of the rich seam of Norse words and idiom that were less familiar to him. He was apparently writing down new words and phrases in his notebook all evening.

After the nets had been shot and the mast lowered, leaving one man on watch, the crew grabbed their usual couple of hours' sleep before starting the long job of hauling the nets back. On this night it was Wilfred Gilbertson's turn to be watchman. Some Shetlanders who, like Wilfred, had been in the merchant navy often used the nautical English they had picked up to emphasise a point or make an important statement. When it was time to call the sleeping crew, he descended the ladder into the cabin, shouting: 'Scaramazoo, let's be having you on deck.' The first man out of his bunk was Grieves, his hair looking even more unruly than normal. Rubbing the sleep from his eyes, he put on his glasses and opened his notebook in a state of excitement. Possibly thinking he had discovered a new Shetlandic sea word, he asked Wilfred to repeat what he had said. Wilfred's rhetorical English flourish had confused Scotland's national bard.

Back up on deck, Grieves settled down to observe the crew hauling and shaking the nets, seeing the first herring coming on board. It inspired his memorable description of the 'herrin' come walking on board . . . as if o' their ain accord', and it was exactly this sight that Josie Simpson described when a crew of experienced drift net men, working as a super coordinated team, hauled back their nets full of herring. Hauling and shaking all night, it looked easy. It even looked, as Grieves wrote, as if the herring were coming aboard by themselves. It was, of course, anything but easy; it was one of those things that only hard work, endless practice and dedicated teamwork can make look effortless.

MacDiarmid's nine years of exile in Whalsay were productive insofar as his writing was concerned. Some believe that this was one of his most creative periods. Perhaps living amongst hard-working and generous people helped him overcome some of his demons. Grounded in the predictable routine of the herring fishing, this was a stable society that contrasted with his chaotic Edinburgh lifestyle. Living in a community that revolved around the daily and weekly rhythm of drift net fishing possibly provided him with the space that he needed to heal, think and write. The rhythm of the herring fishing not only helped MacDiarmid; it also inspired one of Scotland's greatest film-makers.

23

An Epic of Steam and Steel

The evening crowds were bustling outside the Tivoli Picture Theatre on the Strand as George Bernard Shaw, H.G. Wells and other socialists from the London Film Society made their way inside this impressive new cinema. Completed in 1923, it was built from white Portland stone and was a fitting venue for London's intelligentsia, who came there every week to view and discuss avant-garde films. It was November 1929, and the Film Society were in for a treat. Not only were they to watch the much-lauded film *Battleship Potemkin*, but the highly acclaimed Soviet director Sergei Eisenstein would be there himself to answer questions.

Sometimes described as the greatest film ever made, this silent black-and-white masterpiece was based on the actual events of 1905 when sailors on board the *Potemkin* mutinied. An act of political defiance within the Imperial Russian Navy, this became an important symbol of the 1905 revolution that is often described as the dress rehearsal for 1917. It was not only the revolutionary significance of this movie that attracted London's intellectuals, but the film itself was already being hailed as an incredible artistic achievement, with its ground-breaking use of montage. But this was lost on the British establishment. Britain was still reeling from the impact of the 1926 General Strike, and many regarded this film as nothing less than a piece of communist propaganda. Such was the fear that this powerful film might foment further political and industrial unrest in Britain that, following this private screening at the London Film Society, it was banned from public viewing until 1954.

It used to be the case in cinemas that there was a double bill, with the main feature being prefaced by a shorter film. Accompanying *Battleship Potemkin* that evening was a brand new 40-minute film called *Drifters*. Directed by an unknown Scotsman called John Grierson, this was described as a factual film about herring fishing. *Drifters* was a surprising choice to sit alongside Eisenstein's triumph, as it had none of the drama and allure of revolution and was, on the face of it, a potentially dull film. This short film, however, captivated the audience that evening. The following morning, the press reviews enthusiastically described this work as novel, unconventional and impressive. It was, one critic wrote, 'a most original piece of cinema art'. This so-called factual film was the first example of a brand-new type of cinema: documentary.

'An epic of steam and steel' was the caption that Grierson used to preface this film. It tells the story of how large, steam-powered, steel-hulled vessels fished for herring using drift nets. These boats were known as drifters for short, hence the title of the documentary.

By the time Hugh MacDiarmid had spent a night at the herring with the *Valkyrie*, there were hardly any sailboats left. The drift net industry had been transformed by the building of a fleet of steam drifters. Between 25 and 30 metres in length, they were not only much larger than the sailboats but also much more efficient – able to carry more nets, hold a larger catch of herring and operate independently of the prevailing wind conditions.

The first drifters were built in the late 19th century. Herring fishermen on board sailboats had been using steam-powered capstans to haul their bush ropes for many years, so they were comfortable with steam technology and were aware of its potential. Using a large steam engine to power a boat instead of sails was, nevertheless, a step change in technology and ambition. They were also very expensive. A steam drifter cost about four times more to build than a Fifie or Zulu and had a hefty weekly coal bill to meet every week. The greater efficiency of these drifters, however, more than justified the additional capital and operating costs, and many were built in the early years of the 20th century. On the eve of the First World War, the Scottish drifter fleet had grown to 900 vessels, out of a total of 2,500 drift net boats.

There was also a huge investment in drifters in England, mostly by fishing companies based in Lowestoft and Yarmouth. While some Shetland fishermen did invest in drifters, most did not, choosing instead to install engines on board their sailboats. For a community that had been in the vanguard of the expansion of the herring fishing, this is rather surprising. The capital cost may have been too prohibitive for many, and only 34 drifters joined the Shetland fleet. One of these was the *Maid of Thule*. She was built in 1917 for James Shearer, a skipper from Whalsay, who eventually became a founding partner in the herring curing firm of Shearers. Most of the drifters tried to fish for herring all year round, the main fisheries being the Shetland spring and summer season followed by the autumn season off East Anglia.

After the First World War, demand for salt herring from the traditional European markers began its inexorable decline with inevitable consequences for the herring industry. Within a decade the number of Scottish drifters had halved as the profitability of these large coal-hungry boats plunged. A few drifters resumed fishing after the Second World War, but the age of the drifters was past, and the last ones were scrapped in the 1950s.

In many ways, the drifter was the ultimate drift net boat, and they became synonymous with the herring industry at its zenith. It was this boat and this period that Grierson captured so perfectly in *Drifters*.

***

John Grierson grew up in the village of Deanston in Perthshire. Both his parents were teachers, and his mother, who had been a suffragette, was active in the Labour Party. The church played an important part in their lives and, having been imbued with that particularly Scottish combination of socialism and Calvinism, Grierson went on to study in the United States, where he became fascinated by the film industry and its potential to inform and educate.

On returning to Britain, he was employed by the Empire Marketing Board (EMB) to produce a series of films promoting exports, including one that would champion the herring industry. It was a futile task; demand for salt herring had begun a terminal decline that no amount of promotion could stop. But, had EMB not taken this initiative, the world of cinema would have been denied the marvel that is *Drifters*. Very soon after starting work on this commission, Grierson began to see *Drifters* as an artistic endeavour with its own intrinsic value. For him, it was to be more than simply a marketing tool, and this led to conflict over the content of the film: the EMB was insistent that unnecessarily artistic scenes should be removed; Grierson was adamant that there should be no changes. It was a conflict between a utilitarian perspective and an artist wanting to create the best that he could. Fortunately for the world of cinema, Grierson, thrawn Scotsman that he was, prevailed. *Drifters* was the first of many documentaries that he made during his long career in film, and he is now widely acknowledged as the father of the documentary. Writing about his craft many years later, he said that real people and real scenes were always far more powerful than actors and staged sets in telling a story. Some contend that *Drifters* remains the template for all good documentaries, even today.

Like *Battleship Potemkin*, *Drifters* is a silent black-and-white film. In these days of Hollywood blockbusters that assault the senses with colour and noise, it can be difficult to appreciate that these two films, devoid of colour and sound, can continue to be so influential. I have seen *Drifters* many times and never tire of watching it. The opening scene takes place in Hamnavoe, the Shetland fishing village whose natural beauty apparently captivated Grierson. The camera is at ground level and follows the legs of the fishermen leaving their homes and walking to the pier. This innovative filming technique was very different to what was happening in cinema at that time.

While direction and editing were Grierson's responsibility, this film could not have been made without the astounding skill of cinematographer Basil Emmott. With the crisp and clear quality of every shot in near perfect lighting, it is incredible to think it was filmed almost a century ago.

As the drifters get ready to go to sea, there are many close-up shots of the crew, seabirds and waves breaking on the shore. Once the drifters have left port, there are some spectacular shots looking down on two boats rolling around in a heavy sea. These scenes were filmed from a position on top of the wheelhouse of a neighbouring boat; not an easy job from a vessel being thrown about by the sea. Writing many years later, Grierson explained that he lashed the camera and the cameraman to the top of the wheelhouse during a gale and 'let the drifter buck its worst'.

The original musical soundtrack is central to this film. It is deeply atmospheric and is responsible for building up a sense of anticipation as the boat leaves the pier, reaches the fishing grounds and shoots its nets. The music even manages to mimic the mechanical pounding of the steam-driven pistons and the howling groans of the endless wind. A more typical soundtrack at this time would have been the tinkling of a piano accompanying the frolics of Charlie Chaplin or some other early Hollywood star. *Drifters* was utterly different; its soundtrack has stood the test of time.

The film was put together using different boats, various ports and a host of locations around Britain – from Shetland in the north to Lowestoft in the south. Grierson, like Eisenstein, was a pioneer in the use of montage. Carefully selecting and crafting together various shots, he created a beautiful and flowing story. Fishing industry critics point out that the nets are shot off Shetland, but the catch is landed in Lowestoft – something that would never have happened. Likewise, the scenes of the crew in the galley and the cabin do not reflect the motion of a boat at sea; everything is so still that these shots must have been filmed when the boat was safely moored at the pier. These are, however, details that only occur to people with intimate knowledge of the fishing industry. The montage sequence works insofar as telling the story is concerned – and that, ultimately, is all that matters. Grierson was also one of the first to use the technique of superimposing one frame on to another as the scene changes. The result is a smooth flow from one part of the story to another: *Drifters* has none of the jerkiness and sudden changes of scene typical of many of the silent movies of this time.

The *Maid of Thule* is the drifter mostly used throughout the film. Although she was still owned by James Shearer, of Whalsay, her skipper was now Gibbie Goodlad, from Burra. His crew, who worked the *Maid of Thule* for a few years before buying their own drifter, are central to the Grierson narrative. The many close-up shots of the crew tell their own story: the skipper, with his intensive demeanour, in the wheelhouse; the stoker continually shovelling coal into the boiler, only pausing to light a cigarette; and one of the older hands, Lowrie Pottinger, teaching the young cook how to make duff, a type of steam pudding popular at the time.

One of the most interesting scenes in the film is a shoal of herring rising and swimming into the curtain of drift nets. This must have been shot in a fish tank as there were no underwater cameras at this time. Although this now looks very staged to a contemporary audience, it was, for its time, remarkable. In only a few frames this scene was able to explain how a herring shoal rises and then becomes enmeshed in a drift net.

At this stage the soundtrack takes on a haunting, almost eerie, tone as the crew lie sleeping, waiting for the herring to rise. It is then time to start hauling and, one by one, tall men emerge out of tiny bunks. They go up on deck and put on their oilskins while Andy Halcrow, the young cook, climbs down into the rope locker to start coiling the bush rope. He was only 14 years old and wears his cap at a jaunty angle, possibly making his personal bid for a career in film rather than a life at the drift net. As the crew hauls and shakes, the quantity of herring coming on board increases as the wind freshens. As the soundtrack reaches its climax, an image is presented of man against the elements in the middle of the ocean.

After an eight-hour haul the last net comes aboard and the skipper estimates that they have caught 150 crans. Arriving in harbour, the herring are slowly discharged, basket by basket. The cast then changes. Instead of the crew of fishermen in oilskins hauling and shaking, there are now smartly dressed men buying the catch at the herring auction. The all-male cast suddenly disappears when the first gutters appear on screen. Scores of women, first watching the sale and then walking arm-in-arm along the cobbled quayside, make their way to the curing yards, where they gut and pack herring at breakneck speed.

Drifters is a film that can be enjoyed on two levels. It is, first and foremost, a piece of cinematic art made to inform, entertain and to be appreciated for its many unusual qualities. There is no need to know anything about herring fishing, or even to be interested, to feel the force, and enjoy the experience, of this well-made documentary. It can still impress a contemporary audience. In 2017, *Drifters* was again shown in cinemas, this time with the original soundtrack replaced by a live vocal score by sound artist Jason Singh. According to film critic Mark Kermode, this re-release was a huge success with these new sound effects complementing the original film, which remained as powerful as ever. On another level it is the best film ever made of a crew hauling and shaking a drift net. Grierson managed to capture forever on film what Josie Simpson described to me and what Hugh MacDiarmid wrote about in verse – the beauty of a skilled crew hauling and shaking a drift net full of herring.

The steam drifter era, so brilliantly chronicled by Grierson, was over by the 1950s, when diesel-powered boats took over. The drift net, however, continued to endure. It seemed that this method of catching herring would never change; drift nets had been shot and hauled by sailboats, by steam drifters and by diesel powered boats. Shetland still had an active drift net fleet until the early 1970s.

24

A Night at the Drift Net

I was lucky to have experienced the last years of the drift net era. My childhood was immersed in the routine of the herring fishing. The setting was the village of Hamnavoe, on the island of Burra. Located in a perfect natural harbour, it is defined by a single pier, around which most of the houses are clustered in a large semi-circle. When I was growing up, there were around a dozen drift net boats from the village, each with its own evocative name. *Replenish*, *Venture*, *Radiant Star* and *Golden Harvest* are some of the names that still trip off my tongue effortlessly.

I marvel at what I can remember. I can pretty much recall who the crew were on board each boat, what its registration number was, the colour of its wheelhouse and so on. I was not unusual; all the children knew as much as I did. When the fleet was tied up at the pier for the weekend, this was our playground: we'd scramble from boat to boat, fishing off the sterns with homemade lines. The life of the village revolved around the herring season. There was hardly anyone at school whose father was not a fisherman, and most of our mothers had been gutters when they were younger.

I recall pestering my mother to allow me to stay up late so I could hear the drift net skippers speaking on the radio as they searched for herring. Every house had a large wireless, the main purpose of which was to listen to the fishing news on a designated fishing boat channel known as the trawler band. The Home Service or the Light Programme (the forerunners of Radio 4 and Radio 2) were only tuned into when it was known that no one from the boats would be speaking.

Once the nets had been shot, some of the watchmen would sing hymns over the radio. I can recall fighting the sleep that was overpowering me, hearing these men taking turns to sing their favourite hymns. There was no music, just one man singing, making the moment even more special in my memory. Two popular choices were 'Will Your Anchor Hold' and 'The Old Rugged Cross', hymns that are still sung at fishermen's funerals today.

Harry Laurenson, of the *Replenish*, and Charlie Pottinger, of the *Radiant Star*, were both regular singers. Harry was my Sunday school teacher, while Charlie was our next-door neighbour. It always struck me as curious, even remarkable, that I could hear Shetland fishermen singing and speaking, as they pleased, on the airways that were usually the preserve of Home counties accents. The coastguard tried to stop the practice – it was cluttering up the trawler band, they argued – but no one paid any attention; the singing of hymns had become an intrinsic part of the drift net culture.

Around midnight, when the singing stopped, we knew the crews were getting ready to start hauling back their nets. It was then off to bed for me, fully aware that while I slept, hundreds of men were hauling back thousands of crans of herring. My first question at breakfast was how much herring my father's boat had got last night. A skipper spoke on the wireless at eight o'clock every morning with a tally of all the boats catches. Then came the comparisons with my classmates' fathers' boats. Some even kept daily diaries. This may sound obsessive, but this was a time before the internet, before TV even, and we lived in a small village where drift netting for herring dominated our economy and society, even our play.

The season ended when the herring spawned, usually towards the end of August. Herring that had spawned were known as spents and were unsuitable for curing. At first the catches would have a small proportion of spents. That by itself did not mean the boats had to stop fishing, but it was an early sign there was only a few weeks left. By the end of the season, as the owners each decided to stop fishing out of Lerwick, a steady trickle of boats made their way back to Hamnavoe.

At this time, fishermen never received a weekly wage. The boats would 'settle up' at the end of the season, when everyone got paid. With crews arriving back home with a season's wages, there was cause for celebration. Every boat had crates of lemonade for the children, and it was an occasion for a settling present from your dad. The drift nets were taken ashore and spread out on grass fields on the edge of the village, where all traces of salt water would be removed by the rain. When they were cleaned and dry, each owner would take his nets home, where they would be stored over the winter until next year's season.

Before then, each net had to be repaired. This was done by both men and women. Coming home from school, I can remember the dry, musty smell of the drift nets and recall my mum and dad mending as fast as they could. To my eyes, one was as quick as the other, the only discernible difference being the pocketknife that my father used to cut the twine while my mother used scissors attached to a piece of string that hung round her neck. Anxious to help, I was given the job of filling the mending needles, making sure they were always full of twine. Drift nets made from fine cotton or nylon were delicate and soft to handle – so unlike modern trawls which, made of tough synthetic materials, are stiff and hard to the touch. Passing the silk-like meshes through my fingers, I remember wondering how something so fragile could catch so much herring. Their flimsiness was, of course, what made them so effective; unable to see the netting, the herring became firmly enmeshed. Evenly spaced along the top of the net were the corks, some made of synthetic materials, but others really were made of cork. These were uneven to touch, having a beauty of their own, and they'd grow darker with age – some of the oldest ones were black. I recently asked someone who was at school with me if her recollection of net mending was the same as mine. It was, she said. She had loved filling the needles as much as I had, never tiring of watching her parents skilfully repair the complex geometric patterns of a badly torn net.

***

A few years ago, I was in Bermeo, a Basque fishing village that is home to a fleet of sardine purse seiners. It was an exceptionally calm and balmy autumn day as I stood on the pier waiting to meet the manager of the fishers' cooperative. In the distance, I noticed a couple of boats making way through a sea that was so smooth it looked as if it was covered by a sheen of oil. The noise of these boats' diesel engines provided a dull background noise to the vivacious chatter of a team of women sitting on chairs at the edge of the pier mending a large purse seine net. All ages, probably about a dozen or so, they were clearly loving working outside on such a warm day. Despite the cacophony of noise, they never stopped mending: pushing the needles into the net, then pulling back and making a knot before cutting the twine. It all happened at a mesmerising speed.

The tireless energy of the Basques has always impressed me; an observation that was reinforced as I saw how quickly they were repairing the large black net. All the women had brown hair and dark eyes, but their skin colour seemed lighter than the olive complexion that is common in much of Iberia. Some were slim and lithe, others were stockier, but none were tall. The Basques are an attractive and distinctive-looking people, and they are always delighted to be told this, loving to point out that it is not only their language that makes them different from the

Spaniards. Some argue that the Basque language is so different from Spanish that it may have created a cultural barrier around the Basque community. Indeed, recent genetic research suggests that the Basques have barely mixed with other cultures for more than 2,500 years. The Basques are happy with that notion; classic exceptionalists, they define their culture by how different they are.

I was proudly told by the cooperative manager that the Basque country was the only place in the world where women mended nets. With their net-mending expertise, the Basque women were unique, she explained. As much as I like the Basques, they have this slightly annoying belief that they are the centre of the world. Nothing interesting happens anywhere else, especially when it comes to fishing. I was able to tell her that the women of Hamnavoe had been as skilled at mending nets as the women of Bermeo. Smiling to herself, she translated what I had said. The net-mending team immediately erupted into raucous laughter as they raised their heads to look at me. Despite their kindly eyes and warm smiles, I could see they did not believe a word I had said.

***

For as long as I can remember, I had wanted to spend a night at the herring with my father. He always said I was far too young, and I suppose he had a point when I was eight or nine years old. He eventually relented when I was ten.

I recall sitting around the mess room table with the crew having something to eat before we left the pier. It was hot, the men were huge, and I wondered how it had been possible to fit a crew of nine into such a confined space. Everyone's elbows were touching, and I remember thinking that the forks and knives looked tiny in their large hands. Behind our backs were the sleeping bunks built into the hull of the *Golden Harvest*. The cabin filled with hazy blue smoke as some of the crew rolled then smoked their cigarettes. Once the cook had cleared the table, and after we had left the pier, the crew began to disappear into their bunks for a few hours' sleep before we reached the fishing grounds.

It was a fine summer night with a little wind but, as we reached the open sea, the gentle rolling motion first made me feel uneasy then seasick and eventually very tired. My father persuaded me to go to bed and, as I crawled into his bunk, I convinced myself that I would feel much better after a rest. I must have fallen sound asleep as the next thing I heard was the crew speaking to each other as they climbed out of their bunks. Rubbing their eyes, they pulled on thick jumpers and prepared to go up on deck. I was told to stand and watch from the wheelhouse, where I would be out of the way.

The fleet of nets was shot over the side in what seemed to be no time at all; the bush rope flying out of the rope locker, the nets disappearing over the gunwale and the floatation buoys being tied on with relaxed speed and dexterity. It was soon all over. The last thing the crew did was to raise the mizzen, a small sail on the stern mast that kept the boat head to wind, ensuring she did not drift into the fleet of nets. As the engine was switched off, there was total silence and I remember thinking that we were at sea under sail: without the diesel engine turning over, this was what it would have been like to have fished for herring on a sailboat. Our nets were now set and now all we could do was wait and see if the herring rose.

The sun had set as everyone, apart from the watchman, went back to their bunks for a couple of hours' sleep before hauling began. Lying in the watchman's bunk, I listened to the creaks and groans of the boat timbers as the *Golden Harvest* slowly rolled from side to side. This is what wooden boats do at sea, a noise that is only heard when the engine is shut down. Initially alarming, it became strangely soporific, and I realised the crew were all quickly falling asleep. In no time I was fast asleep as well.

Just after midnight the crew assembled on deck again, this time dressed in their oilskins. Back up in the wheelhouse, it was now dark, there was a little more wind and the boat seemed to be rolling more than it had been when the nets were shot. The cook climbed down into the rope locker and, after the crew took their positions, the engine was started, and hauling began. A few herring, glinting bright silver, came aboard. Apart from the hum of the engine driving the winch, it was still remarkably quiet. I could hear the men's voices as they established their steady rhythm of hauling and shaking. Most of the herring fell to the deck, but every now and then a few would fly through the air, some falling into the sea and others hitting the wheelhouse window with a watery slap.

It was clear that some herring were falling out of the net as it was being hauled aboard, such was the feeding frenzy of seabirds. It was the first time I had ever seen gannets diving into the sea at breakneck speed, totally streamlined with their black-tipped wings tucked behind their bodies. Hardly a splash as they plunged below the surface only to remerge after a few seconds with herring in their beaks.

I crept out of the wheelhouse, which smelt of stale tea and fags, and walked forward, to be nearer to the action. Everywhere was wet with salt water being sprayed as the nets were shaken. As I tasted salt on my lips, I noticed that there seemed to be more herring coming on board. Although I was fascinated by what I was seeing, the seasickness returned and, despite the best determination of a ten-year-old, I ended up back in my father's bunk with a promise that he would wake me after a few hours.

When I came back up on deck, the sun was shining out of a blue sky, making the crew's yellow oilskins seem impossibly bright. The wind had completely gone and it was now a beautiful summer morning. Apart from this, everything was the same as it had been before I went to bed. The winch was still taking the strain of the bush rope, which the cook continued to coil in the rope locker. The crew were in their same positions, still hauling and shaking. One of the crew was now in the hold, filling aluminium tins with herring, six to a cran, the aluminium tin having replaced the old wicker basket as the unit of measurement. In the bright sunshine the herring were glinting a colour that was a mixture of blue and silver. As they tumbled to the deck, I could understand why they were called silver darlings.

Making my way forward, the salt spray seemed to be more bearable now, perhaps because it was no longer dark. The crew were laughing and joking, their voices easy to hear in the still morning. I counted three buoys up ahead, meaning there were only three more nets left to haul. In the far distance I saw six other boats hauling up the last of their nets. It was then that I noticed that the sea all around had taken on an unusual, milky green sheen. I was told that this colour was created by the millions of microscopic plankton which had risen to the surface during the night. These are the tiny creatures that the herring eat. Without these plankton enticing the herring to the surface, there would never have been a drift net fishery.

This green sea, the cloudless blue sky and the crew in their yellow oilskins hauling black nets full of silver herring provided a canvas of colour and activity all round me. I remember thinking that this must be one of the finest sights in the world and that it had been going on for hundreds of years. Perhaps I was already aware that I was experiencing the final years of four centuries of drift netting.

When the last net was on board, the cook went into the galley to make breakfast as the rest of the crew cleaned down the deck, hosing away herring scales that had covered everything like snow. I was told that we had caught 37 crans, a total that I would normally have been disappointed in when I heard my classmates bragging that their dads' boat had caught 60 or 70 crans, or maybe more than 100. It could have been worse, my dad reassured me, telling me that, on some nights, boats hardly saw a herring.

Drift netting for herring has been described as a feast or a famine – often catching a lot or not very much. While this is not literally true, as our modest catch that night illustrated, any fishery based on catching a shoaling species was bound to be variable, depending on whether the herring shoal rose to the surface near to where the drift nets had been shot. Occasionally there were so few herring that fishermen would talk about hauling black lint, an expression that spoke of the boredom of black herring nets without any silver darlings to relieve the monotony. In dramatic contrast, herring sometimes filled the nets in huge quantities, often so dense that it was all silver and no black. The first sign of such a catch was the buoys being pulled down by the weight of herring in the net. When the buoys were down so far that they were just visible above the surface, they looked like large dinner plates. Whenever that happened, a long hard haul and a good catch was a certainty.

But certainty could suddenly tip over to disaster if the buoys sank with the weight of herring. John David Henry, from Burra, was 27 years old when he took over as skipper of the *Press On*. It was a normal May night, not much darkness and a good sign of feed in the water when they shot. There were very few herring when they started to haul but, after a few nets, this began to change. Before too long they were hauling a good shot and eventually it seemed that there was a herring in every mesh. It was then that John David looked over the bow and saw the line of dinner plates ahead suddenly disappear. The nets, heavy with herring, plunged to the seabed like a stone, breaking the bush rope. He had never seen nets being lost before, and it was something he would never experience again. It was not, however, unknown. So much so that the crews always tied their drift nets together in rotation, one owner after another, ensuring that no individual lost his entire investment if some of the nets did sink.

As the crew began to take off their oilskins and make their way into the galley, I realised I was hungry, and I wondered if I was getting my sea legs. Back down in the crowded mess room, we all ate a huge breakfast of fried herring, a memorable taste that remains with me even yet.

When I was growing up, I was told, as many of my generation were, that we should work hard at school or else we would end up as a cook at the herring. That exhortation never worked for me. In fact, the prospect of being a cook at the drift net attracted me. I always wanted to be a fisherman, but by the time I was at university and able to get a berth for the summer, the drift net era had finished. I still went fishing and enjoyed many summers working on board white fish boats. Although I regret that I had not been able to spend a season at the herring, I still cherish that first experience of the drift net. I continued to go for a trip to the herring every summer holiday until my father's boat was sold, but the memories of these years are not as vivid as those of my first night at the drift net.

As we landed our catch later that morning, I didn't think that I had experienced anything remarkable. In my small, childish world, I thought most fathers made their living hauling and shaking drift nets. Looking back now, I feel privileged to have seen the last days of the drift net – this ancient method of catching herring that had once been the mainstay of the European fishing industry and whose catch had helped feed much of eastern Europe for hundreds of years. I now appreciate that I had managed to catch the coat-tails of history.

Postscript – What Now for Fishing?

The haaf, the cod smacks and the drift net are now all history. But these great fisheries, which moulded the economy and society of Shetland for hundreds of years, have not entirely disappeared. Much of Shetland's oral history and folklore is still bound up with stories of the sea and all those who worked the fishing industry. The Shetland community now owns and operates the *Vaila Mae* and the *Swan*, two of the most tangible reminders of the islands' fishing heritage. The main legacy of this heritage, however, is the contemporary seafood industry. There are few fishers and fish farmers in Shetland today whose ancestors were not fishermen, beach boys, coopers or gutters.

Although the modern Shetland fishing fleet is smaller than before, employing less fishers, it is now unbelievably efficient and technologically advanced. In that respect it resembles other fishing fleets in the developed world. These modern fleets are now capable of overfishing every fish population in the ocean, such is the devastating efficiency of modern fishing techniques.

With hindsight, it now seems inevitable that fish stocks would be threatened by overfishing, but it nevertheless came as a shock when it happened. Amongst the stocks first overfished to the point of extinction were the two iconic fisheries that had given rise to the huge salt fish trades – North Sea herring and Grand Banks cod.

As the drift net fishery was replaced by much more efficient purse seining and trawling, herring catches at first mushroomed then collapsed. Something that had never happened before then took place – fishing for herring in the North Sea was banned in 1977; a prohibition that would last six years. This fishery, which had first been developed by the Dutch in the 16th century, had been brought to its knees by unregulated catching power.

Even more spectacular was the collapse of the Grand Banks cod fishery in 1992. Like North Sea herring, it had been one of the most productive fisheries in the world. This was where the Basques had first perfected their catching and curing techniques. That these ancient fisheries, previously regarded as inexhaustible, had been decimated, astounded fishing communities and wider society. Even the cod stock on the Faroe Bank, the staple of the Shetland cod fishery, had been so overfished that it was closed in 2008. It was clear that things had to change.

By the turn of the 21st century there was huge public pressure for fisheries to be properly managed. Many environmental NGOs can date their interest in fishing to this period. Fisheries conservation became a political issue, particularly in communities like Newfoundland and Iceland, where fishing was crucial to the local economy. Conservation of fish stocks and sustainable management of fisheries became the new orthodoxy, although different interest groups had quite different understandings of what conservation and sustainable management meant. Fortunately, the MSC was established at this time and was able to bring both scientific rigour and objectivity to the debate. For the first time, it was possible to measure how sustainable a fishery was and whether it was sustainable enough to be certified as such.

There has been remarkable progress in Europe. In 2000, only a handful of fisheries had been certified as sustainable. Today, there are more than 160, with many more in the MSC pipeline. Such dramatic progress has been the result of many factors, not least two decades of constructive dialogue and collaboration between the fishing industry and NGOs. But, just when many fisheries are being managed sustainably, and when the MSC programme is gaining real traction, the fishing industry finds itself the target of an increasingly aggressive campaign by some large NGOs and vociferous individuals. Active on many fronts, their objective is to create huge marine parks where all fishing is prohibited.

In marked contrast to the collaborative approach of only a few years ago, the fishing industry is confused and at a loss as to how to respond to this. Trying to understand what had happened, I spoke to Barrie Deas, the chief executive of the National Federation of Fishermen's Organisations (NFFO). A polite and mild-mannered Scotsman, he has represented fishers for most of his working life. Incredibly knowledgeable, passionate about conserving fish stocks and maintaining viable fishing communities, he is a natural consensus-seeker. His long experience of the reality of managing complex fisheries at both EU and UK levels has taught him that there are no silver bullets. Compromise and goodwill, in his view, are both essential ingredients before meaningful progress can be made.

But he is frustrated and angry at the confrontational approach now taken by some NGOs. His reply when I asked why some had changed direction so dramatically was short and to the point: 'It's all about the money. Billionaires with money to burn, and presumably with guilty consciences, are seeking to solve complex fisheries problems by directing large sums into promoting simple and easily understood solutions such as closed areas.' Fisheries management is complex, and improvements can be slow. This is annoying for rich people who want things to happen quickly. Stopping fishing, in contrast, is easily understood and immediate. It is therefore an attractive solution for impatient people who want uncomplicated answers.

Following the money trail leads to organisations such as the Pew Charitable Trusts in the United States. Founded in 1948 by the deeply conservative Pew family, which made billions from the Sun Oil company, it spends around $400 million every year on various campaigns. Around the turn of the century, Pew turned its attention to the oceans and came up with the disarmingly simple proposition that fish stocks can be best protected if large sea areas are closed. This idea gathered momentum, and professional campaigning groups such as Oceana and Blue Marine are now very active, while journalists like George Monbiot of *The Guardian* peddle a similar narrative. Marine Protected Areas, No Fish Zones and Marine Parks are some of the euphemisms used to describe their vision of stopping fishing.

There are few within the seafood industry who would object to fishing being banned where there are fragile and rare habitats that are endangered by fishing activity. Kelp beds are a good example; these are hugely important in the sequestration of carbon dioxide and are probably as vital as the Amazon rainforest to our global ecosystem. There are also good arguments for separating fishing methods that are incompatible with each other, such as trawling and creeling. Around Europe there are also many fish nursery areas, containing large concentrations of juvenile fish, that are already closed to fishing. Closed areas can, therefore, be an essential component of a well-managed fishery. But to seek fishing prohibitions in huge sea areas as a fisheries management tool, which is now the vision of some NGOs, is neither logical nor practical.

It is not logical because a fishery does not require sea area closures to be managed properly. To be managed sustainably, fishers must only catch what a stock can safely yield. This can be regulated by catch limits, usually on a per-vessel basis. Nets need to be designed with large mesh sizes so that catches of juvenile fish are avoided and by-catches of unwanted species eliminated. This is now largely possible through better gear design and other innovative techniques. All these measures must then be rigorously enforced. This is not some idealistic dream; it is perfectly possible to achieve and is now happening. It may take some time, but the huge increase of MSC-certified fisheries over the past two decades has shown what is possible. This is a major achievement and provides a template for further progress.

The belief that banning fishing from a large area will somehow make the management of fisheries more sustainable is quite irrational. Neither is it practical, since one of the unintended consequences of closed areas will be the displacement of fishing effort to other areas. Behind the attractive veneer of simplicity is an astonishing level of naivety.

Insofar as Scotland is concerned, perhaps there are also hidden motivations. I recently spoke to a young fisher on the west coast of Scotland. In her twenties, she is part of the new generation that is passionate about fisheries conservation. As far as she is concerned, there is no alternative to fishing sustainably and looking after the environment. She is equally passionate about the west coast community she was born into. Worried about the loss of young people and believing that fishing and fish farming offer the best employment prospects for the area, she decided not to go to university but to become a creel fisher instead. Some of her friends took a similar decision, getting jobs on the local fish farm. It is this group of young folks, she explains, who will hopefully be able to bring up a family and keep their remote west Highland community alive. Proud of her industry, she can see a bright future for sustainable seafood but is increasingly exasperated by rich metropolitan men wanting to ban fishing and fish farming in the sea lochs. They claim that their proposed closed areas are needed to preserve marine ecology, but she wonders if the real reason is exclusivity. They want an unimpeded view when they make their occasional visits north. The less activity on the water the better; in fact, the fewer people around the better. They want a wilderness escape from the city, and an active community of fishers and fish farmers spoils that.

The growing concern that the Highlands are becoming a playground for the rich and entitled is often articulated in *The Daily Gael*, a satirical blog written by two activists in the west Highlands. This strikes a chord with the fishers and fish farmers in the area, many of whom are direct descendants of crofters who were cleared from their land by the rich and entitled of the 19th century.

The Daily Gael perspective on Highland affairs is very much in the tradition of playwright John McGrath, who wrote his ground-breaking work *The Cheviot, the Stag and the Black, Black Oil* in the 1970s. This production, and its eventual screening on the BBC, first brought to the attention of a wider audience how successive waves of rich people have exploited the Highlands. A musical satirical romp through Scottish history, it deals in turn with the lairds clearing the land to make way for Cheviot sheep before turning their estates over to stag-hunting parties. The American oil barons then arrived on the scene as Scotland embraced the oil industry. Recently touring Scotland again, playing to packed audiences most of whom had not even been born when it was first written, the production has clearly lost none of its relevance. The lairds have never been on the side of the crofters and fishers, and it now seems as if Scotland is regressing back to these old days. Under the guise of environmentalism, the new green lairds are dictating how local people should live. The inevitable result of their environmental fantasy will be lost jobs and broken communities. Perhaps they do not understand this, or maybe they do not care? Had he still been alive, John McGrath would have despaired.

'Having worked so collaboratively with the NGO community, we now feel like outcasts,' said a weary Barrie Deas, of the NFFO. Such is the power and wealth of the NGO funders that many fishers now feel beleaguered and ignored. It is almost as if the fishing industry is seen an inconvenient nuisance standing in the way of a marine paradise. Fishing voices at meetings to discuss closed areas are often jarring, disrupting the dollar-fuelled consensus on closed areas that has recently emerged.

This growing divergence between the NGO community and the fishing industry was brought home to me at an event I recently attended to discuss the future of the oceans. It was organised by the Ditchley Foundation, a prestigious institution, established to foster understanding and cooperation between the USA and the UK. Bringing together decision-makers and experts from diverse areas of public policy, it aims to find consensus on complex issues through dialogue and discussion. Their model is therefore more than simply having a meeting. Instead, the guests stay together for three days, usually over the weekend, in the extraordinary setting of Ditchley Park.

Near Oxford, Ditchley is a large and beautiful country mansion set in its own impressive estate of 350 acres. Built in 1722 by the Earl of Lichfield, it has hosted aristocrats and royalty over the centuries. It was even Winston Churchill's secret weekend retreat during the Second World War when his official country residence, Chequers, was believed to be too exposed to the risk a German air attack. Central to the Ditchley model is that everyone lives and socialises together throughout the three days. It is a concept that works incredibly well, with plenty of opportunities to network outside the formal discussion sessions. The relaxed nature of the event, together with the expertise of those invited, ensures that there is a high standard of discussion and debate. I really enjoyed the experience and met some incredibly interesting people, both from America and from the UK.

The invited experts, who numbered more than 40, consisted of government advisors, members of think tanks, academics and representatives of various NGOs. There were some very well-known and wealthy individuals present, some of whom had set up their own foundations. All guests were highly competent in their fields, and I was pleased to see as many women as men sitting around the table. I had presumably been asked because I had been doing some work on fisheries sustainability for a conservation charity. But there were no fishers, no skippers and no one from any of the industry associations, either from America or the UK. We were about to start an important session on fisheries management and there was not a single person in the room who made their living from the sea.

When I asked why this was the case, there was initially surprise at my question and then some muted embarrassment. The fishing industry had not been deliberately excluded; it had simply been forgotten about. It was as if the people who catch the fish – and have most to lose if stocks are not fished responsibly – were not visible. This was a metaphor which stayed with me for the rest of the event. It was such a wasted opportunity. The discussion on fisheries was not what it might have been with a key stakeholder – the main stakeholder, many would argue – not present. To discuss the future of fisheries without fishers is as shocking as convening a meeting of white people to discuss racism.

***

The existentialist issue of our age is, of course, climate change. Tony Juniper is a conservationist, environmental activist and author. Recently appointed as chair of Nature England, he first became aware of climate change in the 1980s and is in no doubt that our warming planet is now the most important issue of our time. By nature an optimist, Tony is not, however, confident that we are doing enough. He represented Friends of the Earth at the Rio Summit in 1992, which was the first occasion that most governments publicly acknowledged that climate change was a problem. Looking weary rather than angry, he tells me that we have not addressed the problem – pointing out that we have allowed it to get worse. Thirty years on from Rio, we are emitting 60 per cent more greenhouse gases, a figure that astonishes and alarms me in equal measure. Tony is usually a cheerful man, a smile never far away as he invariably lightens the mood in a room, but he is uncharacteristically despondent when he says that, unless we dramatically reduce these emissions, our planet will continue to get warmer with catastrophic and possibly irreversible consequences.

The spontaneous wildfires in Siberia were my epiphany. They never went out. Something was just not right and, perhaps for the first time, I fully accepted that burning fossil fuels, without any thought of the consequences, cannot continue. The evidence is stark: the ice cap is melting, glaciers are shrinking and unpredictable weather is becoming normal. This has been happening gradually, but many argue there will soon be a tipping point, after which things will deteriorate very rapidly. These tipping points are hard to model and even more difficult to predict, but there is no doubt that the consequences of passing a tipping point will be catastrophic. The Greenland ice sheet might melt, causing sea levels around the globe to rise by seven metres, devastating many coastal cities and submerging much valuable agricultural land. The warm Gulf stream could stop, changing our temperate European weather into a semi-Arctic climate, like that of Labrador.

The amount of greenhouse gases we emit every year is staggering. These gases are measured in tons of carbon dioxide equivalents, and I always struggle to get my mind round how much gas it must take to weigh a ton. When I learned that 50 billion tons of greenhouse gases are released into the atmosphere every year, I thought it had to be a mistake. Fifty billion tons is a jaw-dropping statistic. It is, unfortunately, not an error; it is a depressingly accurate fact. We are all culpable – in heating our homes, driving our cars, in what we consume and even in what we eat. This is called our carbon footprint. At one time it was believed that only governments could tackle big issues like climate change. Many now argue that we must all take responsibility for our personal carbon footprint.

But before it is possible for individuals to decide what they can do, it is important to understand what activities generate the most greenhouse gases. The generation of electricity and heat from fossil fuels is large, estimated to be around 25 per cent of all greenhouse gases. Industrial emissions are also high, at around 24 per cent. Transport stands at something like 16 per cent, with air travel accounting for much of this. To deal with these three large sources of greenhouse gases, we must first reduce, then sever, our dependence on oil, gas and coal and find alternative sources of energy that do not release carbon dioxide. Producing electricity from solar, wind and tidal power are part of the solution, as is hydrogen and nuclear power. All of this is understood and accepted by most people, although many will argue that not enough is being done and the pace of change is far too slow.

Less well understood is the complexity of the carbon footprint of different food production systems. Difficult to calculate, the greenhouse gases associated with producing food range from 25 to 30 per cent of all emissions. I was initially surprised to learn that producing food, which has always been part of our human existence, is responsible for such a large release of greenhouse gases. But food does not grow by itself. Crops need fertiliser, animals need feeding and food is exported around the world – all have a carbon footprint. In contrast to other forms of personal consumption, eating is an essential daily activity we cannot do without; you might buy a jacket every three years, but you eat food three times a day.

Some kinds of food have a much higher carbon footprint than others. The first time I became aware of this was when I attended the annual Seafood Summit a few years ago. Bringing together representatives from the seafood industry and conservation community, this event discusses how the industry can be made more sustainable. It is always well attended with several hundred delegates, mostly from NGOs. The keynote speaker in that particular year was Professor Ray Hilborn, of the Aquatic and Fishery Sciences department at the University of Washington. He began his address by telling the audience that a university colleague was becoming really concerned about global warming. Explaining that he wanted to do his bit to reduce his personal carbon footprint, he was wondering which of the animal proteins produced least greenhouse gases. Hilborn was unable to answer this question, but it prompted him to undertake some of the most important research of his career. Scouring the scientific literature, he calculated how much greenhouse gas was released into the atmosphere when different kinds of protein were produced. His conclusion was as startling as it was concise: 'If you want to do your bit to save the planet then eat fish. Its carbon footprint is far lower than beef, lamb, pork or chicken.'

As he spoke, there was silence. For most of the NGO representatives in the audience, the fishing industry was the problem. According to Hilborn, it was part of the solution. The mood in the room then changed from shocked silence to open hostility. Some of the questions from the floor reflected an unwillingness to even consider what Hilborn had proposed. He was telling people what they did not want to hear, always a difficult task. As I reflected on the response to his interesting and challenging research, I was reminded of an ancient Navajo proverb that says you cannot waken somebody who is pretending to be asleep. Responding with good humour to some of the negative questioning, Hilborn reiterated that sustainably managed fisheries and fish farms can do what no other protein producer can do: provide high-quality food with a minimum carbon footprint. He stressed that he was not making any comment about the state of global fisheries, many of which remain poorly managed and overfished. He was simply saying that eating responsibly sourced seafood, instead of meat, will reduce our carbon footprint.

Since that time, the carbon footprint of food production has been extensively researched by many academics. One of these is a Shetlander, Frances Sandison. When we last spoke, she was in the final stages of writing up her PhD. Growing up in Shetland, she was always aware of how important food from the sea is. This interest became a passion when she first learned that it is possible to reduce our personal carbon footprint by the food choices we make. After graduating she began looking at the carbon footprint of Shetland seafood. This eventually developed into her PhD, which assesses what role seafood consumption can play in delivering a climate smart future. It's her dream research, she says: dealing with the biggest subject of all, our global carbon footprint, but firmly imbedded in the island home she loves.

Her conclusions are arresting. The carbon footprint of producing one kilogram of beef or lamb is around 30 kilograms. Pork is better, ranging from four to 12 kilograms, while chicken is lowest: from three to six kilograms. The contrast with seafood is stark. The carbon footprint of most fisheries is less than three kilograms for every one kilogram of fish produced. The carbon footprint for beef and lamb is so high partly because feed supplements are used but also because ruminants produce emissions as a by-product of their digestive system. Fish, either wild caught or farmed, do not have this problem.

For some fisheries the carbon footprint is stunningly small. Frances has looked in detail at the modern pelagic trawl fleet, which catches both herring and mackerel. Its carbon footprint ranges from 0.3 to 0.7 kilograms, with an almost unbelievable average of 0.5 kilograms. The message is clear: if you want to save the planet, eat more fish and less meat.

Aquaculture is particularly interesting. Because most farmed fish are fed, it has a higher carbon footprint than wild-caught fish. Farmed salmon, for example, has one of the higher seafood carbon footprints, at around four kilograms for every one kilogram of salmon produced. But the winner of the lowest carbon footprint competition is rope-grown farmed mussels. As filter feeders, requiring minimal intervention until they are ready to be harvested, their carbon footprint is only 0.2 kilograms.

A vegetarian or vegan diet is much better than a meat-based diet in terms of carbon footprint, but little different from a pescatarian diet. It is also important to bear in mind that a vegetarian or vegan diet uses land and fresh water, two increasingly scarce resources in our ever more populated world. The catching or growing of fish requires neither land nor fresh water. Many of the items considered essential to a vegan diet, such as avocados, coconut milk and nuts, are flown halfway around the world before they arrive on our supermarket shelves, substantially increasing their carbon footprint.

Returning to Hilborn's keynote address in Vancouver, when he was challenged about the environmental damage to the seabed caused by fishing, he brought up a slide of a small organic farm owned and managed by his wife, Ulrike. Set in a stunningly beautiful location just outside Seattle, he explained that her small-holding produced high-quality organic fruit and vegetables. Allowing the appreciative audience to register their approval for a few seconds, he then pointed out that this farm had been created by destroying the natural habitat of forest when the land was cleared. He accepted this as necessary if the world's growing population is to be fed. The point he wanted to make was that, in comparison, the level of environmental damage caused by fishing and fish farming is very small. Explaining that many methods of fishing (such as mid-water trawling, purse seining and long lining) never touch the seabed at all, he also reminded the audience that, apart from the mooring anchors, fish farms are also located in the water column well above the seabed. Hilborn joked that he regularly helped on Ulrike's organic farm and was not opposed to organic farming. He was simply highlighting the fact that most land-based farming activity has had a far bigger impact on the natural environment than fishing or fish farming ever has.

***

It is not possible to eliminate our personal carbon footprint. Regardless of anything else we do, our need for food adds to the problem of greenhouse gas emissions. As consumers, however, we can make choices. The NGOs campaigning to prohibit fishing and create huge marine parks ignore this fact. Are they oblivious, or are they pretending to be asleep?

One of the most high-profile organisations arguing for no fishing zones is Greenpeace. Always strong on emotion and weak on science, they love criticising the large Dutch freezer trawlers that catch herring in the southern North Sea. These boats are often described as huge industrial trawlers and floating fish factories, the size of cargo ships, that fish with nets bigger than football pitches. To the casual reader this all sounds wrong: the fish can have no chance and the stock must be overfished. The reality is the opposite. The Dutch herring fishery in the North Sea has been certified by the MSC as sustainable. The trawls are towed mid-water, so there is minimal impact on the seabed and there is no by-catch of other species. It is one of the most environmentally responsible and sustainable fishing operations in the world. It is super-efficient and highly profitable but only catches what the herring stock can sustainably yield year on year. And, of course, it has a carbon footprint that is spectacularly low; around 0.5 kilograms, which is 60 times less than beef or lamb. It is inconceivable that Greenpeace are unaware of this. It is far more likely that they figured out a long time ago that a simple story has more impact than a complex one.

Simplistic solutions to complex problems are always appealing. Managing fisheries sustainably is challenging, and it is tempting to suggest a straightforward answer that is easy to explain and easier to understand. When the solution is so obvious, it also helps secure widespread public support and financial backing. George Monbiot, columnist for *The Guardian*, recently wrote that the only way to save life in the oceans is to stop eating fish. This is an easily understood exhortation, but it is dangerous nonsense. What will replace the fish that are no longer eaten? More land-based protein with a much higher carbon footprint that will in turn accelerate climate warming? Or simply letting people in the developing world go hungry, while we, in the rich, well-fed West, create a fantasy marine ecosystem? The reality is that the oceans, which cover 72 per cent of our globe, are where food can be produced with the lowest possible carbon footprint. As Hilborn pointed out, seafood is part of the solution, not the problem.

If world fisheries can be managed to the standard set by MSC then global stocks can rebuild. The global production of seafood is around 180 million tons, comprising 98 million tons from fishing and 82 million tons from aquaculture. Fish stocks that are well managed and sustainable are more productive, yielding a much higher catch than overfished stocks. A few years ago, a think tank called Fishing for a Future tried to quantify this. In their 'Getting to Eden' report, it was estimated that global fish catches could increase by a further 12 million tons if all fisheries were managed sustainably. If, at the same time, the distribution system and supply chain could be improved to eliminate waste, another 15 million tons of fish would become available. In other words, the global fish catch could be increased by more than a quarter (27 million tons) if fisheries were managed sustainably and efficiently. This is not an impossible dream; it is perfectly achievable, as the success of the MSC programme has already demonstrated in some parts of the world.

Hand in hand with proper management should be the prohibition of fishing in areas where there are compelling reasons not to fish, such as kelp forests or fragile habitats that need protection. But simply closing large sea areas, as a tool of fisheries management, is at best a pointless distraction. At worst, it will be a barrier to increasing the global supply of sustainable seafood, whose carbon footprint is a fraction of terrestrial protein production.

Impressive as the potential for increasing the production of fisheries is, it is limited by biology. Once all fisheries are managed to the highest possible standard, there is a biological ceiling as to how much fish can be caught without overfishing the stocks. This ceiling is called the maximum sustainable yield. There is no such limit for aquaculture production, which is expected to overtake the catch of wild fish within the next few years. With the domestication of new species, as technology allows the industry to move further offshore and as ever more innovative and sustainable feeds are used, farmed seafood has the potential to become a huge source of protein with a low carbon footprint. Global production could conceivably double or more over the next decade.

If society accepts that it has a moral responsibility to feed its growing population, then more food needs to be produced. The way to do that without destroying the planet is to use the ocean wisely, though better managed fisheries and sustainable aquaculture.

If you want to save the planet, eat farmed mussels for a starter followed by mackerel as a main course.

Further Reading

Coull, J. *The Sea Fisheries of Scotland. A Historical Geography.* John Donald, Edinburgh, 1996

Coull, J. *Fishing, Fishermen, Fish Merchants and Curers in Shetland.* Shetland Times, Lerwick, 2007

Edmonston, A. *Observations on the Nature and Extent of the Cod Fishery carried on off the coasts of the Zetland and Orkney Islands.* W. Laing, London, 1820

Fenton, A. *The Northern Isles: Orkney and Shetland.* John Donald, Edinburgh, 1978

Goodlad, C. *Shetland Fishing Saga.* Shetland Times, Lerwick, 1971

Goodlad, J. *The Cod Hunters.* Shetland Heritage Publications, Lerwick, 2018

Gray, M. *The Fishing Industries of Scotland, 1790-1914.* Oxford University Press, Oxford, 1978

Halcrow, A. *The Sail Fishermen of Shetland.* Shetland Times, Lerwick, 1950

Henderson, M. *In Search of Willafjord.* Shetland Times, Lerwick, 2016

Hibbert, S. *A Description of the Shetland Islands.* Oliver & Boyd, Edinburgh, 1822

Jakobsen, J. *An Etymological Dictionary of the Norn Language in Shetland.* Moller, Copenhagen, 1928

Joensen, J. *Faeroske Sluppfiskere.* Einars Prent, Torshavn, 1975

Kurlansky, M. *Cod. A biography of the fish that changed the world.* Jonathan Cape, London, 1999

Low, G. *A tour through the islands of Orkney and Schetland.* Melvin Press, Inverness, 1774

March, E. *Sailing Trawlers. The Story of Deep-Sea Fishing with Longline and Trawl.* David & Charles, Devon, 1970

Nicolson, J.R. *Hay and Company, Merchants in Shetland.* Hay and Co., Lerwick, 1982

Ployen, C. *Reminiscences of a voyage to Shetland, Orkney and Scotland in the summer of 1839.* T & J Manson, Lerwick, 1896

Rose, M. *A Merchants Tale: The Life of William Hay (1787 – 1858).* Shetland Times, Lerwick, 1999

Schei, L. and Moberg, G. *The Faroe Islands.* John Murray, London, 1991

Simpson, C. *Water in Burgidale.* Shetland Amenity Trust, Lerwick, 2010

Simpson, C. *Shetlands Heritage of Sail.* Shetland Times, Lerwick, 2011

Smith, H. *Shetland Life and Trade, 1550–1914.* John Donald, Edinburgh, 1984

West, J. *Faroe – The Emergence of a Nation.* Hurst & Co., London, 1972

Index